AN OUTLINE OF CYNIC PHILOSOPHY

Antisthenes of Athens and Diogenes of Sinope

C. D. Yonge

In the ancient world, the Cynic philosopher – following the fourth-century BC teaching of Antisthenes of Athens and Diogenes of Sinope – forsaking home and possessions, dressed in a simple cloak and bearing no more than a staff and a satchel, was a familiar sight on the city streets as he railed against false, shallow, worldly values, in favour of true moral worth and personal integrity. About 600 years later, the Graeco–Roman author Diogenes Laertius devoted part of his large compendium, *The Lives and Opinions of Eminent Philosophers*, to stories and anecdotes about Antisthenes, Diogenes and their followers.

This volume includes the complete text of Book Six of Diogenes' *Lives*. Further ancient writings that discuss the Cynic outlook – by Dio Chrysostom, Epictetus and pseudo-Lucian – are included in the Appendices. The works of the early Cynics have all been lost, and this text by Diogenes Laertius thankfully preserves an important range of quotations and references. Despite the Cynic's extreme stance, this idealistic philosophy still has a valid part to play in the face of the increasing materialism of our modern society, challenging us to re-evaluate our priorities.

The nineteenth-century translation of C. D. Yonge has been substantially revised, and is supported by a new Introduction, Glossary of Names, Notes and Index.

Keith Seddon is a freelance academic and author. He is Professor of Philosophy at Warnborough College Ireland.

By the same author

Epictetus: The Discourses, Handbook and Fragments
[forthcoming]

The Stoic Fragments of Epictetus
[forthcoming]

A Summary of Stoic Philosophy: Zeno of Citium in Diogenes Laertius Book Seven

Stoic Serenity: A Practical Course on Finding Inner Peace

Epictetus' Handbook and the Tablet of Cebes: Guides to Stoic Living

Lao Tzu: Tao Te Ching

Learning the Tao: Chuang Tzu as Teacher

Tractatus Philosophicus Tao: A short treatise on the Tao Te Ching of Lao Tzu

Time: A Philosophical Treatment

AN OUTLINE OF CYNIC PHILOSOPHY

Antisthenes of Athens
and Diogenes of Sinope in
Diogenes Laertius Book Six

Translated
by
C. D. Yonge

Edited and Revised, with a New
Introduction, Notes, Glossary and Index
by
Keith Seddon

Lulu

First edition of C. D. Yonge's translation of Diogenes Laertius'
The Lives and Opinions of Eminent Philosophers published in
London in 1853 by Henry G. Bohn in Bohn's Classical Library.

This revised edition of Book Six published 2008
by Keith Seddon
at Lulu
www.lulu.com

© 2008 Keith Seddon

Typeset in Constantia and Maiandra

All rights reserved. No part of this book may be reprinted
or reproduced or utilised in any form or by any electronic,
mechanical, or other means, now known or hereafter
invented, including photocopying and recording, or in
any information storage or retrieval system, without
permission in writing from the publishers.

ISBN 978–0–9556844-8–7 (hardback)
ISBN 978–0–9556844-4–9 (paperback)

*When he was asked what advantage he had derived
from philosophy, Diogenes replied, 'If no other,
at least this, that I am prepared
for every kind of fortune.'*

Diogenes Laertius, *The Lives and Opinions of
Eminent Philosophers* 6.63

CONTENTS

Plan of Ancient Athens   8 and 9
Preface   11
Preface to Yonge's 1853 Edition   13
Abbreviations   16

Introduction to the 2008 Edition   17

Antisthenes   49
Diogenes   62
Monimus   104
Onesicritus   106
Crates   107
Metrocles   113
Hipparchia   115
Menippus   117
Menedemus   119

Appendix 1 – Dio Chrysostom: Fourth Discourse on Kingship   123
Appendix 2 – Epictetus: Discourse 3.22   155
Appendix 3 – Pseudo-Lucian: The Cynic   175
Glossary of Names   187
Select Bibliography   209
Index   217

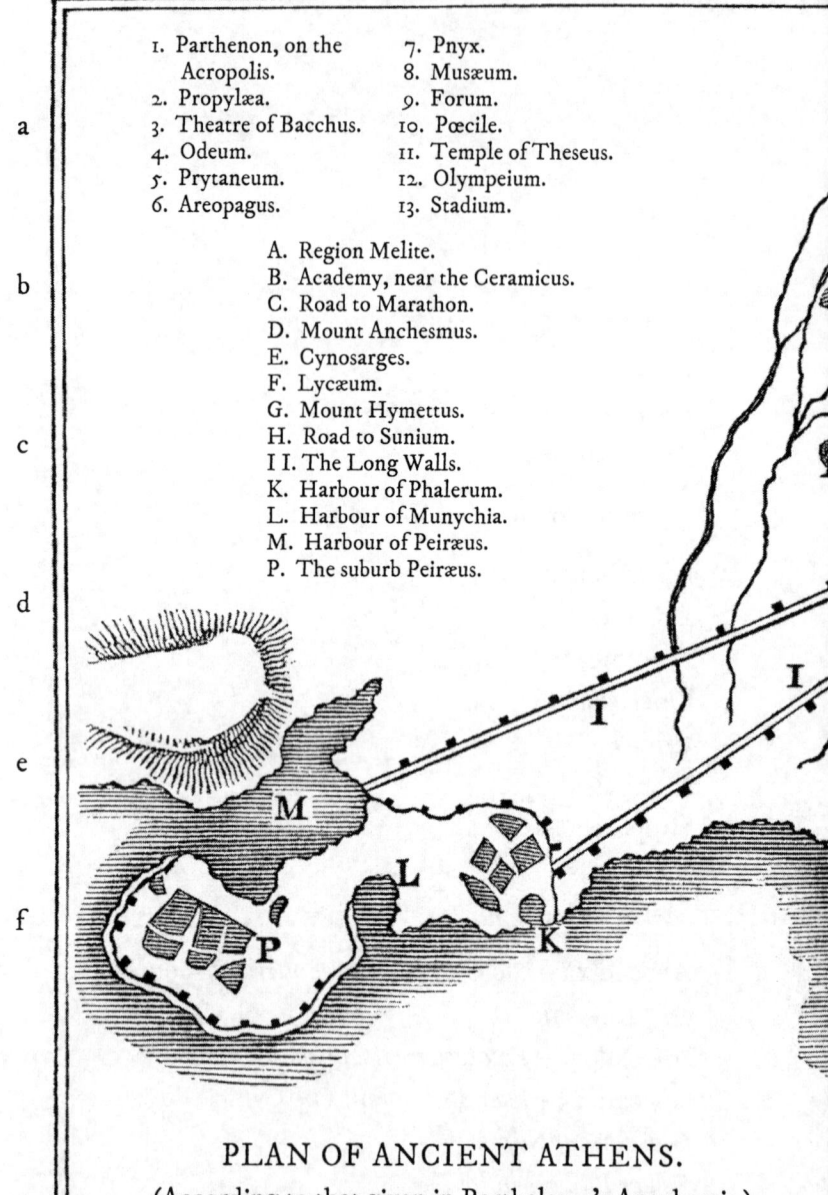

1. Parthenon, on the Acropolis.
2. Propylæa.
3. Theatre of Bacchus.
4. Odeum.
5. Prytaneum.
6. Areopagus.
7. Pnyx.
8. Musæum.
9. Forum.
10. Pœcile.
11. Temple of Theseus.
12. Olympeium.
13. Stadium.

A. Region Melite.
B. Academy, near the Ceramicus.
C. Road to Marathon.
D. Mount Anchesmus.
E. Cynosarges.
F. Lycæum.
G. Mount Hymettus.
H. Road to Sunium.
I I. The Long Walls.
K. Harbour of Phalerum.
L. Harbour of Munychia.
M. Harbour of Peiræus.
P. The suburb Peiræus.

PLAN OF ANCIENT ATHENS.
(According to that given in Barthelemy's Anacharsis.)

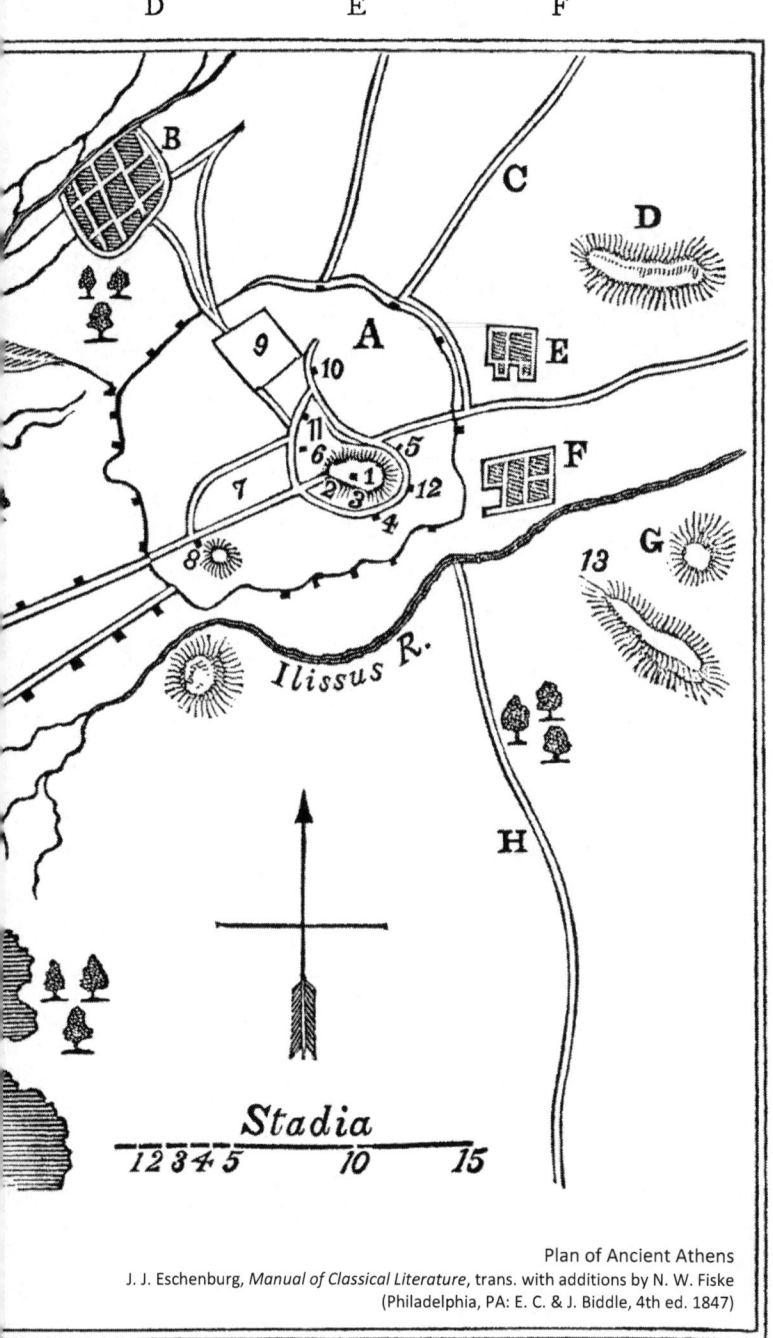

Plan of Ancient Athens
J. J. Eschenburg, *Manual of Classical Literature*, trans. with additions by N. W. Fiske (Philadelphia, PA: E. C. & J. Biddle, 4th ed. 1847)

PREFACE

There have been three translations into English of Diogenes Laertius' third-century Greek compendium *The Lives and Opinions of Eminent Philosophers*; one, a late-seventeenth-century translation which I have not been able to locate,[1] one by R. D. Hicks published in 1925, and a third by C. D. Yonge published in the middle of the nineteenth century.[2] It is from this latter translation that I have already extracted and revised Book Seven, on the Stoics,[3] and from which I offer in this present volume a revised version of Book Six, on

---

[1] Described by Herbert S. Long in his Preface as 'merely quaint' (Hicks 1972, xiii), but lacking a proper bibliographical reference. The British Library catalogue yields this likely possibility for the work in question: *The Lives, Opinions, and Remarkable Sayings of the most famous Ancient Philosophers: Made English by several hands*. Volume 1. (The first book translated by T. Fetherstone, the second book by Samual White, the third book by E. Smith, the fourth book by J. Philips, the fifth book by R. Kippax, the sixth book by William Baxter, and the seventh book by R. M.) Edward Brewster: London 1688. The same title, now listed as having two volumes, was published again in London, this time by R. Bentley in 1696, and has the addition of one further translator, 'P.A.' If this second volume of 1696 completed the project, and included all ten books of Diogenes Laertius, then (assuming that each translator was assigned one book) two further translators are unaccounted for. The second volume appears to make an appearance in the catalogue in its own right, as *A Continuation of Diogenes Laertius: wherein is contain'd the lives of several others of the ancient philosophers*. 1696 (no publisher is listed).

[2] Full bibliographic details are given in the Select Bibliography.

[3] Yonge and Seddon 2007.

the Cynics. To accompany Diogenes' account, I have included in the Appendices three further texts that also discuss Diogenes of Sinope (a *Discourse on Kingship* by Dio Chrysostom) and the Cynic outlook more generally (one of the *Discourses* of Epictetus, and *The Cynic* by pseudo-Lucian).[4]

To make this revised translation I have consulted the Greek of Hicks' Loeb edition – which he says is 'based largely on the Didot edition' (Hicks 1938, xxxvii), published in Paris in 1850, 'bearing the name of Cobet' (xxxiv) and incorporating 'extensive alterations which mark this edition as a great advance upon its predecessors' (xxxv) – as well as Hicks' translation.

ACKNOWLEDGEMENTS

Entries in the Glossary of Names and footnotes incorporating or adapting texts from Wikipedia are licensed under the GNU Free Documentation License <http://www.gnu.org/copyleft/fdl.html>. Links to sources are included immediately following the entries in question.

I am grateful to Steven Paul Hamilton for his usual thoroughness in checking the proofs.

Keith Seddon

Hertfordshire, England
November 2008

---

[4] For brief accounts of Dio Chrysostom and Epictetus, see their entries in the Glossary of Names. For the writer attempting to imitate Lucian in *The Cynic*, known as pseudo-Lucian, we have no biographical knowledge; MacLeod in his introduction to his translation (Loeb, 1967) conjectures that this text 'may well have been written ... in the time of Julian the Apostate', in the fourth century AD, 'but it could be considerably earlier'.

PREFACE

to Yonge's 1853 edition

Diogenes, the author of the following work, was a native (as is generally believed) of Laerte, in Cilicia, from which circumstance he derived the cognomen of Laertius.[5] Little is known of him personally, nor is even the age in which he lived very clearly ascertained. But as Plutarch, Sextus Empiricus, and Saturninus are among the writers whom he quotes, he is generally believed to have lived near the end of the second century AD: although some place him in the time of Alexander Severus, and others as late as Constantine.[6] His work consists of ten books, variously called: *The Lives of Philosophers*, *A History of Philosophy*, and *The Lives of Sophists*. From internal evidence (DL 3.47), we learn that he wrote it for a noble lady (according to some, Arria; according to others, Julia, the Empress of Severus), who

---

[5] The current theory is that 'Laertius' is not derived from the place where Diogenes was born or where he lived, but is a nickname given to him by post-classical scholars to distinguish him from all the other men named Diogenes who populated the ancient world. See Hicks 1972, xv–xvi. [All the footnotes in this Preface are mine. KS]

[6] Modern scholarship is more in agreement with the date that makes Diogenes a contemporary of Alexander Severus (c. AD 209–235): *The Oxford Classical Dictionary* (3rd edition, 1996), for instance, informs us that Diogenes Laertius 'probably lived in the first half of the 3rd century AD'. Constantine, who died in AD 337, appears to give a date that is rather too late for Diogenes Laertius.

occupied herself with the study of philosophy, and especially of Plato.[7]

Diogenes Laertius divides the philosophy of the Greeks into the Ionic, beginning with Anaximander, and ending with Theophrastus (in which class, he includes the Socratic philosophy and all its various ramifications); and the Italian, beginning with Pythagoras, and ending with Epicurus, in which he includes the Eleatics, along with Heraclitus and the Sceptics. From the minute consideration which he devotes to Epicurus and his system, it has been supposed that he himself belonged to that school.[8]

His work is the chief source of information we possess concerning the history of Greek philosophy, and is the foundation of nearly all the modern treatises on that subject; some of the most important of which are little more than translations or amplifications of it. It is valuable because it contains a copious collection of anecdotes illustrative of the life and manners of the Greeks; but he has not always been very careful in his selection, and in some parts there is a confusion in his statements that makes them scarcely intelligible.[9] These faults have led some critics to consider the work as it now exists merely a mutilated abridgment of the original. Breslaeus, who in the thirteenth century, wrote a *Treatise on the Lives and Manners of the Philosophers*, quotes many anecdotes and sayings, which seem to be derived from Diogenes, but which are not to be

---

[7] In his text at DL 3.47, Diogenes Laertius certainly addresses his reader directly in the second person, though does not include any name or any other clues as to who this reader is. Beyond confirming that his reader is indeed a Platonist, there is nothing in the text at this point to suggest either of the women mentioned here, Arria or Julia, as possible candidates.

[8] The general view today is that this supposition is at best rather weak.

[9] It is hard to say exactly what Yonge is getting at here.

found in our present text; whence Schneider concludes that he had a very different and far more complete copy than has come down to us.

The text used in the following translation is chiefly that of Huebner, as published at Leipsic, 1828.

ABBREVIATIONS

DL   Diogenes Laertius
The Lives and Opinions of Eminent Philosophers
(References utilise the standard numbering system adopted by modern scholars, including R. D. Hicks in his Loeb translation.)

Gell.   Aulus Gellius
Attic Nights

OCD   Simon Hornblower and Antony Spawforth
The Oxford Classical Dictionary, 3rd edition

INTRODUCTION

to the 2008 edition*

DIOGENES LAERTIUS: LIFE AND WORK

Virtually nothing is known about Diogenes Laertius apart from the fact that manuscripts of his book, *The Lives and Opinions of Eminent Philosophers*, bear his name,[10] to which we may add a few further sketchy details that can be deduced from the contents of the book itself. Carrying some weight are suppositions concerning the date of the book and the place where its author lived and worked. With respect to the date of composition, since the latest known philosopher that Diogenes Laertius mentions is (the otherwise unknown) Saturninus,[11] listed as a pupil of Sextus Empiricus who is thought to have flourished towards the end of the second century AD, we know that the *Lives* cannot have been written before that time. And because Diogenes Laertius makes no mention of Plotinus (AD 205–269/70), when it is reasonable to expect that he would have done so if he could, we are led to conclude that the *Lives* was written

---

* The early part of the text appearing in this Introduction (up to page 21) is repeated with minor modifications from the companion volume *A Summary of Stoic Philosophy: Zeno of Citium in Diogenes Laertius Book Seven*, Lulu 2007.

[10] For the different forms in which his name appears in the manuscripts and in ancient lexicons see Herbert S. Long's Introduction in Hicks 1972, xv–xvi.

[11] See DL 9.116.

some time during the first half of the third century AD. Modern scholars reject the notion that Laertius indicates the family, city, or region from which our Diogenes came.[12] But there is one phrase in the *Lives* (the opening line to the life of the Sceptic Timon[13]) which *possibly* reveals where Diogenes Laertius lived and worked. The phrase in question has two possible meanings, (1) 'Our Apollonides of Nicaea ...' or (2) 'Apollonides of our Nicaea ...'[14] The second meaning suggests that its author considered himself a native of Nicaea.[15] The conclusion that Diogenes Laertius came from Nicaea thus hangs by two rather frail threads. First, did he mean to say 'our Nicaea'? Mansfeld thinks he did, on the basis of similar usage of this phrase in the manuscripts of Plato's *Sophist*.[16] But even if we feel this reasoning has at least some plausibility, secondly, we now face the possibility that the phrase in question comes not from the pen of Diogenes Laertius, but from some piece of writing by a different author whom he is simply copying into his compendium – and if so, the case for Nicaea obviously collapses.

So far then we can say that probably Diogenes Laertius flourished in the first half of the third century, and possibly he was a native of Nicaea. We know that he wrote a large compendium comprising ten books (almost all of which

---

[12] Again, see Long's Introduction (Hicks 1972, xvi), where he refers to 'the favourite modern thesis' that 'Laertius was a learned nickname of a type familiar in post-classical times, invented to distinguish this Diogenes from the many others, and based upon the Homeric formula διογενὲς Λαερτιάδη used in addressing Odysseus'.

[13] At DL 9.109. See the brief entry for Timon of Phlius in the Glossary of Names, below.

[14] The Greek text is: *Apollônidês ho Nikaeus ho par hêmôn ...*

[15] Nicaea, a city in Bithynia, is now modern-day Iznik. In AD 325 it was chosen by Constantine I for the first great ecumenical Church council, during which the Nicene Creed was formulated.

[16] At *Sophist* at 242d (see Mansfeld 1986, 346–7).

survives[17]), a task possible only for an educated person with, one way or another, access to a substantial library. We know also that he wrote poetry, because he refers to his book of epigrams in various metres (*Pammetros*) on two occasions (though possibly meaning to refer to two separate books),[18] and with respect to three of the Cynic philosophers that he includes in Book Six, he includes verses on the manner of their deaths.[19]

There is no consensus on where Diogenes Laertius' philosophical allegiances lay: he certainly doesn't declare any, or name any teachers. There is no sign in his writing that he had any real competence as a philosopher or that his knowledge of the subject derived from anything more than the enthusiasm of a self-taught and widely read amateur, and he does not seem to have any obvious commitment to any one philosopher or sect over the others (indeed, all are treated with equal consideration and fairness); he has adhered strictly to the role of impartial commentator. It is right, I think, to reject as very feeble the idea (that some have had) that because of the size and quality of Book Ten on Epicurus, Diogenes Laertius was himself an adherent of

---

[17] Unless we are to believe (as some do; see Yonge's Preface, above) that Breslaeus in his thirteenth-century work, *A Treatise on the Lives and Manners of the Philosophers*, was able to quote from Diogenes Laertius a range of sayings we no longer have from more complete manuscripts that have not survived into modern times. That possibility aside, on the basis of a codex in Paris, known as P (dating from about 1300), we can surmise that about half of Book Seven, on the Stoics, has been lost. (There is an index in P which lists the philosophers in Book Seven, indicating that our modern version is missing accounts for nineteen individuals, retaining accounts for only seven; see Hicks 1938, xx.) And this being so, our doubts may be raised as to whether the remainder of the compendium, including Book Six on the Cynics, has survived in its entirety.

[18] At DL 1.39 and 7.31.

[19] See below, DL 6.19 (Antisthenes), 6.79 (Diogenes), and 6.100 (Menippus).

Epicureanism. Some have suggested that Diogenes Laertius' use of the phrase 'Our Apollonides of Nicaea ...' (which we discussed above) means that he, like Apollonides, was a Sceptic, but this idea seems no less feeble (and in any event relies on an interpretation of the 'our' phrase that is not universally accepted). If Diogenes Laertius had an allegiance to any one school, it seems odd that he would not have made this transparently clear. It is therefore likely that he had no such allegiance. In which case we also know that he did not consider himself to be a philosopher, since in the period he was living and throughout the centuries preceding, being a philosopher meant choosing to devote oneself to one particular school over all the others,[20] and modelling one's life according to the precepts and ideals of one's school.[21]

We also do not know how Diogenes Laertius conceived of his own work: we do not know why he wrote it, what purpose he thought it had, or why he thought it would attract readers. Answers to these questions, usually addressed in the author's preface or other preamble, are missing from the manuscripts (though conceivably could have been present in earlier copies) – Book One launches immediately into an account of the early history of philosophy and why the author thinks philosophy was invented by the Greeks. His work is obviously intended to do more than merely inform the reader of beliefs and doctrines, for these can be explained without including any biographical details of the philosophers whose doctrines are being expounded. At one extreme, we might think that Diogenes' main interest is to

---

[20] Indeed, the Greek term that we translate as school is *hairesis*, which means choice or purpose. When a student of philosophy in this era is asked which sect or principles he embraces, he is being asked which philosopher he has chosen to side with (see Algra 1999, 21).

[21] For more on philosophy as a way of life, see especially Hadot 1995.

send up his subjects, including as he does an almost relentless stream of comic and absurd incidents: his intent, at the very least, is to amuse and entertain his reader. If our preference is to be amused, them amused we shall be. But if we want also to learn about the philosophical beliefs adhered to by his subjects, then in this too we will be satisfied, for the specific biographical incidents which are recounted illustrate directly the beliefs and commitments that they held.

The *Lives* is valuable – and attracts our interest today – because it preserves information that otherwise would be lost. It contains 1,186 explicit references to 365 books by about 250 authors, and over 350 anonymous references.[22] And even though its author drew much of his material from secondary and even tertiary sources (from epitomes, digests and summaries), his work all the same allows us to hear at least faint echoes of the voices of a large number of authors who otherwise would now be completely silent under the heavy shroud of the passing centuries. In Book Six, on the Cynics, we find over 40 authors referred to, cited or quoted, over 70 times; see the Glossary of Names to locate them in the text.

In the companion volume to this book, *A Summary of Stoic Philosophy*[23] (comprising Book Seven of the *Lives*), the summary referred to in the title is incorporated directly into Diogenes Laertius' primary text, and any attempt on an editor's part to précis the summary would be superfluous. The situation, however, with Book Six of the *Lives* is rather different, as here we find no corresponding systematic summary of Cynic doctrine. The text instead devotes itself to reporting stories and anecdotes concerning the individual Cynic philosophers (disproportionately focusing on

---

[22] Hicks 1972, xix.
[23] Yonge and Seddon 2007.

Diogenes of Sinope), and although it also records a wide selection of their sayings, this essentially piecemeal approach falls well short of providing the reader with a methodical summary of what the Cynics believed and practised. So for readers new to the Cynics, or for those who would appreciate it, here is my attempt at a concise outline of Cynic doctrine.

CYNICS AND CYNIC PHILOSOPHY

WHY 'CYNIC'? There are two competing accounts of how the philosophical movement founded by Antisthenes of Athens and Diogenes of Sinope came by its name, and why they and their followers were called *kunikos*, 'dog-like'. The first account maintains that *kunikos* derives from *Kunosarges*, the name of the gymnasium set in its own grounds outside Athens, reserved for foreigners and Athenians of illegitimate birth – frequented by Antisthenes because he was not a legitimate Athenian – for it was here in the Cynosarges that Antisthenes met with his students and taught philosophy. Why this gymnasium was called *Kunosarges*, meaning 'white dog', swift dog', or possibly 'dog's meat', we do not know.[24]

The second account holds that there is actually no etymological connection between *Kunosarges* and *kunikos*, and that the similarity that the terms appear to share is mere happenstance. Antisthenes, Diogenes, and their followers were given the designation 'dog' (*kuôn*) as an insult on the part of those who disliked them and wished to disparage their philosophy and their way of life. 'Cynic' was thus used contemptuously, suggests Navia in his book about Antis-

---

[24] See Navia 1998, 52–3; Navia 1996, 15–17; Navia 2001, 26–7; Branham and Goulet-Cazé 1996, 4.

thenes,[25] for, he points out, among the ancient Greeks, dogs were not regarded with affection: they were a fact of life, out on the street causing a nuisance, or kept for their usefulness as working animals. Cynic philosophers were of the former sort, eating and performing natural functions in public, sleeping in the open or in the precincts of public buildings, living off the scraps that people would throw them, and making a nuisance of themselves by begging and pestering people for handouts.

Antisthenes was called the Absolute Dog,[26] and all those who followed him took upon themselves the name Cynic. They snapped at the ankles of those who passed them, so to speak, haranguing and insulting them, not to hurt them, but to awaken them to the truth about human well-being, about why happiness seems to be so elusive to so many, and what needs to be done to secure it.

'DEFACE THE CURRENCY.' This injunction is the foundation stone upon which the whole of Cynic practice rests, the only possible starting place for anyone interested in what the Cynics were trying to do.

Diogenes Laertius' account of Diogenes of Sinope opens with the story of Diogenes' defacing the coins of his home town.[27] It is interesting to note that quantities of Sinopean coins from the time of Diogenes the Cynic have indeed been defaced,[28] though whether Diogenes' father Hicesias did this, whether he and his father acted together, whether Diogenes at first misunderstood Apollo's oracle at Delphi to deface the currency – whether indeed the oracle was really

---

[25] Navia 2001, 99.
[26] DL 6.13.
[27] See DL 6.20–1.
[28] See note 99 (to DL 6.20), p. 62, below.

consulted, or the incident added apocryphally to Diogenes' biography in later years – whether Diogenes fled Sinope or was banished, or whether his leaving really had anything to do with the city's currency, are of course questions whose answers will forever remain unknown. (Even the account that Diogenes became the pupil of Antisthenes can be doubted.[29])

But what we do know is that, whatever the impetus, and however confused Diogenes might at first have been regarding Apollo's injunction, Diogenes committed himself in the most thoroughgoing way imaginable to 'defacing the currency'. His mission was to scratch out, remove, reject and revalue, not the coins themselves, but the values and customs that underpinned all transactions in Greek culture. These values were – and of course they remain to this day – detrimental to human flourishing, and Diogenes' rejection of them had to be visible, public, theatrical and shocking if people were to notice him and learn anything from him.

PHILOSOPHICAL SCHOOL OR JUST A WAY OF LIFE? Hippobotus in his *On Philosophical Sects* lists nine philosophical schools, but omits the Cynics.[30] Indeed, to this day, it is not uncommon for authors writing on the Hellenistic philosophers to disregard the Cynics, sometimes not even bothering to give their reasons for their omission. And Diogenes Laertius himself gives the impression of being

---

[29] See DL 6.21 and the entry for Diogenes of Sinope in the Glossary of Names.

[30] Along with the Sceptic, Dialectician and Elian schools; see DL 1.19–20. See Hippobotus in the Glossary of Names. The 1st-century BC Roman writer Varro, in his lost work *De Philosophia* quoted by Augustine, also denies that the Cynics constituted a genuine school because, along with some other schools, 'they make no mention of the good that is chiefly to be desired...' (*City of God* 19.2, trans. John Healey).

apologetic when at the end of his account of the Cynics in Book Six of the *Lives* (about Menedemus) he hopes that he has not abused the language in referring to the Cynics as an authentic sect, remarking that some contend that the Cynic outlook is nothing more than 'just a way of life'.

To be sure, the Cynics lacked an organisational structure. They had no lasting centre of any kind – building or location – where they taught or promoted their philosophy or where they practised their way of life, in distinct contrast with Plato's Academy, Aristotle's Lyceum, Epicurus' Garden, and Zeno's Stoa. They had no head or principal whose leadership directed the activities of the school or who owned the school's assets. And no less significantly, again in contrast with the other schools, the Cynics possessed no central body of teaching: many Cynics wrote books, of course – Diogenes Laertius lists a notable number of them – but none combined to form a core curriculum that was used by different teachers in different locations at different times (in complete contrast with the works of Chrysippus, say, used by the Stoics to teach a standardised programme).[31]

But the Cynic way of life was not just a way of life, comparable to other ways of life, such as that lived by the farmer or the soldier, say. The farmer does not perfect his humanity by bringing in a harvest, and the soldier does not free himself from the cares of the world by killing on the battlefield. The ideal human being as the Cynics conceived this person does not live that sort of life, but instead seeks the advantages that the philosophic life confers. The philosophic life is that adopted by the person who, having heard of

---

[31] See Aune 2008, 51; Branham and Goulet-Cazé 1996, 21–3. The emperor Julian (4th century AD) remarks that indeed, the Cynics had no treatises with any serious purpose, as opposed to the merely frivolous (*To the Uneducated Cynics* = *Oration* 6.186B).

the injunction KNOW YOURSELF inscribed in the forecourt of the Temple of Apollo at Delphi, or having heard of Socrates' declaration that 'the unexamined life is not worth living',[32] undertakes a personal examination and an investigation of human affairs generally, directed at finding out what sort of life *is* worth living, and then tries to live it. The Cynic way of life does not have as its objective the production of food or the destruction of an enemy army, or any sort of external end, but is itself its own end – a life lived in a certain way, maintained by a special sort of outlook. For someone's life to count as successfully living *this Cynic way of life rather than some other*, it will have to adopt practices of a particular character, and these practices can be seen to rest on specific beliefs and doctrines concerning not what it is that actions produce by way of external goods, but concerning the very nature of the actions themselves. For instance, it is clear that one significant objective of Diogenes of Sinope's taking up the philosophic life is that through his way of living it he might influence others to adopt the same way of life, but his successfully doing so is not the end at which his actions aim: he does not fail if his interlocutor or onlooker fails to cultivate the philosophic life. Diogenes' success rests only upon the manner of his trying.

CYNIC DOCTRINES. As the first-century Roman Stoic teacher Epictetus points out in his presentation on the Cynic philosopher,[33] the person who merely adopts the outward trappings of a Cynic – putting on a cloak, throwing on a little leather bag and picking up a staff, ready now to abuse all whom they meet – does not of course make themselves a Cynic. Their disposition of character, their beliefs

---

[32] Plato, *Apology* 38a.
[33] Epictetus, *Discourses* 3.22.10 in Appendix 2, below.

and convictions must be of the right sort to convert play-acting to authenticity.

The central hub to which all of ancient Greek ethics is connected is the unquestioned assumption that there is an 'end' or 'goal' (*telos*) of human living for whose sake everything in life is done such that it is not itself pursued for the sake of anything else. All the schools of this period,[34] along with the Cynics, accepted the traditional conception of the *telos* being *eudaimonia* ('happiness' or 'flourishing').[35]

The emperor Julian writes:

> Now the end [*telos*] and aim of the Cynic philosophy, as indeed of every philosophy, is happiness [*eudaimonia*], but happiness that consists in living according to nature [*kata phusin*] and not according to the opinions of the multitude.
> (Julian, *To the Uneducated Cynics* 193D, trans. Wright)

The Cynic author whose voice we hear in one of pseudo-Diogenes' Cynic epistles holds that 'happiness ... should be regarded as the most esteemed of all possessions'.[36] And indeed, the Cynics believed that they understood what happiness is, what one needed to do to successfully pursue it

---

[34] With the single exception, that is, of the Cyrenaics who deny that happiness is the end, holding instead that pleasure is the end (see DL 2.86–8).

[35] The firmly established modern trend of translating *eudaimonia* and *eudaimôn* by 'happiness' and 'happy' is far from ideal. '*Eudaimonia* means "supremely blessed", and conveys the notion of someone who is flourishing fully, someone who is happy not just in the sense that they are having a good time, or enjoying some temporary pleasure, but whose happiness is of a special kind: it is stable and enduring, it is a persistence of flourishing that pervades their whole life' (Seddon 2005, 33). Of course, the different schools had differing conceptions as what this flourishing consisted in. Epicureans thought it was pleasure of a particular character, the Sceptics thought it consisted in suspending one's judgement, and the Cynics, along with the Stoics who followed them, thought it was attained by the person who lives in accordance with nature.

[36] Malherbe 1977, 157.

and possess it, and why for the bulk of humanity it would remain forever permanently misunderstood and elusive – for most people pray to the Gods for what they mistakenly believe to be good, then complain of their misfortunes (which follow inevitably, whether or not they get what they prayed for),[37] failing to recognise that the Gods have provided for them an easy life, if only they could see it.[38]

Diogenes of Sinope led this easy life by dispensing with everything, for when everything had gone, all that was left was his freedom (*eleutheria*), and freedom he preferred above everything.[39] He was free of all ties and all commitments, free from anxieties concerning possessions and relationships, free from masters of any kind, beholden to no one, deferring to no one.[40] Even his cloak, bag and staff were not regarded by him as proper possessions – a bit of old cloth, a few stitches in a bit of old leather, a gnarled old stick, these worn-out, throw-away items could be cadged from anyone at any time. His only possessions, if possessions they could be called, were his own self-sufficiency and independence, possessed by those for whom what they hold to and what they do is dependent upon no one but themselves.

This self-sufficiency (*autarkeia*) made Diogenes a king over everyone, just as he was fit to be master over Xeniades' two sons as their tutor, whilst through the lens of convention he was viewed merely as Xeniades' slave.[41] Diogenes is superior even to the celebrated king Alexander the Great,[42] for Alexander, having conquered nations, yet still craves

---

[37] DL 6.42.
[38] DL 6.44.
[39] DL 6.71.
[40] See Epictetus, *Discourses* 3.22.69–72, pp. 166–7 below.
[41] DL 6.30–1.
[42] DL 6.38. See Appendix 1.

more power and dominion, and the more he has the more he fails to have as much as he wants, and for whom success is impossible. His character, his qualities as a human being wither to dust in the glare of Diogenes' excellence, for here is the man who has conquered exile, poverty, his desires for pleasures, luxuries, possessions and status, who basks in his victory, because the less he has the more he attains to the little he wants, and for whom success is unassailable.

Diogenes' dominion over himself at one and the same time gives him dominion over the entire world. Such dominion can be had by anyone who heeds the Cynics' teaching to live according to nature and who undertakes the rigour of Cynic training (*askêsis*), the culmination of which is permanent invulnerability to all vicissitudes and complete happiness (*eudaimonia*).

The expression 'live according to nature', translates the Greek phrase *kata phusin*.[43] 'Nature' (*phusis*) and 'natural' (*phusikos*) refer to a thing's origin, growth, and the form or constitution that it develops in consequence of this growth. Everything thus has its own *phusis*, its own way of growing, behaving and flourishing according to the sort of thing it happens to be. The features that are *phusikos* to something are what are characteristic of the sort of thing it is, qualities that are inherent and innate. Diogenes and the Cynics placed supreme importance on realising what would be truly natural, truly innate in human beings if they were not affected, adulterated and ruined by the *unnatural* influence of the culture in which they grow up and live, holding to the conviction that the *eudaimôn* person must also be the *phusikos* person.

---

[43] The phrase *kata phusin* occurs twice in Book Six of the *Lives*, both at DL 6.71.

Diogenes specifically opposes *nomos* to *phusis*, custom to nature.[44] Thus, to live in accordance with nature, people must expressly reject what is conventional or customary.[45] Otherwise, 'through folly' people will 'make themselves unhappy'.[46] The folly here is to believe in error that happiness lies in what is *nomikos* – in what is conventionally held to confer happiness. For the ancient Greeks, for the whole Graeco–Roman culture that followed, for the vast majority of cultures, and of course for our own culture today, what is *nomikos* in this regard is wealth, possessions, luxury, reputation, status, fame, power. To be sure, some success in pursuing these things may bring momentary pleasures. But such pleasures should not be mistaken for the permanently enduring, unassailable happiness that the ancient philosophers believed was their proper goal. For in these *nomikos* things lie contention, quarrels, calamities and catastrophes of all kinds. For no sooner has one desire for one kind of possession been satisfied than another desire for something else takes its place, and along with it comes a new sense of dissatisfaction, and after that the irritations of fresh frustrations and anxieties under whose influence friend will fall

---

[44] See DL 6.38 and 6.71.

[45] We may note that the Greek term for coinage or currency, which occurs in the opening section on Diogenes (DL 6.20-1) concerning Apollo's injunction to 'deface the currency' is *nomisma*, a cognate of *nomos*, and refers to any custom or anything sanctioned by current or established usage, and therefore means also 'coins' or 'money', with the plural *nomismata* meaning 'pieces of money', 'coins'. Thus, Apollo's injunction to 'deface the currency', which when translated into English gives the impression of being a metaphor, would for Diogenes have had a much more literal meaning. It is interesting to note also that the conceptual equating of money with usage in ancient Greek has at least a partial parallel in the English expression 'ready money' or, more colloquially, 'readies', meaning cash, money that is to hand, ready to spend in the context of actually having a use here and now.

[46] DL 6.71.

out with friend, brother will fight brother for an inheritance, neighbours will harbour resentments and jealousies. Someone who keeps to the road that convention has mistakenly signposted as the way to happiness, as well as becoming a slave to their own desires, is of course prey to the fickle turns of fortune that threaten loss and disappointment at every moment. What has come may just as easily depart. No one is immune to cruel accident or mere serendipity. Acclaim can switch to loathing in a second. The most mighty of fortunes can be snatched away in an instant. How have human beings come to view the most obnoxious of things as the most desirable? Well, in part at least, it suits those with most power and wealth to have those with least believe that power and wealth really do have value and really do have merit as the objects of desire.[47] These false beliefs are the

---

[47] Xenophon (*Symposium* 4.34–8, trans. Todd 1923) records Antisthenes' remarks about wealth: 'I conceive that people's wealth and poverty are to be found not in their real estate but in their hearts. For I see many persons, not in office, who though possessors of large resources, yet look upon themselves as so poor that they bend their backs to any toil, any risk, if only they may increase their holdings; and again I know of brothers, with equal shares in their inheritance, where one of them has plenty, and more than enough to meet expenses, while the other is in utter want. Again, I am told of certain despots, also, who have such a greedy appetite for riches that they commit much more dreadful crimes than they who are afflicted with the direst poverty. For it is of course their want that makes some people steal, others commit burglary, others follow the slave trade; but there are some despots who destroy whole families, kill men wholesale, oftentimes enslave even entire cities, for the sake of money. As for such men, I pity them deeply for their malignant disease; for in my eyes their malady resembles that of a person who possessed abundance but though continually eating could never be satisfied. For my own part, my possessions are so great that I can hardly find them myself; yet I have enough so that I can eat until I reach a point where I no longer feel hungry and drink until I do not feel thirsty and have enough clothing so that when out of doors I do not feel the cold any more than my superlatively wealthy friend Callias here; and when I get into the house I look on my walls as exceedingly warm tunics and the roofs as exceptionally thick

levers and pulleys that work the machinery of our culture to yield to those in temporary control the unimaginably opulent lifestyle they so crave.[48]

Others of course, but especially the Cynics, have seen through the lies. Diogenes' enjoyment of his simple life and the warmth of the sunlight as he confronts Alexander the Great[49] possess a magnificence and grandeur that the petty squabbling and ultimate pointlessness of the great king's life cannot even begin to match. Who matters the most to us today? A king whose empire crumbled to nothing in ancient times, or a philosopher whose ideas and commitment to human flourishing can contribute to both personal and collective conquest of folly?

But there are some who comment on Cynic philosophy who see no value in it. They see the Cynics' wholesale rejection of what is *nomikos*, what is conventional, for something more than it is, and find in this rejection something that both alarms them and something that misrepresents the Cynic position. They mistakenly believe that the Cynics, along with their renunciation of what is *nomikos*, mean also to forsake humanity itself, and hold that the Cynics advo-

---

mantles; and the bedding that I own is so satisfactory that it is actually a hard task to get me awake in the morning.'

[48] Not to mention the destruction of the environment, along with global warming, that are occurring in direct consequence of this outlook. I have heard it said that in the early twenty-first century we are living through the world's worst mass extinction in the entire history of life on earth (this is the sixth mass extinction to occur, and is caused entirely by human activities; see for instance www.massextinction.net). Yet this fact is hardly mentioned. Actions aimed at fixing environmental destruction focus merely on the symptoms, not their causes, and do not address the need for the wholesale abandonment of what until now has been *nomikos*, customary. Only a wholesale change of consciousness, a shift from more to less, and a thoroughgoing drive for simplicity, can save the planet and the human species itself.

[49] DL 6.38, 6.60, and 6.68.

cate a return to primitivism or a descent into bestiality.[50] Indeed, beasts in their wild state live in accordance with nature, but it does not follow from this that for human beings to live in accordance with nature they must also live as beasts do.

When Diogenes takes comfort from seeing a mouse scurrying about 'not seeking for a bed, not afraid of the dark, nor longing for any of those things which appear enjoyable'[51] or remarking (to those who object to his view) that indeed people *can* live like animals, and that the frailty of the human body exhibited by many results from nothing more than soft living,[52] he does not mean that he wants to live *as an animal*, or that to arrive at a state of perfect *eudaimonia* we must all adopt a thoroughgoing animalism. Such an interpretation of the Cynic outlook appears almost wilfully to veer into a bigoted ignorance.

The value of observing animals comes when we realise that, in contrast with almost all human beings, animals *live simply* – without clothes, without contrivances, without desires for more than they need, instinctively aware and trusting that the natural world will provide for them in accordance with the characteristics that they happen to have. Thus, when Diogenes sees a child drinking from their hand, and another scoop up his lentils with a crust, he remarks

---

[50] 'Cynicism was one thing, civilization another. Overwhelmed with the complexities of society, the Cynic took the easy role of over-simplification – disregard for dress and contempt for society. They called this state the state of nature and actually taught that animals were better off than man. The Cynics were anti-social, and confused a return to nature with a return to bestiality' (Riley 2004, 132; modified). 'Cynic ethics may be said to reduce, in its practical outcome, almost wholly to primitivism' (Lovejoy and Boas 1997, 118).

[51] DL 6.22. See note 102 to that section for a more extended account of this incident occurring at Aelian, *Historical Miscellany* 13.26.

[52] Dio Chrysostom, *Sixth Discourse: Diogenes* 26–9.

with respect to the first that he has been beaten in simplicity, and in response to the second he throws away his spoon as something unnecessary.[53]

Simplicity is therefore urged upon us by the very nature of things, denied to us by our own unthinking acceptance of and preference for what is *nomikos*, what is conventional. But of paramount importance is that feature of human beings by which nature has distinguished us from the rest of creation, a defining feature, a feature by which we have named ourselves *homo sapiens* – our reason, described by Diogenes as what we 'most need', and that without it there is no point to being alive. In truth, we need not just reason, but *right reason*,[54] for even the thief, the swindler, the cruel tyrant, as well as the petty pleasure-seeker and the lover of opulence, all make use of their reason to pursue their dubious ends. But their reason is faulty. They cannot tell apart those ends that are by nature proper to human flourishing from those that through convention are unquestioningly but in error put about as being proper.

When reason functions properly, which it may do for those who undertake the appropriate sort of Cynic training, it becomes right reason, bestowing upon those who attain it the ability to see the truth of the Cynic analysis outlined above, directing them in the pursuit of simplicity through living in accordance with nature, and enabling them to deal with the world and with other people through the exercise of those qualities of human character which the ancients referred to as the virtues.[55] And in this the Cynic is fulfilled, for their belief is that virtue is sufficient for happiness

---

[53] DL 6.37.
[54] Translating *dei logos*, DL 6.24.
[55] Translating the Greek *aretai*; singular *aretê*: excellence, applicable generally, but of people referring to their excellence of character, their moral qualities.

(*eudaimonia*), 'needing nothing more than the strength of a Socrates'.[56]

We can say with confidence that many of the ancient Cynics would have addressed the notion of virtue being sufficient for happiness in formal arguments.[57] But alas, as none of their writings survive, we can have no sure idea as to how, in precise detail, these arguments were presented.[58] The same is obviously the case for all the other doctrines that the Cynics held, but with respect to the sufficiency of virtue thesis – and especially because it is of such central importance for the cohesion of the Cynic outlook – it is worthwhile making the attempt to reconstruct it drawing on remarks that Socrates makes in a number of Plato's dialogues. And with equal confidence, we can be sure that this reconstruction will be one with which the Cynics would agree, even if as individuals each may prefer expositions rendered with alternative emphases, and which differ in their sequence of logical steps.

Why does anyone do that they do? Because they think that something good will come of it. Socrates remarks by way of example that seafarers and those engaged in money-making in other ways do not actually want to do what they do, make perilous voyages or suffer troubles of other kinds, but do those things for the sake of something else that they

---

[56] DL 6.11. And further, that virtue is a matter of deeds (6.11), that it can be taught (6.10 and 6.105), that once attained can never be lost (6.105), that it is the same in men as it is in women, that it is a weapon (against all misfortune) that cannot be taken away (6.12), and that it is facilitated by special sorts of both mental and physical training (6.70). (Other instances of *aretê* – virtue – occur at DL 6.54, 6.104 and 6.105.)

[57] Perhaps by Antisthenes in his *On the Good*, or by Diogenes in his *On Virtue*.)

[58] On the scarcity of Cynic literature, see for example Branham and Goulet-Cazé 1996, 3–4; Desmond 2008, 5–6, Navia 1998, 5–8.

do want, namely, wealth.[59] There is a general principle here, that when someone does something, it is done not for the sake of the action itself, but for the sake of what the action results in, and that must be something that is taken to be good. Indeed, all things fall under three headings: those that are at all times good, those that are at all times bad, and those that are 'intermediate' between the two, things that sometimes partake of what is good, sometimes of what is bad, sometimes neither, actions such as sitting, walking, running, sailing the seas, and objects such as sticks and stones. For examples of things not intermediate, but good, Socrates offers wisdom, health, wealth, 'and other such things'; their opposites are bad. And it is for the sake of the good things that people apply themselves to the intermediate things. Socrates is not claiming here that wealth and health and wisdom are always good, but that the fact that people think they are good is required for making sense of why someone would undertake, for example, a sea voyage, something that in itself is neither good nor bad. Whatever actions we undertake for the sake of what we really want (and however many stages there may be in the chain of actions where each is done for the sake of the next[60]), we must eventually arrive at something we desire *for its own sake*, something pursued *not* for the sake of anything else. Thus, there must be something we desire for its own sake, something good in itself that is good *for us*.[61] This is happiness (*eudaimonia*).[62]

---

[59] Plato, *Gorgias* 467d–468b.

[60] When, for instance, someone does a job of work for the sake of a wage, obtained for the sake of buying a car, purchased for the sake of touring Europe...

[61] Plato, *Gorgias* 468b.

[62] See for instance Plato, *Symposium* 204e, *Euthydemus* 280b; Aristotle, *Nicomachean Ethics* 1095a14–20, 1097a15–b21. At *Rhetoric* 1360b4–7,

Socrates believes that it is obviously true that people desire as their ultimate goal happiness, or what he takes to be equivalent expressions, 'living well' and 'doing well'. He remarks to his interlocutor Clinias:

> Do all people wish to do well? Or is this one of those ridiculous questions I was afraid to ask just now? For I suppose it is stupid even to pose the question, since surely everyone must wish to do well?
> Everyone in the world, Clinias agreed.
> Well then, [Socrates continued,] the next question is this: since we all wish to do well, what is required for our doing so? Will we not do so through the having of many good things? Or is this question even more silly than the other one? For surely this too must obviously be the case?
> Clinias agreed.
>
> (Plato, *Euthydemus* 278e–279a)

The dialogue continues with Socrates' attempt to find out what good things are required for happiness.

> Come now, of things that are, what sort do we hold to be really good? Or does it appear to be no difficult matter, and no problem for an important person, to find here too a ready answer? Anyone will tell us that wealth is good, surely?
> Quite true, he said.
> Then it is the same with being healthy and handsome, and having the other bodily endowments in plenty?
> He agreed.
> Again, it is surely clear that good birth and power and honour in one's own country are good things.
> He admitted it.

Aristotle remarks: 'It may be said of each individual person and of all people in common, that there is an end that in what they choose and what they avoid they set as their aim. And this end, to summarise briefly, is happiness [*eudaimonia*] and its constituents.'

Then what have we still remaining, I asked, in the class of goods? What of temperance, justice, and courage? I pray you tell me, Clinias, do you think we shall be right in ranking these as goods, or in rejecting them? For it may be that someone will dispute it. How does it strike you?

They are goods, said Clinias.

Very well, I went on, and where in the troupe shall we station wisdom? Among the goods, or somewhere else?

Among the goods.

(Plato, *Euthydemus* 279a–c, trans. Lamb, modified)

Socrates identifies two distinct types of goods here. Those of the first type, which almost everyone will agree are good, include wealth, health, beauty, 'bodily endowments' (intended to cover features such as strength, good eyesight, intelligence, a good voice, and so on), 'good birth', political power and honours. Many people, to be sure, will think that these types of goods, when possessed to a certain degree, are all that is required for happiness; indeed, they will in all probability believe that their happiness increases in direct proportion to the quantity of such goods that they come to acquire. But Socrates proposes to Clinias that there is a second type of good that should to be considered; and this second type comprises the virtues – Socrates lists just those usually referred to as the four cardinal virtues – temperance, justice, courage, and wisdom. These are qualities of one's character, dispositions to act in specific ways in specific circumstances.

A short while later, Socrates tries to show Clinias how these two types of goods interrelate:

For we agreed, said I [Socrates continues], that if many goods were present to us we should be happy and prosper.

Yes, he said.

Then would we be happy because of our present goods, if they gave us no benefit, or if they gave us some?[63]

If they gave us benefit, he said.

And would a thing benefit us if we merely had it and did not use it? For instance, if we had a lot of provisions, but did not eat them, or liquor, and did not drink it, could we be said to be benefited?

Of course not, he answered.

Well then, if every craftsman found the requisites for his particular work all ready prepared for him, and then made no use of them, would he prosper because of these acquisitions, as having acquired all the things necessary for a craftsman to have at hand? For example, if a carpenter were furnished with all his tools and a good supply of wood, but did no carpentry, is it possible he could be benefited by what he had got?

By no means, he said.

Well now, suppose someone had got wealth and all the goods that we mentioned just now, but made no use of them; would they be happy because of their possessing these goods?

Surely not, Socrates.

So it seems one must not merely have acquired such goods if one is to be happy, but use them too; otherwise there is no benefit to be gained from their possession.

True.

Then have we here enough means, Clinias, for making someone happy – in the possession of these goods and using them?

I think so.

Shall we say, I asked, if they use them rightly, or just as much if they do not?

If rightly.

Well answered, I said, for I suppose there is more mischief when someone uses anything wrongly than when they let it

---

[63] 'Benefit' translates the Greek term *ôphelimos*, meaning helpful, useful, advantageous, beneficial.

alone. In the one case there is evil; in the other there is neither evil nor good. May we not state it so?

He agreed.

(Plato, *Euthydemus* 280b–281a, trans. Lamb, modified)

Clinias concludes by agreeing that the good things that one possesses, and using them well or properly ('rightly') is sufficient to confer happiness. Socrates offers the following conclusion:

To sum up then, Clinias, I proceeded, it seems that as regards the whole lot of things which at first we termed goods, the discussion they demand is not on the question of how they are in themselves and by nature goods, but rather, I conceive, as follows: if they are guided by ignorance, they are greater evils than their opposites, inasmuch as they are more able to minister to the evil principle which rules them; whereas if understanding and wisdom guide them, they are greater goods; but in themselves neither sort is of any worth at all.

I think the case appears, he replied, to be as you suggest.

Now what result do we get from our statements? Is it not precisely that, of all the other things, not one is either good or bad, but of these two, wisdom is good and ignorance bad?

He agreed.

(Plato, *Euthydemus* 281d–e, trans. Lamb, modified)

Socrates says that for conventional goods, such as wealth, health and power to truly benefit their possessor, they must be used properly, 'if understanding and wisdom guide them'. He concludes not just that the conventional goods can confer benefit only if the agent also possesses the second sort of goods, the virtues, or qualities of character, but that the conventional goods have no value at all in themselves. Wealth, for instance, is in itself neither good nor evil, but may be put to good or evil uses (it may benefit its possessor and others, or used to cause harm) according to the disposition (virtuous, or not) of the person who has the wealth at their disposal. Conventional goods, referred to as 'good' only for the sake of common usage, are best regarded as sometimes beneficial, sometimes detrimental – and whether they benefit or harm is determined not by any intrinsic quality or qualities that they have independently of an agent's actions, but by *the nature of the agent's intention alone*.

Someone's happiness, therefore, cannot be affected by the mere presence or possession of 'goods' that sometimes benefit, sometimes harm, because these things lack any sort of intrinsic capacity to so affect people. It is not the presence of the 'good' thing in itself that benefits anyone. We are blessed by happiness, if ever we are, not by the configuration of external events that happens to prevail, but only ever by the manner of our interacting with external events.[64]

These are the sorts of considerations, we may be sure, that interested the Cynics, and not a few of them I would imagine were more competent than I in constructing plausible arguments for virtue being sufficient for happiness. But for those in ancient times who were not convinced by their arguments, and held to the contrary view that conventional goods are necessary (if not also sufficient) for living well and being happy (*eudaimôn*), the Cynics have a simple response: *live simply, in public*. Actions speak louder than words, some people think, and for such people the Cynic is ready to prove practically that what they believe and what they preach can be demonstrated in the business of living well in the midst of austerity and privation.

---

[64] Socrates' arguments receive more comprehensive treatments in Irwin 1995, 52–60 and in Brickhouse and Smith 2000, 123–53. See also Irwin 2007, 13–44.

CYNIC CONDUCT. Of all the schools and sects of the Hellenistic and Roman periods, the Cynics were the most public. To be sure, in contrast with Epicureans who withdrew from society to live in private communities, Stoics would have been encountered teaching in marketplaces or presenting lectures open to the public.[65] But the Cynics went further. Instead of waiting for people to come to them, they took the initiative and did all they could to impose their philosophy on anyone whom they could keep within earshot. In marketplaces and forums, on street corners, at the public baths and in gymnasia, Cynics laboured hard to bring people to their senses, by the example of their very lifestyle – possessing nothing, beholden to no one, free of all encumbrances – seeking to persuade all and sundry that to live happily as nature and Zeus intended, they also should face the world as Cynics.

The Cynic, if they so chose, could of course just as well live unencumbered in solitude, by themselves or in small communities shut away from the world of men, dwelling in forest-built huts or in mountain caves – for such lives are indeed led by some. But such a life lived in solitude, the Cynic spurns, adopting in preference an overarching commitment to live in public, seeing all and being seen by all. Why?

The Cynic rejects the life of quiet solitude beyond the city, in forest hut or hillside cave, either alone in isolation or in a small community of people dedicated to the same outlook because, although such a life, to be sure, may approximate to the Cynic ideal and be free from desires for possessions and wealth, free from all encumbrances, commitments

---

[65] The founder of Stoicism, Zeno of Citium at the beginning of the third century BC for instance, lectured in a public colonnade (the *stoa poikilē*) in Athens' central marketplace (*agora*).

and anxieties, it lacks, for all that, a vital ingredient – constant public exposure.

If the Cynic is to live without fear, then they must live without fearing that in a moment of weakness they may fail their humanity and fail Zeus by bewailing the pain of their illness, say, and make themselves an enemy of nature, failing in their courage. The lure of their old life and the discomfort of their new life may make something that is *nomikos* (something conventionally good) appear desirable: they may long for health whilst in the midst of sickness, or crave food when none is to hand, or yearn for warmer clothes when winter deepens, or curse their rudimentary shelter when the cold rain beats upon their cheeks. Such lapses, if anything more than occasional and fleeting, would cast down their enterprise in ruins.

Alternatively, to live in the city, yet shut themselves away in seclusion as a recluse, carries the very same risks. So the Cynic's best strategy is to reject what is publically *nomikos*, but hold to this rejection and maintain their life of utter simplicity, condemned by the public, *in public*. The privacy of hut or cave, walls and doors, cannot then shield them from the shame of lapsing, and so the fear of failing in public will protect them from such failure.[66] The public, so deluded by what is *nomikos*, so hostile to the Cynic way, so contemptuous of it that they denounce it as 'doglike', thus becomes the Cynic's taskmaster.

No less important than the Cynic's commitment to their own salvation is their undertaking to enlighten others to the truth that human flourishing (*eudaimonia*) is found in living simply, according to nature, holding to virtue. For such a pedagogical mission to succeed, it is necessary that the

---

[66] See for instance Epictetus, *Discourses* 3.22.14–18, p. 157, below.

Cynic live in public. For it must be easy for everyone to see that it is indeed possible to live the simple life that the Cynic espouses, and in seeing that the Cynic does as a matter of fact live this life, that it is possible to live it is of course immediately demonstrated.

Diogenes of Sinope, especially, offers an example of the Cynic who does not simply carry on in the hope that people will glance his way, to notice the man who lives simply and more happily than seems warranted, to then come to him asking in wonder how such a thing is possible. His audience is right there, all the time, ready to be provoked by, attracted by, stimulated by any little thing that he might say or do. So he watches for his opportunities and takes them. Anything to shake anyone out of their lethargy and acceptance of what is *nomikos*, anything to make them think about human flourishing, why it matters, and why they haven't actually got it.

Thus, we see him for instance going about during the day, his lamp lit, saying that he is searching for a man.[67] He knows that in no time at all someone will say that men are all about him, and he will say that that is, alas, not the case, and he may then have the opportunity to explain that he is reserving the term 'man' for the person who lives according to nature, holding that only virtue is good, and that in acquiring virtue one attains *eudaimonia*, the human flourishing that everyone recognises as the proper end (*telos*) for human beings. Or else someone will indignantly respond that they are themselves (of course) a man, and Diogenes will beg to differ – and from that, perhaps sometimes, new understanding will flow.

---

[67] DL 6.41. See also DL 6.27, 6.32, 6.40.

Or, at another time, we see him going into a theatre against the flow of people who are coming out, for the entertainment has already ended.[68] And when he is challenged, he says that he has spent his entire life doing the opposite of what everyone else does, and perhaps someone will be curious enough to want to know what that means, and why someone would want to expose themselves to ridicule and abuse.

If we look at the way the life of Diogenes of Sinope is portrayed in Diogenes Laertius' account, we see that his actions can be allocated to a handful of broad, and frequently overlapping, categories. Diogenes (a) lives simply, and in so doing both (b) opposes what is *nomikos* and (c) exhorts others to likewise adopt simplicity, taking what opportunities come his way to (d) teach philosophy and extol virtue, (e) exposing the folly he sees in those around him, and doing all this in a manner that (f) draws attention to himself such that his actions and antics serve to advertise his mission to cure people of their foolishness.

His way of life is so at odds with what is customary (*nomikos*) that it is inevitable that wearing but a simple cloak, begging in public, doing without cup and spoon, and living in a wine jar will sooner or later attract someone who is bold enough, curious or puzzled or contemptuous enough to ask him why he lives like this. And he will reply that he is free, whilst his interlocutor is not; that he has no desires unfulfilled, whilst his interlocutor carries on with desires unsatisfied; that he is subject to no master, whilst his interlocutor is slave to all who have power over those things they seek or crave.

---

[68] DL 6.64.

THE RELEVANCE OF THE CYNIC OUTLOOK FOR US. For anyone to live the lifestyle of the ancient Cynics in our modern era would of course be difficult, perhaps impossible. Today, a homeless person wandering the streets, begging for food and berating people for their extravagant living would in all likelihood be arrested as mad, or as a troublemaker. In our modern world there are no temple precincts in which to take refuge, no marketplaces with welcoming colonnades for the would-be public speaker to ply his trade or to bed down as night falls. If the spirit of the ancient Cynics is to manifest today, it would have to take a very different form. The political cartoonist, the social satirist, the stand-up comedian, and perhaps also the investigative journalist or the maker of controversial documentaries may all from time to time speak with the voice of the ancient, rebellious Cynic. Closer to the physical aspect of the ancient Cynic is the political protestor or environmental activist, the person who camps out of doors, chains themselves to railings or lies down in the path of bulldozers. For such people are both asserting an opinion about something they see as wrong or misguided, and also urging their audiences to change their opinions, habits, or even their whole way of life.

But for those of us less willing to go to such extremes, if with Socrates we believe that we should concern ourselves less with what we have but with what we are, believing that what really matters for our well-being is not the quantity or value of what we possess but our striving to perfect our own goodness and wisdom[69] – for those of us who believe this, then the ancient Cynics offer inspiration and hope. For like the Cynics, we must reject what is *nomikos* (what is customary) because it is harmful. What society as a whole

---

[69] Plato, *Apology* 36c.

values, we must reject. Instead of being praised and envied for our status, possessions and power, we prefer to be appreciated for our humanity – for our forbearance and self-control, for our magnanimity and just treatment of others, for our courage in the face of troubles and adversities. For we recognise that the craving and struggle for status and possessions is what is most destructive of the human spirit, that what matters is not the satisfaction of vain desires, but the building of inner character. Vexations and troubles of all sorts will come when they will, as will sickness and infirmities, and of course death itself. But the failure of a project, the destruction of property, or the onset of illness or frailty need not overcome our disposition or undermine our good spirits. When nothing is missed, nothing is lacking, and like the Cynics of times long past, we surely fare best when we can 'be content with the works of God',[70] 'prepared for every kind of fortune'.[71]

---

[70] Pseudo-Lucian, *The Cynic* 17, p. 183, below.
[71] DL 6.63, p. 90, below.

ANTISTHENES

[6.1][72] Antisthenes was an Athenian, the son of Antisthenes. It was said, however, that he was not a legitimate Athenian, in reference to which he said to someone who was reproaching him with the circumstance, 'The mother of the Gods too is a Phrygian,'[73] – for he was thought to have had a Thracian mother.[74] On which account, as he had borne himself bravely in the battle of Tanagra,[75] he gave occasion to Socrates to say that the son of two Athenians could not have been so brave. And he himself, when disparaging the Athenians who gave themselves such great airs as having been

---

[72] The section numbering used in this edition is the standard numbering system adopted by modern scholars following that of the Loeb translation by Hicks, and *not* that of Yonge's 1853 edition. [All footnotes in the translation are mine, unless otherwise indicated. KS]

[73] In Greek mythology, the mother of the Olympian Gods and Goddesses was Rhea, wife of Cronus and daughter of Uranus and Gaia. She left her original home in Crete, fleeing to the mountains of Phrygia in Asia Minor to escape the wrath of Cronus after she deceived him in order to save their son Zeus. She was identified with Cybele, the Phrygian Great Mother. See Wikipedia 'Rhea'; Strabo 10.3.12.

[74] Antisthenes is not meaning to imply that Thracia is a part of – or the same place as – Phrygia, only that just as the mother of the Olympian Gods came from a foreign place, so too did *his* mother. If the Gods are acceptable to the Athenians, then so too should he be.

[75] A battle fought in 426 BC during the Peloponnesian War between Athens and Tanagra (which is north of Athens in Boeotia, not far from Thebes); see Thucydides, *History of the Peloponnesian War* 3.91.

born out of the earth itself,[76] said that they were no more noble in this regard than snails and locusts.

Originally he was a pupil of Gorgias the rhetorician, owing to which circumstance he employs the rhetorical style of language in his Dialogues, especially in his *Truth* and in his *Exhortations*. [6.2] And Hermippus says that he had originally intended in his address to the assembly at the Isthmian Games[77] to censure and also to praise the Athenians, and Thebans, and Lacedaemonians, but on the day he abandoned the design when he saw that there were a great many spectators come from those cities.

Afterwards, he attached himself to Socrates and made such progress in philosophy while with him that he advised all his own pupils to become his fellow pupils in the school of Socrates. And as he lived in the Piraeus,[78] he went up forty furlongs to the city[79] every day in order to hear Socrates, from whom he learnt the art of enduring, and of being indifferent to external circumstances, and so became the original founder of the Cynic school. And he used to argue that labour was a good thing, by adducing the examples of the great Heracles, and of Cyrus, the first of which examples

---

[76] The mythical first Athenian king, from whom the Athenians believed they had descended, was Erichthonius, born from the soil when Hephaestus, God of Fire, tried to make love to Athena who repulsed him, causing his semen to fall on her thigh from where she brushed it to the ground. (In another account, Hephaestus' semen ended up on the ground when he was making love to Athena, but didn't realise that she had already left the bed.)

[77] The Isthmian Games (held in honour of Poseidon) were one of the Panhellenic festivals of ancient Greece, named after the isthmus of Corinth where they were held biennially in April or May, both the year before and the year after the Olympic Games.

[78] Piraeus: the great harbour complex of Athens, about 5 miles southwest of Athens. It is labelled M, located at roughly Ae, on the Plan of Ancient Athens.

[79] That is, Athens.

he derived from the Greeks, and the other from the barbarians.

[6.3] He was also the first person who ever gave a definition of the proposition,[80] saying, 'A proposition is that which shows what anything is or was.' And he used continually to say, 'I would rather go mad than feel pleasure.' And, 'One ought to have sex with such women as will thank one for it.' He said once to a youth from Pontus[81] who was on the point of coming to him to be his pupil, and was asking him what things he would need, 'You will need a new book, a new pen, and a new tablet,' meaning a new mind.[82] And to a person who asked him what sort of wife it would be best to marry, he said, 'If you marry a beautiful woman, you won't have her to yourself. If she's ugly, you'll pay the price for it.' He was told once that Plato spoke ill of him, and he replied, 'It is a royal privilege to do well and to have evil spoken of one.'

[6.4] When he was being initiated into the mysteries of Orpheus, and the priest said that those who were initiated enjoyed many good things in Hades, he said, 'Why then don't you die?' Being once reproached as not being the son of two free citizens, he said, 'Neither am I the son of two people skilled in wrestling; but nevertheless, I am a skilful wrestler.' On one occasion he was asked why he had but few disciples, and he said, 'Because I drive them away with a silver rod.' When he was asked why he reproved his pupils with bitter language, he said, 'Physicians too use severe remedies on their patients.' Once he saw an adulterer running away, and said, 'Unhappy man! How much danger

---

[80] Translating the Greek *logos*.
[81] Pontus: a region of northern Asia Minor, having its coast on the Black Sea.
[82] Antisthenes uses an untranslatable pun here: *kainou* means 'new', and *kai nou* means 'a mind too'.

could you have avoided for one obol!'[83] He used to say, as Hecato tells us in his *Anecdotes*, 'It is better to fall among crows than among flatterers; for the first only devour the dead, but the second devour the living.'

[6.5] When he was asked what was the most happy event that could take place in human life, he said, 'To die while prosperous.'[84] On one occasion, one of his friends was lamenting to him that he had lost his notes, to which he remarked, 'You should have inscribed them on your mind instead of on paper.' A favourite saying of his was that, 'Envious people are devoured by their own disposition, just as iron is eaten away by rust.' Another was that, 'Those who wish to be immortal ought to live piously and justly.' He used to say too that, 'Cities were ruined when they were unable to distinguish worthless citizens from virtuous ones.' On one occasion he was being praised by some wicked men, and said, 'I am dreadfully afraid that I must have done some wicked thing.'

[6.6] One of his favourite sayings was that, 'The fellowship of brothers of one mind is stronger than any fortified city.' He used to say that, 'Those things are the best for a man to take on a journey which would float with him if he were shipwrecked.' He was once reproached for being intimate with wicked men, and said, 'Physicians also live with those who are sick, and yet they do not catch fevers.' He used to say that, 'It is an absurd thing to clear a corn field of weeds, and in war to get rid of unfit soldiers, and yet not to exclude wicked citizens from service to the state.' When he

---

[83] He means the price of a prostitute.

[84] Hicks translates this, 'To die happy.' The Greek term *eutuchês*, 'successful, fortunate', derives from *eu-tuchê*, 'good-fortune/fate', and refers less to the prosperity that one may earn through personal striving, and more to the advantages that fortune bestows regardless of any effort expended trying to secure such benefits.

was asked what advantage he had derived from philosophy, he replied, 'The advantage of being able to converse with myself.' At a drinking party, a man once said to him, 'Give us a song,' and he replied, 'Then you must accompany me on the flute.' When Diogenes asked him for a coat, he bade him to fold his cloak double.[85] [6.7] He was asked on one occasion what learning was the most necessary, and he replied, 'How to throw off having anything to unlearn.' And he used to exhort those who suffered slander to endure it more courageously than if someone were throwing stones at them.

He used to laugh at Plato for being conceited. Accordingly, once when there was a fine procession, seeing a horse neighing, he said to Plato, 'It seems to me that you would have made just such a proud and showy steed,' and he said this all the more because Plato kept on praising the horse. At another time, he had gone to see Plato when he was ill, and when he saw there a dish in which Plato had vomited, he said, 'I see your bile there, but I do not see your conceit.' [6.8] He used to advise the Athenians to pass a vote that asses were horses; and when they deemed this absurd, he said, 'Why, those whom you make generals have never learnt to be really generals – they have only been voted such.' A man said to him one day, 'Many people praise you.' 'Why, what evil have I done?' he asked. When he turned the rent in his cloak outside, Socrates seeing it, said to him, 'I

---

[85] See DL 6.13, where we learn that Antisthenes was the first person to adopt the custom of doubling his cloak – that is, fold it so as to make two layers of cloth. But see DL 6.22, where we are told that some people held that it was Diogenes of Sinope himself who initiated the practice of doubling the cloak.

see your vanity through the hole in your cloak.'[86] On another occasion the question was put to him by someone, as Phanias relates in his treatise *On the Philosophers of the Socratic School*, what he could do to show himself an honourable and a virtuous man,[87] and he replied, 'You must attend to those who understand the subject, and learn from them that you ought to shun the bad habits which you have.' Someone was praising luxury in his hearing, and he said, 'May the children of your enemies live in luxury.'

[6.9] Seeing a young man model for an artist in a carefully studied pose, he said, 'Tell me, if the bronze could speak, on what would it pride itself?' And when the young man replied, 'On its beauty,' he said, 'Are you not then ashamed to rejoice in the same thing as an inanimate piece of bronze?' A young man from Pontus[88] once promised to treat him with great consideration as soon as his vessel of salt fish arrived. And so he took him with him, along with an empty bag, and went to a woman who sold flour, and filling his sack he went away. When the woman asked him to pay for it, he said, 'The young man will pay you, when his vessel of salt fish arrives.'

He it was who appears to have been responsible for Anytus' banishment, and for Meletus' death. [6.10] For having met with some young men of Pontus who had come to Athens on account of the reputation of Socrates, he took them to Anytus, telling them that in moral philosophy he was wiser than Socrates. And those standing by were indignant at this, and drove Anytus out of the city. And whenever he saw a woman beautifully adorned, he would go off

---

[86] The Cynic endures hardship, and happens to endure it in public, but does not set out to make a deliberate show of it. To do so, thinks Socrates, would be vain, and would detract from one's true purpose.

[87] Translating the Greek *kalos kai agathos*.

[88] See note 81 to DL 6.3, above.

to her house and bid her husband to bring out his horse and his arms; and then if he had such things, he would give him leave to indulge in luxury, seeing that he possessed the means of defending himself. But if he did not have these things, then he would bid him strip his wife of her ornaments.

And his favourite themes were these. He used to insist that virtue can be taught, and that nobility belongs only to those virtuously disposed. [6.11] And he held that virtue was of itself sufficient for happiness, and was in need of nothing more than the strength of a Socrates. And he looked upon virtue as a matter of deeds, needing neither words nor learning. He taught that the wise man was sufficient for himself, for everything that belonged to others belonged to him. He considered ill repute a good thing,[89] and equally good with suffering.[90] And he used to say that the wise man would regulate his conduct as a citizen, not according to the established laws of the state, but according to the law of virtue.[91] And that he would marry for the sake of having children, selecting the most beautiful woman for his wife. And that he would love her, for the wise man alone knows what is deserving of love.

---

[89] This is the ill repute that the virtuous Cynic has in the eyes of the vicious non-Cynic who does not understand what virtue is, or where true well-being for human beings is to be found. To be ridiculed, insulted, or otherwise badly treated by vicious people reminds the Cynic that they are on the right path; see DL 6.5 above, for instance, where Antisthenes is worried that because some wicked men are praising him he must have done something wrong.

[90] Translating the Greek *ponos*: meaning toil, exertion, labour, but also trouble, distress, and suffering (including physical pain). Suffering is the material upon which the Cynic's virtue exercises and strengthens itself.

[91] One's conduct should not be regulated by the laws of one's community, but by one's own excellence (*aretê*, virtue), that is by the qualities perfected in one's own good character.

[6.12] Diocles also attributes the following sayings to him. To the wise man, nothing is strange and nothing difficult. The good man deserves to be loved. Good men are friends. It is right to make allies of the brave and just. Virtue is a weapon that cannot be taken away. It is better to fight with a few good men against all the wicked, than with many wicked men against a few good men. One should attend to one's enemies, for they are the first to detect one's faults. One should consider a just man as of more value than a kinsman. Virtue is the same in a man as in a woman. What is good is honourable, and what is bad is shameful. Think everything wicked as foreign and alien. [6.13] Wisdom is the most secure stronghold, for it can neither fall to pieces nor be betrayed. One must prepare for oneself a fortress in one's own impregnable thoughts.

He used to lecture in the gymnasium called the Cynosarges,[92] not far from the gates, and some people say that it is from this place that the Cynic school got its name. And he himself was called *Haplokuôn*.[93] He was the first person to set the fashion of doubling his cloak, as Diocles says, and he wore no other garment. And he used to carry a staff and a wallet; and Neanthes too says that he was the first person who wore a cloak doubled over. But Sosicrates, in the third book of his *Successions*, says that Diodorus of Aspendos was the first to do this, also letting his beard grow, and carrying a staff and a wallet.

[6.14] He is the only one of all the pupils of Socrates whom Theopompus praises and speaks of as clever, and able to persuade whomsoever he pleased by the sweetness of his

---

[92] *Kunosarges*: literally, 'white dog', or possibly 'swift dog' (see Navia 1998, 53), or perhaps 'dog's meat' (see Branham and Goulet-Cazé 1996, 4). (See also Morison 2006.) It is labelled E, located at roughly Fb, on the Plan of Ancient Athens.

[93] Literally 'Absolute Dog'.

conversation. And this is plain, both from his own writings, and from the *Symposium* of Xenophon. He appears to have been the founder of the more manly section of the Stoic school, on which account Athenaeus[94] the epigrammatist speaks thus of them:

> Ye, who learned are in Stoic fables,
> Ye who consign the wisest of all doctrines
> To your most sacred books; you say that virtue
> Is the sole good, for that alone can save
> The life of man, and strongly fenced cities.
> But if some fancy pleasure their best aim,
> One of the Muses 'tis who has convinc'd them.

[6.15] He was the original cause of the dispassion of Diogenes, the temperance of Crates, and the patience of Zeno, having himself, as it were, laid the foundations of the city which they afterwards built. And Xenophon says that in his conversation and society, he was the most delightful of men, and in every respect the most temperate.

Ten volumes of his writings are extant.

The first volume includes:

> *On Expression*, or *On Styles of Speaking*
> *Ajax*, or *The Speech of Ajax*
> *Odysseus*, or *Concerning Odysseus*
> *A Defence of Orestes*, or *Concerning Forensic Writers*
> *Isography* ['similar writing'], or *Lysias and Isocrates*
> *A reply to the Speech of Isocrates*, entitled *The Absence of Witnesses*

---

[94] This is not Athenaeus of Naucratis, the author of (the probably satirical) *The Deipnosophists* ('The Banquet of the Learned'): see Smith 1867, 1.400–2, where we find Diogenes' Athenaeus accorded a separate entry on page 400, stating that he was an epigrammatic poet mentioned in the DL text here, and also at DL 7.30.

The second volume includes:

> [6.16] *On the Nature of Animals*
> *On the Procreation of Children*, or *On Marriage* (an essay on love)
> *On the Sophists*, an essay on physiognomy
> *On Justice and Courage* (an hortative work in three books)
> *On Theognis* (making a fourth and a fifth book)

The third volume contains:

> *On the Good*
> *On Courage*
> *On Law*, or *Political Constitutions*
> *On Law*, or *On Goodness and Justice*
> *On Freedom and Slavery*
> *On Good Faith*
> *On the Guardian*, or *On Persuasion*
> *On the Mastery of Thrift*

The fourth volume contains:

> *Cyrus*
> *The Greater Heracles*, or *On Strength*.

The fifth volume contains:

> *Cyrus*, or *On Sovereignty*
> *Aspasia*

The sixth volume contains:

> *Truth*
> *On Discussion* (a handbook on debate)

> *Satho*, or *On Contradiction* (three books)
> *On Speech*

The seventh contains:

> [6.17] *On Education*, or *Names* (five books)
> *On the Use of Names* (a controversial work)
> *On Questions and Answers*
> *On Opinion and Knowledge* (four books)
> *On Dying*
> *On Life and Death*
> *On Those in the Underworld*
> *On Nature* (two books)
> *Questions in Natural Philosophy* (two books)
> *On Opinions*, or *The Contentious Man*
> *On Problems about Learning*

The eighth volume includes:

> *On Music*
> *On Commentators*
> *On Homer*
> *On Injustice and Impiety*
> *On Calchas*
> *On the Scout*
> *On Pleasure*

The ninth book contains:

> *On the Odyssey*
> *On the Staff*[95]

---

[95] Translating the Greek *rabdos*, which can be a magic wand, a staff of office, a rod for chastisement, or a shepherd's crook; also used for streaks and stripes on the skins of animals, the fluting of a column, and shafts of light.

> *Athena*, or *On Telemachus*
> *On Helen and Penelope*
> *On Proteus*
> *Cyclops*, or *On Odysseus*
> [6.18] *On the Use of Wine*, or *On Drunkenness*, or *On the Cyclops*
> *On Circe*
> *On Amphiaraus*
> *On Odysseus, Penelope, and the Dog*

The tenth volume contains:

> *Heracles*, or *Midas*
> *Heracles*, or *On Wisdom* or *On Strength*
> *Cyrus* or *The Beloved*
> *Cyrus*, or *The Scouts*
> *Menexenus*, or *On Ruling*
> *Alcibiades*
> *Archelaus*, or *On Kingship*

Those then are the titles of his works.

And Timon, rebuking him because of their great number, called him a prolific babbler. He died of some disease, and while he was ill Diogenes came to visit him and asked of him, 'Have you need of a friend?' Once too when Diogenes came to see him with a dagger in his hand, and Antisthenes said, 'Who can deliver me from this suffering?' he pointed to the dagger and said, 'This can.' But Antisthenes replied, 'I said from suffering, not from life;' [6.19] for he seemed to show some weakness in bearing his disease through his love of life. And there is an epigram which I have written on him, which runs thus:

> In life you were a bitter dog, Antisthenes,

> Born to bite people's minds with sayings sharp,
> Not with your actual teeth. Now you are slain
> By fell consumption, passers-by may say,
> Why should he not; one wants a guide to Hades.

There were also three other people having the name Antisthenes. One was a disciple of Heraclitus, the second was from Ephesus, and the third was a historian from Rhodes. And since we have spoken of those who proceeded from the school of Aristippus and Phaedo,[96] we may now go on to the Cynics and Stoics,[97] who derived their origin from Antisthenes. And we will take them in the following order.

---

[96] In Book Two of the *Lives*.

[97] The Cynics occupy Book Six of the *Lives* (included in this present volume), and the Stoics occupy Book Seven of the *Lives* (see Yonge and Seddon 2007).

DIOGENES

[6.20] Diogenes was a native of Sinope, the son of Hicesias, a banker. And Diocles says that he was forced to flee from his native city, as his father kept the public bank there, and had defaced[98] the currency.[99] But Eubulides, in his essay on Diogenes, says that it was Diogenes himself who did this, and that he was banished with his father. And, indeed, he himself, in his *Pordalus*, says of himself that he had defaced the public money. Others say that he was one of the curators, and was persuaded by the artisans employed, and that

---

[98] Translating *paracharassô*, meaning to re-stamp, re-value, or debase the currency, probably referring in this instance to putting counterfeit coins out of circulation.

[99] Numismatic research reveals some interesting facts. Navia (1998, 23) reports that it is known that a man named Hicesias was indeed responsible for the minting of coins in Sinope sometime around the first half of the 4th century BC, and that around the year 350 BC a large proportion of defaced and counterfeit coins were in fact in circulation. Many Sinopean coins from this period show the city's seal on the front side and the engraver's name on the reverse side, and this name is ΙΚΕΣΙΟ, the name Diogenes Laertius records as the name of Diogenes of Sinope's father. Furthermore, many of these coins show signs of having been deliberately defaced or damaged, suggesting the possibility that someone made a concerted effort to put a large number of coins out of circulation. Further evidence as to the possible truth behind any of the various accounts that Diogenes Laertius offers in this opening paragraph is sadly lacking. The intriguing possibility is that Diogenes was indeed, in one way or another, intimately connected to the defacing of Sinope's coins, if not as perpetrator himself, then as his father's accomplice or accessory.

he went to Delphi, or else to the oracle at Delos, and there consulted Apollo as to whether he should do what people were trying to persuade him to do; and that, as the god gave him permission to do so, Diogenes, not comprehending that the god meant that he might change the political customs[100] of his country if he could, ruined the coins; and being detected, was banished, as some people say, but as other accounts have it, took the alarm and fled away of his own accord. [6.21] Some again say that he spoilt the money which he had received from his father, and that his father was thrown into prison and died there, but that Diogenes escaped and went to Delphi and asked not whether he should tamper with the coinage, but what he should do to gain the greatest reputation, and that in consequence he received the oracle's answer which I have mentioned.

And when he came to Athens he attached himself to Antisthenes who [at first] drove him away, because he did not take on pupils, but through sheer persistence Diogenes wore him down. And once, when Antisthenes raised his stick to him, Diogenes put his head under it and said, 'Strike, for you will not find any stick hard enough to drive me away as long as I think you have something to say.'[101] And from that time forward Diogenes was one of his pupils;

---

[100] The passage is not free from difficulty; but the thing which misled Diogenes appears to have been that *nomisma*, the word here used, meant both 'a coin, or coinage,' and 'a custom' [Yonge].

[101] Cf. Aelian (*Historical Miscellany* 10.16, trans. Wilson): 'When Antisthenes had pressed many people to take up philosophy and they paid no attention, he finally became angry and would receive no one. So he even dismissed Diogenes from his company. But when Diogenes became rather tenacious and insistent, he went so far as to threaten him with his stick, and once even struck him on the head. Diogenes did not go away, and persisted still more energetically, as he was very anxious to follow his lectures, saying: "Hit me if you wish, and I shall lay my head in front of you; but you will not find a stick hard enough to drive me away from your lectures." Antisthenes was delighted with him.'

and being an exile, he naturally set out upon a simple way of life.

[6.22] And when, as Theophrastus tells us in his *Megarian* dialogue, he saw a mouse running about and not seeking for a bed, nor afraid of the dark, nor longing for any of those things which appear enjoyable, he found a remedy for his own circumstances.[102] He was, according to the account of some people, the first person who doubled up his cloak out of necessity, and who slept in it; and who carried a wallet in which he kept his food; and who used whatever place was near at hand for all sorts of purposes – for eating, and sleeping, and conversing in. In reference to which habit he used to point to the Colonnade of Zeus and to the Hall of Processions,[103] saying that the Athenians had built him places to live in. [6.23] He did not support himself with a staff until he became infirm; but afterwards, he carried it continually, not in the city to be sure, but whenever he was walking on the roads, together with his wallet, as Olympiodorus (who was once an Athenian magistrate), and Polyeuctus the orator, and Lysanias the son of Aeschrio, all tell. He had written to someone asking that they provide a small house for him, but because this person was a long

---

[102] This incident is also reported by Aelian (*Historical Miscellany* 13.26, trans. Wilson): 'Diogenes of Sinope lived alone and rejected by the world. He was too poor to entertain anyone, and no one invited him. He was avoided because of his carping manner and his dissatisfaction with everything that was said or done. So Diogenes was miserable and ate barley-bread and green shoots – that was what he had. A mouse used to come and take crumbs of his bread. Diogenes watched closely what was happening, smiled and became more cheerful and contented than he had been, remarking: "This mouse does not need any of the luxuries of the Athenians, but you, Diogenes, are annoyed at not dining with Athenians." And he provided himself with timely comfort.'

[103] The public storehouse in which were keep the vessels employed in processions. Presumably Diogenes did not find shelter inside the building itself, but camped out in the portico.

time going about it, he took a large wine jar[104] which he found in the Metroön,[105] and used it for his house, as he himself tells us in his letters. And during the summer he used to roll it over the hot sand, whilst in winter he would embrace statues all covered with snow, training himself at every opportunity to endure anything.

[6.24] He was vehement in expressing his disdain of others. He said that the school of Euclides was bilious, and he used to call Plato's lectures a waste of time. It was also a saying of his that the Dionysian Games were a great marvel to fools; and that popular leaders[106] were merely the lackeys of the mob.[107] He used to say likewise that when in the course of his life he beheld pilots, and physicians, and philosophers, he thought man the wisest of all animals; but when again he beheld interpreters of dreams, and soothsayers, and those who listened to them, and men puffed up with glory or riches, then he thought that there was not a more foolish animal than man. He also used to say repeatedly that what was most needed in the course of life was either right reason or a noose.

[6.25] On one occasion, when he noticed Plato at a very lavish entertainment tasting some olives, he said, 'O you wise man! Why, after having sailed to Sicily for the sake of

---

[104] Translating the Greek *pithos*. Such a jar, sometimes as tall or taller than a person, was usually made of earthenware, moulded from clay supported on a wooden frame (the frame would burn away during firing). The story of Diogenes living in one suggests that sometimes they were made of such a size that a man could easily get inside – and indeed, some archaeological remains suggest volumes of up to two cubic metres could be attained, which is more than adequate for a *pithos*-dweller to rest in comfort for long periods.

[105] *Mêtrôon*: the Temple of Cybele at Athens, used as the depository for the state archives.

[106] Translating *dêmagôgos*.

[107] This phrase is repeated again at DL 6.41.

such a feast, do you not now enjoy what you have before you?' And Plato replied, 'By the Gods, Diogenes, while I was there I ate olives and all such things a great deal.' Diogenes rejoined, 'What then did you want to sail to Syracuse for? Did not Attica at that time produce any olives?' But Favorinus in his *Miscellaneous History* attributes this story to Aristippus. At another time he was eating dried figs when Plato met him, and he said to him, 'You may have a share of these.' And as Plato took some and ate them, he remarked, 'I said that you might have a share of them, not that you might eat all of them.'

[6.26] On one occasion Plato had invited some friends who had come to him from Dionysius, and Diogenes trampled on his cushions,[108] saying, 'Thus I trample on the empty pride of Plato.' And Plato answered him, 'How much arrogance you display, Diogenes, when you think that you are not arrogant at all!' But, as others tell the story, what Diogenes said was, 'Thus I trample on the arrogance of Plato,' And Plato rejoined, 'Yes, Diogenes, with quite as much arrogance of another sort.' (Sotion, however, in his fourth book[109] states that the Cynic addressed his remark directly to Plato.[110]) Diogenes once asked him for some wine, and then for some dried figs, so Plato sent him an entire jar full; and Diogenes said to him, 'Will you, if you are asked how many two and two make, answer twenty? In this way, you neither give with any reference to what you are asked for, nor do you answer with reference to the question put to you.' He used also to ridicule him as an interminable talker.

---

[108] Translating the Greek *strôma*, used of anything spread or laid out for lying or sitting on, including as well as cushions, the coverings of dinner-couches, bedclothes, mattress, bed, and so forth.

[109] In his *Succession of the Philosophers*.

[110] Rather than to the visiting friends, presumably.

[6.27] When he was asked where in Greece he saw good men, he said, 'Men – nowhere; but I see good boys in Lacedaemon.' On one occasion, when no one came to listen to him while he was discoursing seriously, he began to whistle. And then when people flocked round him, he reproached them for coming with eagerness to folly, but being lazy and indifferent when the theme was serious. One of his frequent sayings was that men contended with one another in punching[111] and kicking, but that no one showed any effort in the pursuit of an excellent[112] character. He used to express his astonishment at the grammarians who investigated the misfortunes of Odysseus whilst being ignorant of their own, and also at the musicians who tuned the strings of their lyres properly but left all the habits of their souls discordant, [6.28] and at the mathematicians who kept their eyes fixed on the sun and moon but overlooked what was under their feet, and at orators who were anxious to speak about justice but not at all about practising it, and at the avaricious who spoke out against money whilst being inordinately fond of it. He often condemned those who praise the just for being superior to money, but who at the same time are eager themselves for great riches. He was also very indignant at seeing men sacrifice to the Gods to procure good health, and yet at the sacrifice eating in a manner injurious to health. He often expressed his surprise at slaves, who, seeing their masters eating in a gluttonous manner, still do not themselves lay hands on any of the food. [6.29] He would frequently praise those who were about to marry,

---

[111] Translating *parorussô*, which Hicks thinks should be translated 'digging'. His note to this word reads: 'From Epictetus [*Discourses*] 3.15.4 it is evident that competition in digging trenches formed a part of the course of preparation which athletes underwent at Olympia.'

[112] Translating *kalokagathos*, denoting a character and conduct that is noble, good, and honourable.

and then did not marry; or who were about to take a voyage, and then did not take a voyage; or who were about to engage in affairs of state, and did not do so; and those who were about to rear children, then did not rear any; and those who were preparing to live with rulers, and then did not go to them. One of his sayings was that one ought to hold out one's hand to a friend without closing the fingers.[113] Hermippus,[114] in his *Sale of Diogenes*, says that he was taken prisoner and put up to be sold, and when asked what he could do, he answered, 'Govern men.' And so he told the auctioneer to announce that if anyone wanted to purchase a master for himself, there was one here for him. When he was ordered not to sit down, he said, 'It makes no difference, for fish are sold in whatever position they lie.' [6.30] He used to say that he wondered at men always ringing a dish or jar before buying it, but being content to judge of a man on his looks alone. When Xeniades bought him, he said to him that he ought to obey him even though he was his slave, for a physician or a pilot would find men to obey them even though they also might be slaves. And Eubulus says in his essay entitled *The Sale of Diogenes*, that he taught the children of Xeniades, after their other lessons, to ride, and shoot with the bow, and sling stones, and throw javelins. And then in the gymnasium he did not permit the trainer to exercise them after the fashion of athletes, but exercised them himself to just the degree sufficient to give them a good colour and good health.

---

[113] Meaning, presumably, that is, one should give magnanimously to others no less enthusiastically than one receives from them.

[114] The Greek text of the Didot edition (Paris, 1850) has the name Menippus here, and not that of Hermippus, which appears in the Huebner edition (Leipsic, 1828) upon which Yonge based his translation. Hermippus may be the better option, as a book titled *Sale of Diogenes* does not appear in the list of books by Menippus at DL 6.101, below.

[6.31] And the boys learned by heart many passages from poets and prose writers, and of Diogenes himself; and he used to give them concise summaries of everything that were easily remembered; and at home he used to teach them to wait upon themselves,[115] contenting themselves with plain food, and drinking water. And he accustomed them to cut their hair close, and to avoid ornament, and to go without tunics or shoes, and to keep silent, looking at nothing except themselves as they walked along. He used also to take them out hunting; and they paid the greatest attention and respect to Diogenes himself, and spoke well of him to their parents. And the same author affirms that he grew old in the household of Xeniades, and that when he died he was buried by his sons. And that while he was living with him, Xeniades once asked him how he should bury him; and he said, 'On my face.' [6.32] And when he was asked why, he said, 'Because, in a little while, everything will be turned upside-down.' And he said this because the Macedonians were already attaining power, and becoming a mighty people from having been insignificant. Once, when a man had conducted him into a magnificent house, and had told him that he must not spit, after hawking a little, he spat in his face, saying that he could not find a meaner receptacle. (But some tell this story of Aristippus.) Once, he called out, 'Come, men!' And when some people gathered round him in consequence, he drove them away with his staff, saying, 'I called for men – not dregs.' This anecdote I have derived from Hecato, in the first book of his *Anecdotes*. They also relate that Alexander said that if he had not been Alexander, he would have liked to have been Diogenes.

---

[115] That is, to do without the services of slaves.

[6.33] He used to call disabled, not those who were dumb and blind, but those who had no wallet.[116] On one occasion he went half shaved into an entertainment of young men, as Metrocles tells us in his *Anecdotes*, and so was beaten by them. And afterwards he wrote on a white tablet the names of all those who had beaten him, and went about with the tablet round his neck, so as to expose them to insult, and thus brought upon them condemnation and reproach for their conduct. He used to say that he was the hound that everyone praised, but that none of those who praised him dared to go out hunting with him. A man once said to him, 'I defeated men at the Pythian Games,' to which he said, 'I defeat men, but you only defeat slaves.'[117]

[6.34] When some people said to him, 'You are an old man, and should rest for the remainder of your life,' he replied, 'Why is that? Suppose I had run a long distance, ought I to stop when I was near the end, and not rather press on?' Once, when he was invited to a banquet, he said that he would not come, for the last time he had gone, the host had not thanked him for coming. He used to go barefoot through the snow, and to do a number of other things which have been already mentioned.[118] Once he attempted to eat raw meat, but he could not digest it. On one occasion he found Demosthenes the orator dining in an inn, and as he tried to duck out of sight, Diogenes said to him, 'Thus all

---

[116] 'Disabled' translates *anapêros*, and 'wallet' translates *pêra*. There is a pun here that cannot be rendered in English. All those who are not Cynics (who do not carry a wallet), Diogenes calls 'disabled'. Facetious though his remark is (in keeping, to be sure, with the Cynic attitude), it makes the serious point that those who do not understand the true nature of the good and virtue are handicapped in character.

[117] Diogenes makes a similar retort about Dioxippus at DL 6.43.

[118] We have already learned that Diogenes would endure the summer heat in his *pithos*, and in winter embrace frozen statues (DL 6.23).

the more will you be inside the inn.'[119] Once, when some strangers wished to see Demosthenes, he stretched out his middle finger, and said, 'This is the great demagogue of the Athenians.' [6.35] When someone had dropped a loaf, and was ashamed to pick it up again, he, wishing to give him a lesson, tied a cord around the neck of a bottle and dragged it all through the Ceramicus.[120]

He used to say that he imitated the teachers of choruses, for they set the note a little high, in order that the rest might reach the right note. Another of his sayings was that most men were within a finger's breadth of being mad. If, then, anyone were to walk along stretching out his middle finger, he will seem to be mad; but if he puts out his forefinger, he will not be thought so.[121] Another of his sayings was that things of great value were often sold for nothing, and vice versa. Accordingly, a statue can fetch three thousand drachmas, and a bushel of meal only two obols.

[6.36] And when Xeniades had bought him, he said to him, 'Come, do what I order you to do.' And when Xeniades said in reply:

---

[119] *pandokeion*: inn, tavern, literally 'receive-all' suggests Desmond, possibly 'a rough place where customers could get cheap wine, prostitutes, fleas, black eyes and worse' (2008, 109). To avoid a scandal, Demosthenes tries to avoid being spotted in the inn by concealing himself in the inn. Another version of this incident is reported by Aelian (*Historical Miscellany* 9.19, trans. Wilson): 'Diogenes was having a meal in a bar one day, and called out to Demosthenes as he passed by. When the latter did not listen, he said, "Demosthenes, are you ashamed to enter a bar? Yet your master comes in here every day," referring to the public and individual citizens. He was making it plain that politicians and public speakers are slaves of the people.'

[120] Ceramicus: large, loosely defined area of north-west Athens, incorporating the potters' quarter. The name is sometimes intended to refer to the famous extramural cemetery, including the *Demosion Sema* (public burial-ground). See OCD 'Ceramicus'.

[121] It would seem that holding out one's middle finger was no less rude and offensive in Diogenes' time than it is in our own.

> The streams of sacred rivers now
> Run backwards to their source!¹²²

Diogenes replied, saying, 'Suppose you had been sick, and had bought a physician, would you refuse to be guided by him, and tell him "The streams of sacred rivers now run backwards to their source"?'

Once a man came to him, and wished to study philosophy as his pupil; and he gave him a fish to carry, and made him follow him. And from shame he threw it away and departed, but soon afterwards [Diogenes] met him and, laughing, said to him, 'A fish has broken your friendship for me.' But Diocles tells this story in the following manner, that when someone said to him, 'Charge me with a task, Diogenes,' he took him off and gave him a half-obol worth of cheese to carry. And as he refused to carry it, Diogenes said, 'See, a half-obol worth of cheese has broken our friendship.'

[6.37] On one occasion he saw a child drinking out of its hands, and so he threw away the cup which he kept in his wallet, saying, 'That child has beaten me in simplicity.' He also threw away his spoon, after seeing a boy who had broken his bowl, take up his lentils with a crust of bread. And he used to argue thus, 'Everything belongs to the gods; and wise men are the friends of the gods. All things are in common among friends; therefore everything belongs to wise men.' Once he saw a woman falling down before the Gods in an unbecoming attitude; wishing to cure her of her superstition, as Zoilus of Perga tells us, he came up to her and said, 'Are you not afraid, woman, to be in such an indecent

---

¹²² Euripides, *Medea* 410. It would have been appropriate for Xeniades to quote also the very next line, which reads: 'Tradition, order, all things are reversed' (trans.Vellacott), for Diogenes the slave believes that he is now the master.

attitude, when some God may be behind you? For every place is full of him, and you might disgrace yourself.' [6.38] He consecrated a man to Asclepius, who was to run up and beat all those who prostrated themselves with their faces to the ground. And he was in the habit of saying that all the curses of tragedy had come upon him, for he was

> Houseless, without a city, a piteous exile
> From his dear native land; a wandering beggar,
> Scraping a pittance poor from day to day.[123]

And another of his sayings was that he opposed courage to fortune, nature to convention, and reason to passion.[124] Once, while he was sitting in the sun in the Craneum, Alexander was standing by, and said to him, 'Ask of me any favour you choose.' And he replied, 'Stop casting your shadow over me.' On one occasion a man was reading some long passages, and when he came to the end of the book and showed that there was nothing more written, Diogenes exclaimed, 'Be of good cheer, my friends! There's land in sight!' A man once proved to him syllogistically that he had horns, so he put his hand to his forehead and said, 'I do not see them.' [6.39] And in a similar manner he replied to someone who had been asserting that there was no such thing as motion, by getting up and walking away. When a man was talking about the heavenly bodies and meteors, he said to him, 'Tell us – how many days has it been since you came down from heaven?' A eunuch of bad character had written upon his own door, 'Let no evil thing enter here.' 'How, then,' asked Diogenes, 'is the master of the house going to get in?' After having spread ointment over his feet, he said that the perfume from his head rose up to heaven,

---

[123] Cf. Aelian, *Historical Miscellany* 3.29.
[124] Translating *tharsos/tuchê, phusis/nomos, logos/pathê*. See DL 6.71.

whereas that from his feet rose up to his nose. When the Athenians entreated him to be initiated in the Eleusinian mysteries,[125] saying that in the shades below the initiated had the best seats, he replied, 'It will be an absurd thing if Agesilaus and Epaminondas are to live in the mud, whilst some miserable wretches, just because they have been initiated, are to dwell in the Isles of the Blessed.'[126]

[6.40] Some mice crept up to his table, and he said, 'See, even Diogenes maintains his hangers-on.' Once, when he was leaving the public baths and a man asked him whether

---

[125] The Eleusinian Mysteries, the most famous of the secret religious rites of ancient Greece, were based on the myth of the earth goddess Demeter who descended to the underworld in search of her daughter Persephone who had been abducted by Hades. The sacred rites which comprised the Mysteries lasted for several days, and culminated when the initiates went in procession from Athens to Eleusis (a journey of some 14 miles), where in the Telesterion (Hall of Initiation) they performed rites which have, for all time, remained secret. 'Something was recited, something was revealed, and acts were performed, but there is no sure evidence of what the rites actually were ... It is clear, however, that neophytes were initiated in stages and that the annual process began with purification rites at what were called the Lesser Mysteries held at Agrai (Agrae) on the stream of Ilissos, outside of Athens, in the month of Anthesterion (February–March). The Greater Mysteries at Eleusis was celebrated annually in the month of Boedromion (September–October). It included a ritual bath in the sea, three days of fasting, and completion of the still-mysterious central rite. These acts completed the initiation, and the initiate was promised benefits of some kind in the afterlife' ('Eleusinian Mysteries' in *Encyclopædia Britannica. Encyclopædia Britannica 2007 Deluxe Edition*. Chicago: Encyclopædia Britannica, 2007). The story of Demeter and Persephone is recounted by Hesiod in *The Homeric Hymn to Demeter* (see Hine 2005, 98–114).

[126] Zeus created a fourth generation of mankind, a race of heroes, most of whom died in a series of wars (including the Trojan war), but some did not die, and these

Others, however, the son of Cronus decided to grant a
Dwelling place far from men at the furthermost ends of the earth, and
There they continued to live, their consciousness perfectly carefree,
There in the Isles of the Blessed, beside deep-eddying Ocean...
(Hesiod, *Works and Days* 161–4, trans. Hine)

many men were bathing, he said, 'No.' But to someone else who asked if there was a great crowd of bathers, he confessed that there were indeed a great many. When Plato called him a dog, he said, 'Undoubtedly, for I have come back to those who sold me.' Plato defined man as a bipedal, featherless animal, and was much praised for the definition; so Diogenes plucked a cock and brought it into his school, and said, 'Here is Plato's man.' In consequence of which this addition was made to the definition: 'With broad, flat nails.' A man once asked him what was the proper time for supper, and he answered, 'If you are a rich man, whenever you please; and if you are a poor man, whenever you can.'

[6.41] When he was at Megara he saw some sheep carefully covered over with skins,[127] and the children running about naked; and so he said, 'It is better at Megara to be a man's ram, than his son.'[128] A man once struck him with a beam of wood, and then said, 'Watch out!' 'What,' he said, 'are you going to strike me again?' He used to say that popular leaders[129] were merely the lackeys of the mob;[130] and the garlands with which they were crowned were like erupting pustules. He lit a lamp and went about in broad daylight looking this way and that, saying, 'I am searching for a man.' On one occasion he stood under a fountain, and as the bystanders were pitying him, Plato, who was present, said to them, 'If you really wish to show your pity for him, come away,' intimating that he was only acting in this way out of a desire for notoriety. Once, when a man had struck

---

[127] Hicks includes this note: 'Where the wool was of fine quality ... the fleeces were protected by coverings of skin, partly against damage from brambles and partly to preserve the colour.'

[128] Cf. Aelian, *Historical Miscellany* 12.56.

[129] Translating *dêmagôgos*.

[130] This phrase is repeated from DL 6.24 (the Greek is *tous men dêmagôgous ochlou diakonous*).

him with his fist, he said, 'O Heracles, what a strange thing that I should be walking about with a helmet on without knowing it!' [6.42] When Midias struck him with his fist and said, 'There are three thousand drachmas for you,' the next day Diogenes put on the cestus[131] of a boxer and beat him soundly, and said, 'There are three thousand drachmas for you.'[132] When Lysias the drug-seller asked him if he believed in the Gods, he said, 'How can I help thinking so, when I consider you to be hated by them?' (But some attribute this reply to Theodorus.) Once he saw a man purifying himself by washing, and said to him, 'Oh, wretched man, do you not know that just as you cannot wash away blunders in grammar by purification, neither can you efface the errors of conduct in the same manner?' He used to say that men were wrong to complain of their fortune, for they pray to the Gods for what appear to be good things, not for what are really so. [6.43] And of those who were frightened by their dreams, he said that while they care nothing for what they do while they are awake, they make a great fuss about what they fancy they see while they are asleep. Once, at the Olympic Games, when the herald proclaimed, 'Dioxippus is the conqueror of men,' he said, 'He is the conqueror of slaves. I am the conqueror of men.'[133]

He was greatly loved by the Athenians. Accordingly, when a youth had broken his jar[134] they beat him, and gave Diogenes another one. And Dionysius the Stoic says that

---

[131] cestus (a Latin word, translating the Greek *imantion*): a tough thong of leather wound around the wrists and hands of boxers.

[132] This is probably an allusion to a prosecution instituted by Demosthenes against Midias, which was afterwards compromised by Midias paying Demosthenes thirty minæ, or three thousand drachmæ. See Dem. Or. cont. Midias [Yonge].

[133] Diogenes makes the same retort about somebody else at DL 6.33.

[134] Translating the Greek *pithos*. This is presumably the same jar that has already appeared at DL 6.23.

after the battle of Chaeronea he was taken prisoner and brought to Philip;[135] and being asked who he was replied, 'A spy, here to spy upon your insatiability,' for which Philip admired him, and let him go.

[6.44] Once, when Alexander had sent a letter to Athens to Antipater, by the hands of a man named Athlios, Diogenes, being present, said,

> Wretched son of wretched sire to wretched wight by wretched squire.[136]

When Perdiccas threatened that he would put him to death if he did not come to him, he replied, 'That's not so very impressive, for a scorpion or a tarantula could do as much: you would do better to threaten me that, if I were to keep away, you would be very happy.' He used constantly to repeat with emphasis that an easy life had been given to man by the Gods, but that it had been laid aside by their seeking for honey, cheese-cakes, and unguents, and things of that sort. On which account he said to a man whose shoes were being put on by his servant, 'You are not thoroughly happy unless he also wipes your nose for you; and he will do this, when you have lost the use of your hands.'[137]

[6.45] On one occasion, when he had seen the officials leading away one of the stewards who had stolen a goblet,

---

[135] This is Philip II of Macedonia who, in 388 BC at the battle of Chaeronea, won a decisive victory over the Greek alliance led by Athens and Thebes, in effect bringing to an end the era of the independent Greek *polis*.

[136] Following Hicks, who, however, prefers 'graceless' to 'wretched' for the Greek *athlios*, which means unhappy, miserable, wretched, pitiful. The Greek for this quotation is: *athlios par' athliou di' athliou pros athlion*, which makes fun of Athlios' name being the same as the Greek adjective *athlios*. Diogenes means '*athlios*' to refer respectively to the son (Alexander), his father (Philip), the recipient (Antipater), and the messenger (Athlios).

[137] He means through lack of use, not old age or disease.

he said, 'The great thieves are carrying off the little thief.' At another time, seeing a young man throwing stones at a gallows, he said, 'Well done! You will be sure to reach the mark.'[138] Once, too, some boys got round him and said, 'We are taking care that you do not bite us,' to which he said, 'Be of good cheer, my boys, a dog does not eat beetroot.'[139] He saw a man giving himself airs because he was clad in a lion's skin, and said to him, 'Do not go on dishonouring such an excellent garment.'[140] When people were speaking of the happiness of Callisthenes, and saying what splendid treatment he received from Alexander, he replied, 'The man then is wretched, for he is forced to breakfast and dine whenever Alexander chooses.'

[6.46] When he was in need of money, he did not ask for alms from his friends, but instead demanded back from them what was his due. On one occasion he was working with his hands[141] in the marketplace, and said, 'I wish I could rub my stomach in the same way, and so avoid hunger.' When he saw a young man going with some wealthy men[142] to supper, he dragged him away and led him off to his relations, and bade them take care of him. He was once addressed by a youth beautifully adorned, who asked him

---

[138] He means that the boy will himself one day die.

[139] The use of the term 'beetroot' is, I suspect, a euphemistic obscenity. It occurs again, below, at DL 6.61.

[140] The mythological hero Heracles, much revered by the Cynics, is depicted as wearing a lion's skin.

[141] This is a literal translation of the Greek *cheirourgeô*, meaning to do something with the hand, make something by hand, or more generally practise some art, or even operate (on a patient), and appears to be a reference to masturbation, which is why Hicks renders this verb, 'behaving indecently'. (See also DL 6.69, below.)

[142] Translating the Greek *satrapês*, 'satrap', literally a Persian governor of a province. The term is probably used here derogatorily, consistent with the general Cynic outlook of disapproving of wealth and disapproving especially of people who think it important.

some question; and he refused to give him any answer until he had lifted his clothes to prove whether he was a man or a woman. And on one occasion, when a youth was playing *cottabos*[143] in the bath, he said to him, 'The better you do it, the worse you do it.' Once at a banquet, some of the guests threw him bones, as if he had been a dog; so as he went away, he put up his leg against them as if he really was a dog.[144]

[6.47] He used to call the orators, and all those who speak for fame 'thrice human',[145] meaning thereby 'thrice wretched'.[146] He said that a rich but ignorant man was like a sheep with a golden fleece. When he saw a notice on the house of a profligate man, TO BE SOLD, he said 'I knew that after such drunken revelry, you would soon vomit up your owner.' To a young man who was complaining of the number of people who sought his acquaintance, he said, 'Do not make such a show of your availability.' Having been in a very dirty bath, he said, 'I wonder where the people who bathe here clean themselves.' When all the company was finding fault with an overweight harp-player, he alone praised him, and being asked why he did so, he said, 'Because, although he is of such a size as he is, he plays the harp and does not steal.' [6.48] He saluted a harp player who was always deserted by his audience with, 'Greetings,

---

[143] *cottabos*: a sort of drinking game originating in Sicily which had several different forms, its main component being the throwing of the dregs of one's glass or cup at a metal bowl serving as a target (see Liddell and Scott 1996, '*kottabos*'; and Smith 1870, 366–7). In order to make ready the dregs, the players would have to drain their cups first. The inevitable outcome was that players would get drunk. Thus Diogenes' comment: 'the better you do it' meaning 'the more you drink', and 'the worse you do it' meaning 'the less often you hit the target'.

[144] That is, he urinated on them.

[145] *trisanthrôpoi*.

[146] *trisathlioi*.

cockerel!' And when the man asked him why he did so, he said, 'Because when you sing, you make everyone get up.' When a young man was one day making a speech, Diogenes, who was standing right opposite, having filled the folds of his robe with lupins, began to eat them; and when he had drawn everyone's attention, he remarked on his surprise that they should have abandoned the young man to look at him instead. And when a man, who was very superstitious, said to him, 'With one blow I will break your head,' he replied, 'And I, with one sneeze through my left nostril will make you tremble.'[147] When Hegesias asked that he lend him one of his books, he said, 'You are very foolish, Hegesias, for you would not take painted figs, but real ones; and yet you overlook genuine training,[148] and seek for what is merely written.'

[6.49] A man once reproached him with his banishment, and his answer was, 'You wretched man, that is what made me a philosopher!' And when, on another occasion, someone said to him, 'The people of Sinope condemned you to banishment,' he replied, 'And I condemned them to remain where they were.' Once he saw a man who had been victor at the Olympic Games tending sheep, and he said to him, 'Too quickly, my good friend, have you left Olympia for Nemea.'[149] When he was asked why athletes are insensible

---

[147] Left was the direction of ill omen, 'because to a Greek, looking northward, unlucky signs came from the left' (Liddell and Scott 'ἀριστερός 3.'). See for instance Homer, *Odyssey* 20.240–6, where Amphinomus, after an eagle flew across from the left, urged the abandoning of the plot to slay Telemachus.

[148] Translating *askêsis*.

[149] This is a reference to the Nemean Games, reorganized as a Panhellenic festival in 573 BC and held in July every second and fourth year in each Olympiad in the sanctuary of Zeus at Nemea (in the north-eastern Peloponnese), possibly held to commemorate Heracles' legendary killing of the Nemean lion. The Nemean Games it seemed lacked the prestige of

to pain,¹⁵⁰ he said, 'Because they are built up of pork and beef.' He once begged alms from a statue; and being questioned as to his reason for doing so, he said, 'I am practising being disappointed.' When begging for alms (for he did this at first out of actual want), he used to say, 'If you have given to anyone else, give also to me; and if you have never given to anyone, then begin with me.'

[6.50] On one occasion he was asked by a tyrant as to what sort of bronze was the best for a statue, to which he replied, 'That of which the statues of Harmodius and Aristogiton are made.' When he was asked how Dionysius treats his friends, he said, 'Like bags. Those which are full he hangs up, and those which are empty he throws away.' A man who was recently married put an inscription on his house,

> The son of Zeus, victorious Heracles
> Lives here; let no evil enter in.

And so Diogenes wrote in addition, 'After war, alliance.'¹⁵¹ He used to say that avariciousness was the metropolis of all evils.¹⁵² Seeing on one occasion a spendthrift in an inn

---

the Olympic Games. There is a pun here on the Greek verb *nemô* (tend, pasture, graze) and *Nemea*.

¹⁵⁰ 'insensible to pain' translates the Greek *anaisthêtos*, which can mean 'without sense' or 'without feeling', but also 'without perception', 'without common sense', or 'stupid' – the latter being favoured by Hicks. The noun, *anaisthesia*, is of course the origin for our modern English usage of 'anaesthesia'.

¹⁵¹ Desmond (2008, 93) remarks that 'Perhaps Diogenes is comparing the period of "courting" to a war, in which the grooms' and brides' families manoeuvre and scheme for maximum advantage before coming to close quarters, as it were. ... Thus, after a struggle for advantage, the groom wins his bride, like some conquering Heracles, and the two then unite for the further promotion of their household: a marital, if not a martial, alliance.'

¹⁵² *Metropolis* means 'mother-city' – and in Diogenes' metaphor, he means that greed is the origin of all evil. Cf. 1 Tim 6:10, 'For the love of

eating olives, he said, 'If you had breakfasted thus, you would not have dined thus.'[153]

[6.51] One of his apophthegms was that good men were the images of the Gods; another, that love was the business of those who had nothing to do. When he was asked what was wretched in life, he answered, 'A destitute old man.'[154] And when the question was put to him as to what beast inflicts the worst bite, he said, 'Of wild beasts, the sycophant; and of tame animals, the flatterer.' On one occasion he saw two Centaurs very badly painted, and he said, 'Which of the two is Chiron?'[155] He used to say that a speech, the object of which was solely to please, was a honeyed halter.[156] He called the stomach livelihood's Charybdis.[157] Having heard

---

money is the root of all evil,' and also Matt 19:23, Mark 10:23–5, Luke 16:13, 18:22–5. Desmond (2008, 98) conjectures that this Christian view probably originated with this Cynic saying.

[153] If the profligacy demonstrated by the man had occurred earlier with respect to his breakfast, he would not now have an appetite to eat more, or would now have lacked funds sufficient for his dinner.

[154] Diogenes did not believe himself to be destitute, but were he to be so, that is what would make his life miserable; but his lifestyle was such that no circumstance could fall upon him that would make him destitute. Possessing nothing, and wanting nothing, his immunity was assured.

[155] There is a pun here on Chiron's name, since *cheirôn* means 'worse'. Chiron was the most celebrated of the Centaurs, the teacher of Achilles.

[156] That is, a noose which strangles.

[157] That is, the stomach consumes all we labour to produce. In Greek mythology, Charybdis was a nymph-daughter of Poseidon and Gaia until Zeus turned her into a sea monster having the form of a single, gaping mouth. She creates whirlpools in the Strait of Messina between Italy and Sicily by alternately sucked in and belching out huge quantities of water. On the opposite side of the channel living on a perilous rock which bears her name, is the monster Scylla, a creature with six heads, ready to devour passing sailors (see Homer, *Odyssey* 12.101–26). The expression 'Between Scylla and Charybdis' refers to seeking to avoid the danger of one evil at the risk of falling into another, and may be the origin of the phrase 'Between a rock and a hard place;' 'hard' being meant here in the sense of 'difficult' – the phrase as a whole alluding to avoiding on the one hand

once that Didymon the flute-player had been caught in adultery, he remarked, 'His name alone is sufficient to hang him.'[158] When the question was put to him as to why gold is of a pale colour, he said, 'Because it has so many people plotting against it.' When he saw a woman being carried in a litter, he said, 'The cage is not suited to the animal.'

[6.52] And seeing a runaway slave sitting on the edge of a well, he said, 'My boy, take care you do not fall in.' Another time, he saw a little boy who was stealing clothes from the baths, and said, 'Do you do this for a little unguent, or for another garment?'[159] Seeing some women hanged from an olive tree, he said, 'I wish every tree bore similar fruit.' At another time, he saw a clothes-stealer, and addressed him thus:

> What moves thee, say, when sleep has closed the sight,
> To roam the silent fields in dead of night?
> Art thou some wretch by hopes of plunder led,
> Through heaps of carnage to despoil the dead?[160]

When he was asked whether he had any girl or boy to wait on him, and he answered, 'No,' his questioner asked

---

the dangerous rock of Scylla, and on the other, the whirlpools of Charybdis that are hard to navigate.

[158] Didymon's immorality was obviously notorious in his day, but the records of his exploits have not survived into our modern era, and nothing further is known of him.

[159] There is a pun here on *aleimmation* (unguent) and *all' imation* (another garment).

[160] The Greek text of this quotation has only two lines:
tipte su ôde, pheriste;
ê tiva sulêsôn nekuôn katatethnêôtôv;
rendered by Hicks:
What mak'st thou here, my gallant?
Com'st thou perchance for plunder of the dead?
The second line of which comes from Homer, *Iliad* 10.343 = 10.387. Yonge renders this quote (using Pope's translation) in its wider context, including the lines for *Iliad* 10.385-7.

further, 'Then if you die, who will bury you?' And he replied, 'Whoever wants my house.'

[6.53] Seeing a handsome youth sleeping whilst exposing himself, he nudged him, and said, 'Wake up!'

> Mix'd with the vulgar shall thy fate be found,
> Pierced in the back, a vile, dishonest wound?[161]

And he addressed a man who was buying delicacies at a great expense:

> Not long, my son, will you on earth remain,
> If such your dealings.[162]

When Plato was discoursing about his 'ideas', and using the nouns 'tableness' and 'cupness', Diogenes interrupted, saying, 'I, Plato, see a table and a cup, but I see no tableness or cupness.' Plato answered, 'That is natural enough, for you have eyes, by which a cup and a table are seen; but you do not have intellect, by which tableness and cupness are perceived.' [6.54] On one occasion, he[163] was asked by a certain person, 'What sort of a man is Diogenes?' And he said, 'A Socrates gone mad.'[164]

Another time, the question was put to him[165] as to what was the right time to marry, and he replied, 'For young men,

---

[161] The Greek here reads: *mê tis toi pheugonti metaphrenô ev doru pêxê*, from Homer: 'Watch out that as you flee some man does not plant his spear in your back.' (*Iliad* 8.95, trans. Murray and Wyatt). Yonge quotes Pope's translation, including the line that appears immediately before (though which does not feature in the Greek of Diogenes Laertius' text). See also Homer, *Iliad* 5.40.

[162] This is a parody on Homer, *Iliad* 18.95, which reads: 'Doomed then to a speedy death, my child, will you be, from what you say.' (trans. Murray and Wyatt); Diogenes changes the end of the line from *oi' agoreueis* ('if such be your language') to *oi' agorazeis* ('if you buy such things').

[163] That is, Plato.

[164] This epithet occurs also in Aelian, *Historical Miscellany* 14.33.

[165] That is, Diogenes.

not yet; and for old men, never.' When asked what he would take to let a man give him a blow on the head, he replied, 'A helmet.' Seeing a youth smartening himself up with great care, he said to him, 'If you are doing that for men, you are miserable; and if for women, you are profligate.' Once he saw a youth blushing, and addressed him, 'Take courage, my boy, for that is the complexion of virtue.' Having once listened to two lawyers, he condemned them both, saying that the one had stolen the thing in question, and that the other had not lost it. When asked what wine he liked to drink, he said, 'That which belongs to someone else.' A man said to him one day, 'Many people laugh at you.' 'But I am not laughed down,' he replied.

[6.55] When a man said to him that it was a bad thing to live, he said, 'Not to live, but to live badly.' When some people were advising him to go in pursuit of his slave who had run away, he said, 'It would be absurd for Manes to be able to live without Diogenes, but for Diogenes not to be able to live without Manes.'[166] While he was dining on olives, a cheese-cake was brought in, which he threw away, saying:

> Off the road with you, stranger! Make way for a king![167]

And on another occasion he said:

> He whipped an olive.[168]

---

[166] This incident is also reported by Aelian, *Historical Miscellany* 13.28.

[167] Euripides, *Phoenician Women* 40 (trans. Davie 2005).

[168] This is a pun on the phrase *mastixen d' elaan*, from lines in Homer's *Iliad*: *par de hoi Iris ebaine kai hênia lazeto chersi, mastixen d' elaan, tô d' ouk aekonte petesthên*, '...and Iris climbed beside her, seized the reins, whipped the team to a run and on the horses flew, holding nothing back' (5.365–6, trans. Fagles = 5.411–13), and *mastixen d' elaan: tô d' ouk aekonte petesthên messêgus gaiês te kai ouranou asteroentos*, 'A crack of the lash – the team plunged to a run and on the stallions flew,

When he was asked what sort of a dog he was, he replied, 'When hungry, I am a Maltese; when satisfied, a Molossian; breeds which most people who praise do not like to take out hunting with them, because of the effort of keeping up with them; and in like manner, you cannot live with me, from fear of the discomfort I give you.'

[6.56] The question was put to him as to whether wise men ate cakes, and he replied, 'They eat all sorts, just like everyone else.' When asked why people give to beggars and not to philosophers, he said, 'Because they think it possible that one day they themselves may become lame or blind, but they do not expect that they will ever to turn to philosophy.' He once begged of a covetous man, and as he was slow to give, he said, 'Man, I am asking you to provide for some food, not pay for my funeral.'[169] When someone reproached him for having tampered with the coinage, he said, 'There was a time when I was such a person as you are now; but such as I am now, you will never be.' And to another person who reproached him on the same grounds, he said, 'There were times when what I did was stupid, but that is not the case now.'

[6.57] When he went to Myndus,[170] he saw some very large gates, but the city was a small one, and so he said, 'Oh men of Myndus, shut your gates, lest your city should make off.' On one occasion, he saw a man who had been detected stealing purple, and so he said:

---

holding nothing back as they winged between the earth and starry skies...' (8.45–6, trans. Fagles = 8.52–4). Diogenes is making a pun on the similarity of the word 'olive' (*elaan*), to the verb 'to drive, whip, strike' (*elaan*).

[169] There is a pun here on *eis trophên* ('maintain me') and *eis taphên* ('bury me').

[170] Myndus: ancient Greek city on the south-west coast of Asia Minor, modern-day Gümüslük in Turkey.

A purple death, and mighty fate o'ertook him.[171]

When Craterus entreated him to come and visit him, he said, 'I would rather lick up a few grains of salt at Athens than enjoy the extravagance of Craterus' table.' On one occasion, he met Anaximenes the orator, who was a fat man, and thus accosted him: 'Pray give us, who are poor, some of your belly; for by so doing you will provide relief for yourself, and assistance to us.' And once, when he[172] was discussing some point, Diogenes held up a piece of salt fish, and drew off the attention of his audience; and as Anaximenes was indignant at this, he[173] said, 'See, one pennyworth of salt fish has put an end to the lecture of Anaximenes.'

[6.58] Being once reproached for eating in the marketplace, he answered, 'That I did, for it was in the marketplace that I felt hungry.' Some authors also attribute the following story to him. Plato saw him washing vegetables, and so, coming up to him, he quietly accosted him thus: 'If you had paid court to Dionysius, you would not have been washing vegetables.' And he replied, with equal quietness, 'If you had washed vegetables, you would not have paid court to Dionysius.' When a man said to him once, 'Most people laugh at you,' he replied, 'And very likely the asses laugh at them; but they do not pay attention to the asses, and neither do I pay any attention to them.' Once he saw a youth studying philosophy, and said to him, 'Well done! You are diverting admirers of your bodily charms to contemplate instead the beauty of your mind.'

[6.59] A certain person was admiring the offerings in the

---

[171] Homer, *Iliad* 5.82–3.
[172] That is, Anaximenes.
[173] That is, Diogenes.

temple at Samothrace,[174] and he said to him, 'They would have been much more numerous if those who were lost had offered them instead of those who were saved.' But some attribute this speech to Diagoras of Melos. Once he saw a handsome youth going to a banquet, and said to him, 'You will come back worse.' And when the next day, after the banquet, he said to him, 'I went to the banquet, and am no worse for it,' he replied, 'You were not Chiron, but Eurytion.'[175] He was begging once of a very ill-tempered man, and as he said to him, 'If you can persuade me, I will give you something,' he replied, 'If I could have persuaded you, I would have persuaded you to hang yourself.' He was on one occasion returning from Lacedaemon to Athens, and when someone asked him, 'Where are you going, and from where do you come?' he said, 'I am going from the men's apartments to the women's.'

[6.60] Another time he was returning from the Olympic Games, and when someone asked him whether there had been a great multitude there, he said, 'A great multitude, but very few men.' He used to say that debauched men resembled figs growing on a precipice, the fruit of which is not tasted by men, but devoured by crows and vultures.

---

[174] Samothrace: (modern-day Samothraki) a mountainous island in the northern Aegean, settled by Greeks from about 700 BC [KS]. The Samothracian Gods were Gods of the sea, and it was customary for those who had been saved from shipwreck to make them an offering of some part of what they had saved; and of their hair, if they had saved nothing but their lives [Yonge].

[175] Chiron: the most wise and most just of the Centaurs, the instructor of Achilles. There is a pun here on Chiron's name. When Diogenes remarked earlier, 'You will come back worse,' 'worse' translates the Greek *cheirôn*. Eurytion was a Centaur who got drunk and misbehaved at Pirithous' wedding-feast, and began a quarrel between Centaurs and men, and was later killed by Heracles. If the youth did not come back as Chiron (*cheirôn*, worse), then he came back as Eurytion (dissolute).

When Phryne[176] had dedicated a golden statue of Aphrodite at Delphi, it is said that he wrote upon it, 'From the licentiousness of the Greeks.' Once, Alexander the Great came and stood by him, and said, 'I am Alexander, the great king.' 'And I,' he said, 'am Diogenes the dog.' And when he was asked as to why he merited being called a dog, he said, 'Because I fawn upon those who give me anything, bark at those who give me nothing, and sink my teeth into the worthless.'[177]

[6.61] On one occasion he was gathering some of the fruit of a fig-tree, when he was told by its keeper that a man had hung himself on this tree not long before. 'Then I will now purify[178] it,' he said. Once he saw a man who had been a victor at the Olympic Games casting repeated glances upon a courtesan. 'Look,' he said, 'at that ram, once full of warlike frenzy, now taken prisoner by the first girl he meets.'[179] One of his sayings was that good-looking courtesans were like poisoned mead. On one occasion he was eating his dinner in the marketplace, and the bystanders kept constantly calling out, 'Dog!' But he answered back, 'It is you who are the dogs, who stand around me while I am eating my dinner.'

---

[176] Phryne: one of the most celebrated courtesans (*hetaira*) of ancient Athens. See Glossary of Names.

[177] 'worthless' translates the Greek *ponêros*: bad, wicked, villainous, useless, ill, distressed, painful, dangerous.

[178] Translating the Greek *kathairô*, cleanse, purify (in a religious sense), but also purge, evacuate (in the medical sense, used also of menstruation). The meaning here is unclear, or possibly intentionally ambiguous. Possibly Diogenes was signalling his plan to urinate against the tree (bearing in mind that he is *kunikos*, dog-like, Cynic), or possibly he meant to make an allusion to figs and their purgative effect. Alternatively, he might have used the verb *kathairô* with another meaning, that of 'prune', as in pruning a tree to clear it of superfluous wood: he cleared the tree of its superfluous fruit.

[179] This athlete concerned, according to Aelian (*Historical Miscellany* 12.58), was the Athenian Dioxippus.

When two effeminate fellows were getting out of his way, he said, 'Do not be afraid. A dog does not eat beetroot.'[180] Being once asked about a debauched boy, as to what country he came from, he said, 'He is from Tegea.'[181] [6.62] Seeing an unskilled wrestler practising on someone as a physician, he said, 'What is this? Are you hoping now to overthrow those who formerly defeated you?' On one occasion he saw the son of a courtesan throwing stones at a crowd, and said to him, 'Take care, lest you hit your father.'

When a boy showed him a dagger that he had received from an admirer,[182] he told him, 'The blade is fair, but the handle is ugly.' And when some people were praising a man who had given him something, he said to them, 'And do not you praise me who was worthy to receive it?' He was asked by someone to give him back his cloak, and he replied, 'If you gave it me, it is mine; and if you only lent it me, I am still using it.' Someone's supposititious son once said to him that he had gold in his cloak. 'No doubt,' he said, 'that is the very reason why you sleep with it under your head.'[183] [6.63] When he was asked what advantage he had derived from philosophy, he replied, 'If no other, at least this, that I am prepared for every kind of fortune.' When asked where he

---

[180] The term 'beetroot' has already occurred at DL 6.45, and is, I suspect, a euphemistic obscenity.

[181] There is a pun here. Diogenes answers simply, '*Tegeatês*,' which in Greek is the same word meaning 'from a brothel' ('brothel' being *tegos*).

[182] Following Hicks. The Greek word here is *erastos*, lover, which Yonge translates 'someone for whom he had done some discreditable service', obviously uncomfortable with the homosexual implication of the sentence.

[183] There is a pun here: 'supposititious son' (that is, a child substituted for the genuine person, set up to displace the real heir or successor) translates *hupobolimaios*, and 'under your head' translates *hupobeblêmenos*.

6.63

came from, he replied, 'I am a citizen of the world.'[184] Some men were sacrificing to the Gods to prevail on them to send them sons, and he said, 'And do you not sacrifice to procure sons of a particular character?' Once when he was asked by the president of a society for a contribution, he said to him:[185]

Despoil all the rest, but keep your hands from Hector.[186]

He used to say that the courtesans of kings were queens, for they make the kings do their bidding. When the Athenians had voted that Alexander be given the title of Dionysus, he said to them, 'Vote, too, that I am Serapis.'[187] When a

---

[184] Translating the Greek *kosmopolitês*. Hicks has a footnote which reads: 'If this answer is authentic, it apparently shows that the famous term "cosmopolitan" originated with Diogenes.'

[185] The Greek is *eranon pot' apaitoumenos pros ton eranarchên ephê* – *eranos* was not only a subscription or contribution for the support of the poor, but also a club or society of subscribers to a common fund for any purpose, social, commercial, or charitable, or especially political [Yonge].

[186] Hicks includes the following footnote on this line: 'There is no such line in our mss. of Homer; it is unknown to the Scholiasts and to Eustathius. Joshua Barnes, in his edition of the *Iliad*, introduced it as xvi. 82a. Pope rendered it, about 1718, as follows (*Il.* xvi. 86):

Rage uncontrolled through all the hostile crew,
But touch not Hector, Hector is my due.

In Clarke's edition of 1740 it is expelled from the text and relegated to a footnote. J. H. Voss, however, making a German translation of the *Iliad*, probably between 1781 and 1793, still regarded it as Homeric, but found a fresh place for it, after xvi. 90.'

Diogenes likens the president to someone who scours a battlefield for corpses to rob. He identifies himself as Hector, the greatest of the Trojan heroes, whose body was desecrated by Achilles when in rage he dragged it behind his chariot before the gates of Troy and around the tomb of Patroclus.

[187] Dionysus was the survivor-hero of a Greek mystery cult. When the Ptolemies went to Egypt they adopted an Egyptian mystery cult of Isis and Osiris to form a new cult of Isianism with Osiris transformed into a combination of Apis and Osiris to form a God similar in many ways to Dionysus. Diogenes is both criticising the absurdity of giving a God's

man reproached him for going into unclean places, he said, 'The sun too penetrates into privies, but is not defiled by them.'

[6.64] When dining in a temple and some dirty loaves were set before him, he took them up and threw them away, saying that nothing dirty ought to come into a temple; and when someone said to him, 'You philosophise without being possessed of any knowledge,' he said, 'If I only pretend to wisdom, that is philosophising.' A man once brought him a boy, and said that he was naturally gifted and had an excellent character. 'What need then,' said Diogenes, 'does he have of me?' He used to say that those who utter virtuous sentiments but do not do them, are no better than harps, for a harp, like them, has neither hearing nor understanding. Once he was going into a theatre while everyone else was coming out of it; and when asked why he did so, 'It is,' said he, 'what I have been doing all my life.'

[6.65] Once when he saw a young man putting on effeminate airs, he said to him, 'Are you not ashamed to have worse plans for yourself than nature had for you? For she has made you a man, but you are trying to force yourself to be a woman.' When he saw an ignorant man tuning a psaltery, he said to him, 'Are you not ashamed to be arranging concordant sounds on a wooden instrument, yet fail to harmonise your soul to a proper life?' When a man remarked to him, 'I am not suited for philosophy,' he said, 'Why then do you live, if you have no desire to live properly?' To a man who treated his father with contempt, he said, 'Are you not ashamed to despise him to whom you owe it that you have it in your power to give yourself airs at all?' Seeing a handsome young man chattering in an unseemly

---

name to someone like Alexander, and declaring that he himself is worthy of bearing the title of a new sort of God.

manner, he said, 'Are you not ashamed to draw a dagger made of lead from of a scabbard made of ivory?'

[6.66] Being once reproached for drinking in a vintner's shop, he said, 'I have my hair cut, too, in a barber's.' At another time, he was attacked for having accepted a cloak from Antipater, but he replied:

> Refuse not thou to heed
> The gifts which from the mighty Gods proceed.[188]

A man once came at him with a broom, and said, 'Take care!' So he struck him with his staff, and said, 'Take care!' He once said to a man who was addressing anxious pleas to a courtesan, 'What can you hope to gain by doing that, you wretched man, when it would be better for you to fail?' Seeing a man reeking all over with unguents, he said to him, 'Have a care, lest the fragrance of your head give a bad odour to your life.' Just as slaves obey their masters, he said, so wicked men are slaves to their desires.

[6.67] On being asked why slaves were called *andrapoda*,[189] he replied, 'Because they have the feet of men,'[190] but souls such as you have, you who are asking this question.' He once asked a spendthrift for a mina, and when he put the question to him, as to why he asked others for an obol, and him for a mina,[191] he said, 'Because I hope to get something from the others another time, but the Gods alone know whether I shall ever extract anything from you again.' Once he was reproached for asking favours, while Plato never asked for any, and he said,

> He asks as well as I do, but he does it

---

[188] Homer, *Iliad* 3.65.

[189] *andrapodon*: someone taken captive in war, and sold as a slave.

[190] 'Feet of men' translates the Greek *tous podas andôn*.

[191] A mina had a value 600 times greater than that of an obol. Six obols made a drachma, and 100 drachmas made a mina. See OCD 'weights'.

Bending his head, that no one else may hear.[192]

One day he saw an unskilful archer shooting, so he went and sat down by the target, saying, 'Now I shall be out of harm's way.' He used to say that those in love derived their pleasures from their misfortune.

[6.68] When he was asked as to whether death was an evil, he replied, 'How can it be an evil if, when it is present, we have no awareness of it?' When Alexander was once standing by him, and said, 'Do you not fear me?' he replied, 'Why – what are you? Something good or something evil?' And as he said that he was good, Diogenes asked, 'Who, then, fears what is good?' He used to say that education was a restraint for the young, consolation for the old, riches for the poor, and decoration for the rich. When Didymon the adulterer was once trying to cure the eye of a young girl, he said, 'Take care, lest when you are treating the girl's eye, you do not ruin the pupil.'[193] A man once said to him that his friends were plotting against him. 'What then,' he said, 'is to be done, if you have to treat both friends and enemies alike?'

[6.69] On one occasion he was asked as to what was the most excellent thing among men, and he said, 'Freedom of speech.'[194] He once went into a school and saw many statues of the Muses, but very few pupils, and said to the schoolmaster, 'With the help of the Gods, you have plenty of

---

[192] Cf. Homer, *Odyssey* 1.156–7 and 4.69–70:

... Telemachus spoke to bright-eyed Athene, with his head close to hers so that the others could not hear (trans. Rieu).

... then Telemachus spoke to the son of Nestor, holding his head close to him, that the others might not hear (trans. Murray and Dimock).

[193] There is a pun here: *korê* means both 'girl' and 'pupil of the eye'; and *phtheirô*, 'ruin, destroy', also means 'seduce'.

[194] Translating the Greek *parrhêsia*: outspokenness, frankness, freedom of speech – claimed by the Athenians as their privilege.

pupils.' He was in the habit of doing everything in public, whether in respect of Demeter or Aphrodite alike.[195] And he used to put his conclusions in this way to people: 'If there is nothing absurd in dining, then it is not absurd to dine in the marketplace. But it is not absurd to dine, therefore it is not absurd to dine in the marketplace.' And as he was continually doing manual work[196] in public, he said one day, 'I wish that by rubbing my belly I could as easily get rid of hunger.' Other sayings are also attributed to him, which it would take a long time to enumerate as there is such a multiplicity of them.[197]

[6.70] He used to say that there are two kinds of training,[198] that of the mind, and that of the body; and that the latter of these, if continuously practised, creates in the mind such quick and agile impressions,[199] so as to very much facilitate the practice of virtue; but that one is incomplete without the other, since the health and vigour necessary for the practice of what is good depend equally on both mind and body. And he used to allege as proofs of this, and of the ease which practice imparts to acts of virtue, that people could see that in the case of mere common working trades, and other employments of that kind, the artisans arrived at no inconsiderable competence by constant practice; and

---

[195] Demeter is the Goddess of cereals, and Aphrodite is the Goddess of love. This is a reference to eating, and to sexual activity.

[196] 'Manual work' translates *cheirourgeô*, 'do with the hand', 'make by hand', which is probably being used here euphemistically to refer to masturbation, and is translated by Hicks using the phrase, 'Behaving indecently in public...' (See also DL 6.46.)

[197] Some of them, however, feature in the following sections, DL 6.70-3. Section DL 6.74 appears to run on from DL 6.69, suggesting that the digest of Cynic maxims commencing in the next section was inserted later than the time of original composition.

[198] Translating *askêsis*.

[199] Translating *phantasiai* (singular, *phantasia*).

that anyone may see how much one flute-player, or one wrestler, is superior to another, by his own continued practice. And that if these men transferred the same training to their minds they would not labour in a profitless or imperfect manner.

[6.71] He used to say also that there is nothing whatever in life which can be accomplished successfully without practice,[200] and that practice alone is able to overcome every obstacle; and that instead of toiling uselessly people should abide in accordance with nature[201] and thereby live happily, yet through folly they make themselves unhappy. For the very contempt of pleasure, if we can only habituate ourselves to it, is very pleasant; and just as those who are accustomed to a life of pleasure are forced unwillingly to forego their pleasures, so those who have been hardened to go without pleasures feel a sort of pleasure in the contempt of pleasure. This used to be the language which he maintained, and which he sustained in practice, defacing the currency[202] to be sure, and deferring in all things to what is in accordance with nature rather than to what is in accordance with convention,[203] saying that he was adopting the same way of life as had Heracles, preferring freedom above everything.

[6.72] And he maintained that everything belonged to the wise, and advanced arguments such as those mentioned above. For instance: everything belongs to the Gods, and the Gods are friends to the wise, and all the property of friends is held in common, therefore everything belongs to the

---

[200] Translating *askêsis*.

[201] Translating *kata phusin*.

[202] Translating *nomisma*, meaning not only currency in the sense of actual coinage, but also custom, anything sanctioned by current or established usage.

[203] Translating *kata phusin* and *kata nomos*. See DL 6.38.

wise. He also argued about the law, saying that without it, it would be impossible for society to exist, for without a city no benefit can be derived from what is civilised. But the city is civilised, and there can be no advantage in law without a city; therefore law is something civilised. And he would ridicule good birth, and reputation, and all such distinctions, saying that they were all showy ornaments of vice. The only true commonwealth he said, was that which comprised the whole cosmos. Another of his doctrines was that all women ought to be shared in common, that marriage was invalid, but that every man should live with any woman whom he can persuade to consent. And on the same principle he said that children also should be held in common.

[6.73] And there was no impropriety either in stealing anything from a temple, or eating any animal whatever, and there was no impiety either in tasting even human flesh, as is plain from the customs of foreign nations; and he said that this principle might be correctly extended to every case and every people. For he said that in reality everything is a combination of all things. For not only is meat a constituent of bread, but bread is also a constituent of vegetables, and so there are some particles of all other bodies in everything, penetrating by invisible passages in the form of vapour. He explains this theory clearly in the *Thyestes*, if indeed the tragedies attributed to him are really his composition, and not rather the work of his friend Philiscus of Aegina, or of Pasiphon,[204] the son of Lucian, who is stated by Favorinus in

---

[204] Hicks remarks in his footnote that it has been conjectured that the Pasiphon mentioned here is the philosopher of Eretria, to whom Persaeus attributed the composition of spurious Socratic Dialogues (v supra, ii. 61), and that modern scholars are inclined to regard him as the author of the *Pinax* ('Tablet') attributed to Cebes at DL 2.195 (for a translation of *The Tablet of Cebes*, and bibliographical references to further translations, see Seddon 2005).

his *Miscellaneous History* to have written them after Diogenes' death. Music and geometry, and astronomy, and all things of that kind, he neglected as useless and unnecessary. [6.74] But he was a man very happy to engage in argument, as is plain from what we have already said.

And he bore being sold as a slave with a most magnanimous spirit. For when he was sailing to Aegina[205] and taken prisoner by some pirates under the command of Scirpalus, he was carried off to Crete and put up for sale; and when the auctioneer asked him in what craft he was proficient, he said, 'That of governing men.' And presently pointing out a Corinthian, dressed in a robe with a fine purple border (the same Xeniades whom we have mentioned before[206]), he said, 'Sell me to that man, for he needs a master.' Accordingly, Xeniades bought him and carried him away to Corinth; and then he made him tutor of his sons, and committed to him the entire management of his house. And he conducted himself in every affair in such a manner that Xeniades, when looking over his property, said, 'A good genius has come into my house.'

[6.75] And Cleomenes, in his book entitled *The Schoolmaster*, says that Diogenes' friends wanted to pay a ransom for him, but Diogenes said that they were all simpleminded; for lions do not become the slaves of those who keep them, but, on the contrary, it is those who provide for lions who are *their* slaves: for fear is the mark of the slave, but not that of the wild beast who induces fear in men. And the man had the gift of persuasion to a wonderful degree, so that he could easily overcome anyone by his arguments. Accordingly, it is said that Onesicritus of Aegina, who had

---

[205] One of the Saronic Islands in the Saronic Gulf, 17 miles south-west of Athens.

[206] Xeniades has already been mentioned at DL 6.30, 6.31 and 6.36.

two sons, sent the one whose name was Androsthenes to Athens, and that after he had heard Diogenes lecture, he remained there as his pupil; and that after that he sent the elder son, Philiscus (who has been already mentioned[207]), and that Philiscus was also charmed in the same way. [6.76] And last of all, he came himself, and then he too remained there, no less than his sons, joining in the love and pursuit of wisdom, so magical was the spell which the discourses of Diogenes exerted. Another pupil of his was Phocion, who was called the Good; and Stilpo of Megara, and a great many other men who were eminent as statesmen.

He is said to have died when he was nearly ninety years of age, but there are different accounts given of his death. For some say that he ate raw octopus, and in consequence was seized with a bilious attack, of which he died; others, of whom Cercidas of Megalopolis (or of Crete) is one, say that he died by voluntarily holding his breath; and Cercidas speaks thus of him in his *Meliambics*:

> He, that Sinopian who bore the staff,
> Wore his cloak doubled, and in th' open air
> Dined without washing, would not bear with life
> [6.77] A moment longer: but he shut his teeth,
> And held his breath. He was truly Diogenes,
> The son of Zeus, heaven's dog.

Others say that whilst he was trying to divide up an octopus between his dogs, he was bitten by them through the tendon of his foot, and so died. But his own friends, as Antisthenes tells us in his *Successions*, rather sanction the story of his having died from holding his breath. For he used to live in the Craneum, which was a gymnasium at the

---

[207] Philiscus of Aegina has been mentioned two paragraphs earlier, at DL 6.73.

gates of Corinth. And his friends came according to their custom, and finding him wrapped in his cloak, they supposed that he was asleep, although he was by no means given to drowsiness or lethargy. And so they drew away the cloak from his face, and found that he was no longer breathing; and they thought that he had done this on purpose, wishing to escape the remaining portion of his life.

[6.78] On this there was a quarrel, as they say, between his friends, as to who should bury him, and they even came to blows; but when the elders and chief men of the city came there, they say that he was buried by them at the gate which leads to the Isthmus. And they erected over him a pillar, and placed upon it a dog in Parian marble. And at a later time his fellow citizens honoured him with bronze statues, and put this inscription on them:

> E'en brass by lapse of time doth old become,
> But there is no such time as shall efface
> Your lasting glory, wise Diogenes;
> Since you alone did teach to men the art
> Of a contented life and the surest path
> To self-sufficiency and a lasting happiness.

[6.79] We ourselves have also written an epigram on him in the proceleusmatic metre:

> A. Tell me, Diogenes, tell me true, I pray,
> How did you die; what fate to Hades bore you?
>
> D. The savage bite of a dog did kill me.

Some, however, say that when he was dying he ordered his friends to throw his corpse away unburied so that every wild beast might feed on it, or else to throw it into a ditch and sprinkle a little dust over it. And others say that his instructions were that he should be thrown into the Ilissus;[208] that so he might be useful to his brethren.[209]

Demetrius, in his treatise *On Men of the Same Name*, says that Diogenes died in Corinth on the very same day that Alexander died in Babylon. And he was already an old man as early as the hundred and thirteenth [6.80] Olympiad.[210]

The following books are attributed to him.

Diologues:

> *Cephalion*
> *Icthyas*
> *Jackdaw*
> *Leopard*
> *The Athenian Demos*
> *Republic*
> *Art of Ethics*
> *On Wealth*

---

[208] 'Ilissos' names both the river that ran south of Athens' defensive walls (in modern times mostly confined to conduits below ground level; see Plan of Ancient Athens), and the river-god who dwelt in its waters, the son of Poseidon and Demeter. If the account given of Diogenes' death at DL 6.77 is correct, that he died in Corinth, then this instruction, that his body be thrown into the Ilissos at Athens, makes little sense. It seems unlikely that he meant for his body to be transported 50 miles to Athens... And how could his body being thrown into the Ilissos 'be useful to his brethren'? Useful to only his Cynic followers? To the citizens of Corinth? To everyone? Perhaps this passage means only that Diogenes' wish to have his corpse disposed of like any old piece of rubbish would further emphasise his contempt of death and his insistence that material things – his body included – have no value.

[209] Cf. Aelian (*Historical Miscellany* 8.14, trans. Wilson): 'Diogenes of Sinope, when suffering his last illness, dragged himself with difficulty to a bridge and threw himself down on it. This was near a gymnasium, and he told the guardian to throw his body into the Ilissus when he could see that he was dead. So little did Diogenes care about death and burial.'

[210] 324–321 BC.

> *On Love*
> *Theodorus*
> *Hypsias*
> *Aristarchus*
> *On Death*
> *Letters*

Seven Tragedies:

> *Helen*
> *Thyestes*
> *Heracles*
> *Achilles*
> *Medea*
> *Chrysippus*
> *Oedippus*

But Sosicrates, in the first book of his *Successions*, and Satyrus, in the fourth book of his *Lives*, both assert that none of these are genuine compositions of Diogenes. And Satyrus affirms that the tragedies are the work of Philiscus of Aegina, who was a friend of Diogenes. But Sotion, in his seventh book, says that these are the only genuine works of Diogenes:

> *On Virtue*
> *On the Good*
> *On Love*
> *The Beggar*
> *Tolmaeus*
> *Leopard*
> *Cassandrus*
> *Cephalion*
> *Philiscus*
> *Aristarchus*
> *Sisyphus*

Ganymede
Anecdotes
Letters

[6.81] There were five people who had the name Diogenes. The first a native of Apollonia, a natural philosopher; and the beginning of his treatise on Natural Philosophy is as follows: 'It appears to me to be well for everyone who commences any kind of philosophical treatise, to lay down some undeniable principle to start with.' The second was from Sicyon, who wrote an account of Peloponnesus. The third was the man of whom we have been speaking. The fourth was a Stoic, a native of Seleucia, but usually called a Babylonian, from the proximity of Seleucia to Babylon. The fifth was a native of Tarsus, who wrote on the subject of some questions concerning poetry which he endeavours to solve.

Athenodorus, in the eighth book of his *Conversations*,[211] says that the philosopher[212] always had a shining appearance, from his habit of anointing himself.[213]

---

[211] Translating the Greek *Peripatôn*, 'walking', referring in this context to walking about while teaching, meaning by extension 'discourse' or 'conversation', the latter expression favoured by Yonge.

[212] That is, Diogenes of Sinope.

[213] See Epictetus, *Discourses* 3.22.86–8: 'And yet such a man [the Cynic philosopher] needs also a certain kind of body, since if a consumptive comes forward, thin and pale, his testimony no longer carries the same weight. For he must not merely, by exhibiting the qualities of his soul, prove to the laymen that it is possible, without the help of the things which they admire, to be a good and excellent man, but he must also show, by the state of his body, that his plain and simple style of life in the open air does not injure even his body: "Look," he says, "both I and my body are witnesses to the truth of my contention." That was the way of Diogenes, for he used to go about with a radiant complexion, and would attract the attention of the common people by the very appearance of his body' (trans. Oldfather). See this passage in the context of the whole chapter, in Appendix 2, p. 170, below.

MONIMUS

[6.82] Monimus of Syracuse was a pupil of Diogenes,[214] but also a slave of some Corinthian money-changer, as Sosicrates tells us. Xeniades,[215] who bought Diogenes, used often to come to him, extolling the excellence of Diogenes both in actions and words, until he excited a great affection for the man in the mind of Monimus. For he immediately feigned madness, and threw about all the money and all the coins that were on the table, until his master dismissed him, and then straightaway he went to Diogenes and became his pupil. He also followed Crates the Cynic a good deal, and devoted himself to the same studies as he did; and his master, seeing this conduct made him all the more think that he was mad.

[6.83] And he was a very eminent man, so that even Menander the comic poet speaks of him accordingly in one of his plays, that is in *The Groom*,[216] where he mentions him, saying:

> There is a man, Philo, named Monimus,
> A wise man, though but little known, and one
> Who bears a wallet at his back, and is not
> Content with one but three. He never spoke

---

[214] This is Diogenes of Sinope.
[215] Xeniades appears above, at DL 6.30–1, 6.36, 6.74.
[216] Not bridegroom, but *ippokomos*, someone who looks after horses.

> A single sentence, by great Zeus I swear,
> Like this one, 'Know thyself,' or any other
> Of the oft-quoted proverbs: all such sayings
> He scorned, as he did beg his way through dirt;
> Teaching that all opinion is but vanity.

But he was a man of such gravity that he despised opinion, and sought only for truth.

He wrote some nonsense[217] mixed with serious treatises, and two essays: *On Impulses*, and an *Exhortation to Philosophy*.

---

[217] Translating the Greek *paignia*; Yonge has 'jests', and Hicks favours 'trifles'. The suggestion is of writing that is playful and humorous, for entertainment and amusement.

ONESICRITUS

[6.84] Onesicritus is called by some authors an Aeginetan, but Demetrius of Magnesia affirms that he was a native of Astypalaea. He was also one of the most eminent of the disciples of Diogenes. And he appears in some points to resemble Xenophon. For Xenophon joined in the expedition of Cyrus, and Onesicritus joined in that of Alexander; and Xenophon wrote the *Education of Cyrus*, and Onesicritus wrote an account of the education of Alexander. Xenophon, too, wrote a Panegyric on Cyrus, and Onesicritus one on Alexander. They were also both similar to one another in style, except that a copyist is naturally inferior to the original.

Menander, too, who was surnamed Drymus[218] (a great admirer of Homer), was a pupil of Diogenes: and so was Hegesias of Sinope, who was nicknamed Clocus,[219] and so too was Philiscus of Aegina who was mentioned before.[220]

---

[218] *Drumos* means copse or thicket.

[219] *Kloios* means dog-collar, and can refer also to the wooden collar used to restrain prisoners.

[220] Philiscus of Aegina has been mentioned above at DL 6.73, 6.75 and 6.80.

CRATES

[6.85] Crates was a Theban by birth, and the son of Ascondus. He also was one of the eminent disciples of the Cynic.[221] But Hippobotus asserts that he was not a pupil of Diogenes, but of Bryson of Achaea. The following playful lines are attributed to him:

> The waves surround fair Pera's[222] fruitful soil,
> And fertile acres crown the sea-born isle;
> Land which no parasite e'er dares invade,
> Or lewd seducer of a hapless maid;
> It bears figs, bread, thyme, garlic's savoury charms,
> Gifts which ne'er tempt men to detested arms,
> They'd neither fight for gold nor glory's dreams.

[6.86] There is also an account-book of his much spoken of, which is drawn up in such terms as these:

> Put down the cook for minas half a score,
> Put down the doctor for a drachma more:
> Five talents to the flatterer; some smoke
> To the adviser; for the willing nymph,
> A talent; and three obols
> For the philosopher.[223]

---

[221] Diogenes of Sinope.
[222] *pêra*: the Greek word that names the Cynic's leather wallet or satchel. In adopting the Cynic lifestyle, wherever they may roam each Cynic dwells perpetually in Pera's idyllic realm.

He was also nicknamed 'Door-opener', because he used to enter every house and give the inhabitants advice. These lines, too, are his:

> All this I learnt and pondered in my mind,
> Drawing deep wisdom from the Muses kind,
> But all the rest is vanity.

There is a line, too, which tells us what he gained from philosophy:

> A peck of lupins, and to care for nobody.

This, too, is attributed to him:

> Hunger checks love; and should it not, time does.
> If both should fail you, then a halter[224] choose.

He flourished about the hundred and thirteenth Olympiad.[225]

[6.87] Antisthenes, in his *Successions*, says that he first turned to Cynic philosophy after having once seen Telephus in a certain tragedy holding a little basket, and in a miserable plight in other respects; and having converted his property into money (for he came from a distinguished family), and acquiring by this means two hundred talents, he divided the sum among the citizens. And after that he devoted himself to philosophy with such eagerness that even Philemon the comic poet mentions him. Accordingly he says:

---

[223] This is intended satirically. It is supposedly taken from the account-book of someone lacking philosophical, specifically Cynic, insight. One talent equals 60 minae; one mina equals 100 drachmas; and one drachma equals six obols. To the keeper of this account-book, a prostitute has a value 12,000 times greater than that of a philosopher's instruction.

[224] That is, a noose by which one may end one's life.

[225] 328–324 BC.

And in the summer he'd a shaggy gown,
To inure himself to hardship: in the winter
He wore mere rags.

But Diocles says that it was Diogenes who persuaded him to discard all his estate and his flocks, and to throw his money into the sea; [6.88] and he says further that Alexander stayed in the house of Crates, as Philip once lodged in Hipparchia's.[226] Very often when his relations would visit and try to dissuade him from his purpose, he would drive them away with his staff – and his resolution remained unshakable.[227] Demetrius of Magnesia relates that he deposited his money with a banker, making an agreement with him that if his sons turned out ordinary men, he was then to restore it to them; but if they became philosophers, then he was to divide it among the people, for if they were philosophers they would have no need of anything. And Eratosthenes tells us that he had by Hipparchia, whom we shall mention hereafter, a son whose name was Pasicles, and that when he grew up, he took him to a brothel kept by a female slave, and told him that that was all the marriage that his father intended for him; [6.89] for marriages which resulted in adultery were themes for tragedians, and had exile and bloodshed for their prizes; and the marriages of those who lived with courtesans were subjects for the comic poets, and often produced madness as the result of debauchery and drunkenness. (He had a brother also named Pasicles, a pupil of Euclides.)

Favorinus, in the second book of his *Memorabilia*, relates a witty saying of his, for he says that once when he was begging a favour of the master of a gymnasium on behalf of

---

[226] This is Alexander the Great and his father Philip; Hipparchia is going to become Crates wife – see below, DL 6.96–8.

[227] His purpose and resolution to live the philosophic life, that is.

some acquaintance, he touched the man's hips, and in response to the indignation that this caused, he said, 'What, are not these hips just as much yours as your knees?'[228] He used to say that it was impossible to find a man who had never done wrong, in the same way as there was always some worthless seed in a pomegranate. On one occasion he provoked Nicodromus the harp-player, and received a black eye from him; so he put a plaster on his forehead and wrote upon it, 'Nicodromus did this.' [6.90] He deliberately insulted prostitutes with the intention of habituating himself to enduring the abuse that he provoked from them.

When Demetrius of Phalerum sent him some loaves and wine, he attacked him for his present, saying, 'If only the springs would yield bread as well as water!' For he was notorious for being a water-drinker.

He was once reproved by the city officials of Athens for wearing fine linen, and so he replied, 'I will show you Theophrastus also clad in fine linen.' And as they did not believe him, he took them to a barber's shop and showed him to them as he was being shaved. At Thebes he was once flogged by the master of the gymnasium (though some say this was done by Euthycrates at Corinth), and dragged out by the feet; but he did not care, and quoted the line:

> I feel, mighty chief, your matchless might,
> Dragged, foot first, downward from th' ethereal height.[229]

[6.91] But Diocles says that it was Menedemus of Eretria who dragged him in this manner, for as he was a handsome

---

[228] Instead of patting the man on his shoulder, or shaking his hand as we might do today, or even patting him on the knee, which would have been appropriate for men sitting down, Crates patted his hip, which would have had – as it does for us – sexual overtones. This he did to show his disregard for convention.

[229] A parody of Homer, *Iliad* 1.591.

man, and supposed to be very intimate with Asclepiades the Phliasian, Crates touched his thighs and said, 'Is Asclepiades within?' And Menedemus was very much offended, and dragged him out, as has been already said; and then Crates quoted the line already cited above.

Zeno of Citium, in his *Anecdotes*, says that in a fit of heedlessness he once sewed a sheepskin into his cloak. He was a very ugly man, and such as to excite laughter when he was taking exercise. And he used to say to himself, as he threw up his hands, 'Take courage, Crates, for this concerns the good of your eyes and the rest of your body; [6.92] for you shall see those who now ridicule you convulsed with disease and envying your happiness, and accusing themselves of indolence.' One of his sayings was: 'A man ought to study philosophy to the point of looking on generals as nothing more than donkey-drivers.' Another was that those who live with flatterers are as desolate as calves when in the company of wolves; for neither the one nor the other are with those whom they ought to be, nor with their own kindred, but only with those who are plotting against them. When he felt that he was dying, he intoned verses over himself, saying:

> You're going, noble hunchback, you are going
> To Hades' realms, bent double by old age.

For his age had made him hunchbacked.

[6.93] When Alexander asked him whether he wished to see his native city rebuilt, he said, 'What would be the use of it? For perhaps some other Alexander would come at some future time and destroy it again.'

> But poverty and dear obscurity,
> Are what a prudent man should think his country;
> For these e'en fortune can't deprive him of.

He also said that he was:

> A fellow countryman of wise Diogenes,
> Whom even envy never had attacked.

Menander, in his *Twin Sisters*, mentions him thus:

> For you will walk with me wrapped in your cloak,
> As with the Cynic Crates his wife used to do.
> His daughter too, as he himself used to say,
> He gave in marriage for a month on trial.

We now come to his pupils.

METROCLES

[6.94] Metrocles of Maroneia was the brother of Hipparchia, and although he had formerly been a pupil of Theophrastus the Peripatetic, he had profited so little by his instruction that once, thinking that whilst listening to a lecture on philosophy he had disgraced himself by breaking wind, he fell into despondency and shut himself up in his house, intending to starve himself to death. Accordingly, when Crates heard of this he came to him, as he had been asked, and deliberately preparing a meal of lupins, he persuaded him by a number of arguments that he had done no harm; for it would be a wonder for a man not to take the natural means of releasing wind. And by reproducing the action himself,[230] he lifted Metrocles from his dejection. And from that time onwards, Metrocles became Crates' pupil, and became proficient in philosophy.

[6.95] He burnt all his writings, as Hecato tells us in the first book of his *Anecdotes*, saying:

> These are the phantoms of infernal dreams,

as if he meant that they were all nonsense. But some say that it was the notes he had taken of the lectures of Theophrastus which he burnt, quoting the following verse:

---

[230] Revealing why Crates had chosen lupins for their meal. Lupins, like many types of bean, are known for causing wind.

> Hephaestus, draw near, 'tis Thetis asks your aid.

He used to say that some things could be bought with money, such as, for instance, a house; whereas others could be obtained only with time and effort, such as education. Wealth, he said, was harmful unless it was used properly.

He died at a great age, having suffocated himself.

His disciples were Theombrotus and Cleomenes. And for his pupil, Theombrotus had Demetrius of Alexandria, while Cleomenes instructed Timarchus of Alexandria and Echecles of Ephesus. Not that Echecles was not also a pupil of Theombrotus, whose lectures were attended by Menedemus, of whom we shall speak shortly. Menippus, of Sinope, too, was someone very eminent in his school.

HIPPARCHIA

[6.96] Hipparchia, the sister of Metrocles, among others, was captivated by the doctrines of this school. Both she and Metrocles were born at Maroneia.

She fell in love with both the doctrines and demeanour of Crates, and could not be diverted from her regard for him, by either the wealth or high birth, or personal beauty of any of her suitors, but Crates was everything to her; and she even threatened her parents that she would do away with herself if she were not given in marriage to him. Crates accordingly, being implored by her parents to dissuade her from this resolution, did all he could; and at last, as he could not persuade her, he got up, and taking off all his clothes in front of her, he said, 'This is the bridegroom whom you are choosing, and this is the whole of his property; consider these facts, for it will not be possible for you to become his partner if you do not also apply yourself to the same studies and conform to the same habits that he does.'

[6.97] But the girl chose him; and assuming the same dress that he wore, went about with him as her husband, and appeared with him in public everywhere, and went to all entertainments in his company. And once when she went to dinner with Lysimachus, she attacked Theodorus, who was called the Atheist, proposing to him the following sophism: 'What Theodorus could not be called wrong for doing, that same thing Hipparchia ought not to be called wrong for doing. But Theodorus does no wrong when he beats himself; therefore Hipparchia does no wrong when she beats Theodorus.' He made no reply to what she said, but only pulled her clothes about; but Hipparchia was neither offended nor ashamed, as many a woman would have been; [6.98] but when he said to her,

> Who is the woman who has left the shuttle
> So near the warp?[231]

she replied, 'I, Theodorus, am that person; but do I appear to you to have come to a wrong decision, if I devote that time to philosophy, which I otherwise should have spent at the loom?' And these and many other sayings are reported of this female philosopher.

There is also extant a volume of Crates' *Letters*, containing the most excellent philosophy in a style sometimes resembling that of Plato.[232] He also wrote some tragedies, which are imbued with a very sublime spirit of philosophy, of which the following lines are a specimen:

> 'Tis not one tower that is my country, nor a single roof,
> But in every land each city and each house seems to me
> To be my dwelling-place, ready-made.

And he died at a great age, and was buried in Boeotia.

---

[231] Euripides, *The Bacchae* 1236.

[232] The fact that this last paragraph abandons Hipparchia's story and returns to Crates, suggests the possibility that Diogenes Laertius' chapters on Crates, Metrocles, and Hipparchia may originally have been combined into a single chapter.

MENIPPUS

[6.99] Menippus was also a Cynic, a Phoenician by descent, and a slave by birth, as Achaicus tells us in his *Ethics*. And Diocles informs us that his master was a native of Pontus, and was named Baton; but that subsequently, in consequence of his resolute begging and miserly habits, he became rich, and obtained the rights of citizenship at Thebes.

He never wrote anything serious, but his books are full of absurdities, and in some respects they are similar to those of Meleager, who was his contemporary.

And Hermippus tells us that he was a man who lent money at daily interest, and that he was called a usurer; for he used to lend on nautical usury,[233] and take security, so that he amassed a large fortune. [6.100] But in the end he fell victim to a plot and lost everything, and in a fit of despair he hung himself, and so ended his life. And we have written a playful epigram on him:

> Phoenician by birth, but a Cretan hound,
> A money-lender, so he was called,

---

[233] Also referred to as bottomry or bottomage, 'a maritime contract ... by which the owner of a ship borrows money for equipping or repairing the vessel and, for a definite term, pledges the ship as security – it being stipulated that if the ship be lost in the specified voyage or period, by any of the perils enumerated, the lender shall lose his money' ('bottomry' in *Encyclopædia Britannica*. *Encyclopædia Britannica 2007 Deluxe Edition*. Chicago: Encyclopædia Britannica, 2007).

> Perhaps you know Menippus.
> At Thebes one time men broke into his house
> And stole everything he had.
> But not understanding what it is to be a Cynic,
> He hanged himself.

But some say that the books attributed to him are not really his work, but are the composition of Dionysius and Zopyrus of Colophon, who wrote them for a joke, and then gave them to him as a man well able to gain some advantage by them.

[6.101] There were six persons of the name of Menippus. The first was the man who wrote a *History of the Lydians*, and made an abridgment of Xanthus. The second was this man of whom we have been speaking. The third was a sophist of Stratonicea, a Carian by descent. The fourth was a sculptor, and the fifth and the sixth were painters, and they are both mentioned by Apollodorus.[234]

The writings left by Menippus the Cynic amount to thirteen volumes:

> *Necromancy*
> *Wills*
> *Letters* (fictitious compositions as if written by the gods)
> *Replies to Physicists, Mathematicians, and Grammarians*
> *On the Birth of Epicurus*, and
> *On the School's Observance of the Twentieth Day*
> (And others.)

---

[234] Apollodorus was a common Greek name, and it is not possible to make any sensible conjectures as to whether this particular individual appears in modern compendia and dictionaries, or (if he does), which one he is. See Smith 1867, 1.232–6 for the options.

MENEDEMUS

[6.102] Menedemus was a disciple of Celotes of Lampsacus. According to Hippobotus, he attained such a degree of audacity in wonder-working that he went about in the guise of a Fury,[235] saying that he had come from Hades to take notice of all who did wrong, in order that he might descend thither again and make his report to the deities who abide there. And this was his attire: a tunic of a dark colour reaching to his feet, and a purple girdle round his waist, an Arcadian hat on his head with the twelve signs of the zodiac embroidered on it, tragic buskins, a preposterously long beard, and an ashen staff in his hand.

[6.103] These then are the lives of each of the Cynics; and we shall also append some of the doctrines which they all held in common, if indeed it is not an abuse of language to call this an authentic sect of philosophy, instead, as some contend that it should be termed, just a way of life. They

---

[235] The translation here follows Hicks. In Greek mythology the *Erinyes* (plural of *Erinys* – literally, 'the angry ones') or *Eumenides* (plural of *Eumenis* – literally 'the gracious ones') or Furies in Roman mythology, were female, chthonic deities of vengeance or supernatural personifications of the anger of the dead. They represent regeneration and the potency of creation, which both consumes and empowers. A formulaic oath in the *Iliad* (3.278 ff., 19.260 ff.) invokes them as 'those who beneath the earth punish whosoever has sworn a false oath' (adapted from the opening to the article 'Erinyes' at Wikipedia <http://en.wikipedia.org/wiki/Erinyes> accessed 2008-09-13).

wished to abolish the subjects of logic and natural philosophy, like Aristo of Chios,[236] and thought that men should study nothing but ethics. And what some people assert of Socrates was described by Diocles as a characteristic of Diogenes, for he said that his doctrine was that a man ought to investigate

> Only the good and ill that takes place
> Within our houses.

They also discard the ordinary subjects of education. At any rate, Antisthenes said that those who had attained discretion had better not study literature, lest they should be perverted by adverse influences; [6.104] they also wish to abolish geometry and music, and everything of that kind. In any case, Diogenes once said to a person who was showing him a clock, 'It is a very useful thing to save a man from being too late for supper.' And once when a man made an exhibition of musical skill before him, he said:

> Cities are governed, so are houses too,
> By wisdom, not by harp-playing and whistling.[237]

Their doctrine is that the end[238] of mankind is to live according to virtue, as Antisthenes says in his *Heracles*, exactly like the Stoics. For those two sects have a good deal

---

[236] Aristo of Chios was a heterodox Stoic. See the Glossary of Names.
[237] Yonge includes the following note:
This is a parody on two lines in the *Antiope* of Euripides:

Gnômêi gar andros eu men oikountai poleis.
Eu d'oikos eis t' au polemon ischuei mega.

Which may be translated:
Wisdom it is which regulates both cities
And private citizens, and makes their lot
Secure and happy; nor is her influence
Of less account in war.
[238] Translating the Greek *telos*.

in common with one another, on which account they themselves say that Cynic philosophy is a short road to virtue; and in this way lived Zeno of Citium.

They also teach that men ought to live simply, using only plain food in moderate quantities, wearing nothing but a single cloak, and despising riches, and glory, and nobleness of birth; accordingly, some of them feed upon nothing beyond herbs and cold water, living in any shelter that they can find, or in tubs as Diogenes did; for he used to say that it was the peculiar property of the Gods to want nothing, and that, therefore, when a man wished for nothing he was like the Gods.

[6.105] Another of their doctrines is that virtue can be taught, as Antisthenes maintains in his *Heracles*; and that when it has once been attained it can never be lost. They also say that the wise man deserves to be loved, and cannot commit error, and is a friend to everyone who resembles him, and that he leaves nothing to fortune. And everything which is unconnected with either virtue or vice they call indifferent, agreeing in this with Aristo of Chios.

These then were the Cynics; and now we must pass on to the Stoics, of which sect the founder was Zeno, who had been a disciple of Crates.[239]

---

[239] The Stoics (Zeno of Citium, Chrysippus and others) appear in Book Seven of Diogenes Laertius' *Lives and Opinions of Eminent Philosophers*. See Yonge and Seddon 2007.

APPENDIX 1

Dio Chrysostom: *Fourth Discourse on Kingship*[240]

[1] They tell us that once upon a time Alexander when not over busy met Diogenes,[241] who had an abundance of time on his hands. For the one was king of Macedonia and many other countries beside, while the other was an exile from Sinope;[242] and there are many who in speaking and writing of this encounter give no less admiration and credit to Alex-

---

[240] The text of Appendix 1 is taken from volume 1 of the Harvard University Loeb edition of *Dio Chrysostom*, with an English translation by J. W. Cohoon (in five volumes), first published in 1932. The *Fourth Discourse on Kingship* is reprinted here in its entirety with the permission of Harvard University Press. With some omissions, the footnotes in this Appendix are those of J. W. Cohoon in the Loeb edition, with occasional additions of my own, indicated by initials [KS]. Cohoon commences his translation with this brief preamble:

In the fourth Discourse Alexander the Great is represented as conversing with Diogenes, who tells him that the real king is a son of Zeus even as Homer says. Then he goes on to give the Cynic doctrine that this sonship is evidenced by qualities of mind and character, not by military power and wide dominion. He concludes by picturing graphically the spirit of avarice, the spirit of love of pleasure, and the spirit of ambition, which rule the lives of ordinary men.

The reference at the very end to the happy fortune of those who received a good *daimon* or *genius* at their birth has led to the reasonable conjecture that this address was delivered before Trajan on his birthday, September 18th in AD 103.

[241] The famous Cynic philosopher, discussed by Diogenes Laertius above, pp. 62–103 (DL 6.20–81) [KS].

[242] An important town on the southern shore of the Euxine or Black Sea.

ander than to Diogenes because, although he was ruler over so many people and had greater power than any other man of his day, he did not disdain to converse with a poor man who had intelligence and the power of endurance. [2] For all men without exception are naturally delighted when they see wisdom honoured by the greatest power and might; hence they not only relate the facts in such cases but add extravagant embellishments of their own; nay more, they strip their wise men of all else, such as wealth, honours, and physical strength, so that the high regard in which they are held may appear to be due to their intelligence alone. [3] And so I should like on this occasion to tell what in all likelihood was the nature of their conversation, since it happens too that I have nothing else that demands my attention.

[4] Now it should be explained that Alexander was by common report the most ambitious of men and the greatest lover of glory. He was anxious to leave his name the greatest among the Greeks and barbarians and longed to be honoured, not only – as one might put it – by mankind the world over, but, if it were at all possible, by the birds of the air and the beasts of the mountains. [5] Moreover, he looked down upon all other men and thought that no one was a dangerous rival in this matter – neither the Persian king nor the Scythian nor the Indian nor any man or city among the Greeks. [6] For he perceived that they had all been wellnigh ruined in soul by luxury and idleness and were the slaves of money and pleasure. But as to Diogenes, when Alexander heard of the words which this man spoke and of the deeds which he did and how he bore his exile, though at times he despised the man for his poverty and shabbiness, quite naturally, as he himself was young and had been reared in royal luxury, [7] yet often he would admire and envy the man for his courage and endurance, and especially

for his great reputation, because all the Greeks knew and admired him for what he was, and no one else could match him in point of distinction. [8] He himself needed his Macedonian phalanx, his Thessalian cavalry, Thracians, Paeonians, and many others if he was to go where he wished and get what he desired; but Diogenes went forth unattended in perfect safety by night as well as by day whithersoever he cared to go. [9] Again, he himself required huge sums of gold and silver to carry out any of his projects; and what is more, if he expected to keep the Macedonians and the other Greeks submissive, must time and again curry the favour of their rulers and the general populace by words and gifts; [10] whereas Diogenes cajoled no men by flattery, but told everybody the truth and, even though he possessed not a single drachma, succeeded in doing as he pleased, failed in nothing he set before himself, was the only man who lived the life he considered the best and happiest, and would not have accepted Alexander's throne or the wealth of the Medes and Persians in exchange for his own poverty.

[11] Therefore Alexander, being nettled to think that anyone living so easy and care-free a life was going to surpass himself and in addition should be no less famous, and thinking perhaps too that he would receive some benefit from an interview with the man, had long desired to behold him and converse with him; [12] and when he had come to Corinth and had received the Greek embassies and regulated the affairs of the allies as well, he told his attendants that he wished to have a little leisure and went off – I will not say to the court[243] of Diogenes, for he had no court

---

[243] θύραι means literally 'doors, or gate'. From the Eastern custom of receiving petitions at the gate of the palace the gate came to mean 'the royal court'. Cf. the expression, 'The Sublime Porte', which meant 'The Ottoman court', or the Government of the Turkish empire.

either great or small, nor house nor hearth of his own as the well-to-do have, [13] but he made the cities his home and used to live there in the public buildings and in the shrines, which are dedicated to the gods, and took for his hearthstone the wide world, which after all is man's common hearth and nourisher. [14] On that day it happened that Diogenes was all alone in the Craneion,[244] for he had no pupils at all nor any such crowd about him as the sophists and flue-players and choral masters have. So the king came up to him as he sat there and greeted him, whereat the other looked up at him with a terrible glare like that of a lion and ordered him to step aside a little, for Diogenes happened to be warming himself in the sun. [15] Now Alexander was at once delighted with the man's boldness and composure in not being awestruck in his presence. For it is somehow natural for the courageous to love the courageous, while cowards eye them with misgiving and hate them as enemies, but welcome the base and like them. And so to the one class truth and frankness are the most agreeable things in the world, to the other, flattery and deceit. The latter lend a willing ear to those who in their intercourse seek to please, the former, to those who have regard for the truth.

[16] Then after a brief pause Diogenes asked the king who he was and what object he had in coming to him. 'Was it,' he said, 'to take some of my property?'[245]

'Why, have you any property?' replied the other; 'do you own anything that you might share with one?'

---

[244] A cypress grove and a gymnasium in a suburb of Corinth. Here it evidently means the gymnasium.

[245] Cahoon runs these exchanges of dialogue into single paragraphs (intending to mirror the format of the Greek text, presumably). I hope I have assisted the reader is amending the typesetting of Cahoon's original text by allowing each participant his own indented paragraph, in the style usually encountered in contemporary typography [KS].

'Much indeed,' he replied, 'and very valuable, in which I do not at all feel sure that you will ever be able to have a share. Yet it is not glaives or cauldrons or mixing-bowls or couches and tables such as Darius[246] is reported by some writers to possess in Persia that I happen to own.'

[17] 'What,' retorted the other, 'do you not know Alexander the king?'[247]

'I hear many speak his name, to be sure,' said he, 'like so many jackdaws flitting about, but the man I know not, for I am not acquainted with his mind.'

'But now,' came the answer, 'you shall know his mind also, since I have come for the very purpose of letting you know me thoroughly and of seeing you.'

[18] 'Well, it would be hard for you to see me,' rejoined the other, 'just as it is for men with weak eyes to see the light. But tell me this: are you the Alexander whom they call a bastard?'

At this the king flushed and showed anger, but he controlled himself and regretted that he had deigned to enter into conversation with a man who was both rude and an impostor, as he thought. [19] Diogenes, however, marking his embarrassment, would fain change his throw just like men playing at dice. So when the king said, 'What gave you the idea of calling me a bastard?' he replied, 'What gave it? Why, I hear that your own mother says this of you. Or is it not Olympias[248] who said that Philip is not your father, as it happens, but a dragon or Ammon or some god or other or

---

[246] Darius Codomannus, the last king of Persia, who soon after this was defeated by Alexander.

[247] Alexander is annoyed that Diogenes has selected Darius as an example of a wealthy person, and not himself [KS].

[248] Wife of Philip II, king of Macedon and mother of Alexander the Great [KS].

demigod or wild animal? And yet in that case you would certainly be a bastard.'

[20] Thereupon Alexander smiled and was pleased as never before, thinking that Diogenes, so far from being rude, was the most tactful of men and the only one who really knew how to pay a compliment. 'Well then,' said he, 'do you think the story is true or false?'

[21] 'It is uncertain,' was the reply; 'for if you are self-controlled and know the royal art of Zeus, nothing prevents your being a son of Zeus; [22] for this is what they claim Homer says: that Zeus is the father, not only of gods but of men as well, though not of slaves nor of any mean and ignoble man. If, however, you are cowardly and love luxury and have a servile nature, then you are in no way related to the gods or to good men. [23] Why, methinks of old the "Sown men", as they were called, of Thebes[249] had what seemed a spear mark on their bodies as a sign of their origin, and he who did not have this mark was not regarded as one of the "Sown men". And do you not think that in the souls of the offspring of Zeus also a sign is to be found by which those who have the power to judge will know whether they are of his seed or not?'

Of course Alexander was greatly delighted with this thought. [24] Hereupon he put the following question to Diogenes. 'How,' said he, 'could one be the best king?'

At this the other, eyeing him sternly, answered, 'But no one can be a bad king any more than he can be a bad good man; for the king is the best one among men, since he is most brave and righteous and humane, and cannot be over-

---

[249] From the dragon's teeth sown by Cadmus sprang up, according to the myth, fully armed men, who fought with one another until only five remained. These were made citizens of Thebes and with their reputed descendents were called Sown Men.

come by any toil or by any appetite. [25] Or do you think a man is a charioteer if he cannot drive, or that one is a pilot if he is ignorant of steering, or is a physician if he knows not how to cure? It is impossible, nay, though all the Greeks and barbarians acclaim him as such and load him with many diadems and sceptres and tiaras like so many necklaces that are put on castaway children lest they fail of recognition. Therefore, just as one cannot pilot except after the manner of pilots, so no one can be a king except in a kingly way.'

[26] Then Alexander in alarm, lest after all he might be found ignorant of the science of kingship, said, 'And who, think you, imparts this art, or where must one go to learn it?'

[27] To which Diogenes replied, 'Well, you know it if the words of Olympias are true and you are a son of Zeus, for it is he who first and chiefly possesses this knowledge and imparts it to whom he will; and all they to whom he imparts it are sons of Zeus and are so called.'[250] [28] Or do you think that it is the sophists who teach kingship? Nay, the most of them do not even know how to live, to say nothing of how to be king. [29] Do you not know,' he continued, 'that education is of two kinds, the one from heaven, as it were, the other human? Now the divine is great and strong and easy, while the human is small and weak and full of pitfalls and no little deception; and yet it must be added to the other if everything is to be right. [30] This human sort, however, is what most people call "education" – meaning thereby something for children,[251] I suppose – and they have the notion that he who knows the most literature, Persian or

---

[250] Homer calls kings διογενεῖσ (sprung from Zeus).
[251] So Plato puns on the Greek word for education. τὴν περὶ τὰς Μούσας παιδείαν τε καὶ παιδιάν, *Laws* 656c – 'The education and play for children in the Muses.' See also Plutarch, *Moralia* 80c. μὴ παιδιᾶς ἀλλὰ παιδείας ἕνεκα, 'Not for the play of children but for education.'

Greek or Syrian or Phoenician, and has read the most books is the wisest and best educated person; but again, when people find any knaves or cowards or avaricious men among these, then they say the fact is as insignificant as the individual.[252] The other kind men sometimes call simply education, at other times, "true manhood" and "high-mindedness". [31] And it was for that reason that men of old called those persons "sons of Zeus" who received the good education and were manly of soul, having been educated after the pattern of the great Heracles. Whoever, then, being noble by nature, possesses that higher education, readily acquires this other also, having only to learn a few things in a few lessons,[253] merely the greatest and most important things, and is already initiated and treasures them in his soul. [32] And thenceforth nothing can rob him of any of these things, neither time nor any tricky sophist, nay, not even one who would fain burn them out by fire. But if the man were burned, as Heracles is said to have burned himself, yet his principles would abide in his soul just as, I believe, the teeth of bodies that have been cremated are said to remain undestroyed though the rest of the body has been consumed by the fire. [33] For he does not have to learn but merely to recall; after that he at once knows and recognises, as having had these principles in his mind at the beginning. And furthermore, if he comes upon a man who knows the road, so to speak, this man easily directs him, and on getting the information he at once goes his way. If, however, he falls in with some ignorant and charlatan sophist, the fellow will wear him out by leading him hither and thither, dragging him now to the east and now to the west and now to the south, not knowing anything himself but merely guessing,

---

[252] *i.e.*, neither proves anything against the 'human' education.
[253] A compliment to Trajan, who had little interest in letters.

after having been led far afield himself long before by impostors like himself. [34] It is just the same as in hunting. When dogs that are untrained and unruly catch no scent and do not pick up the trail, they mislead others by barking and behaving as if they knew and saw, and many, chiefly the most foolish, follow those dogs that bark at random, [35] and of this pack those which make no outcry and keep silent are merely deceived themselves, but the most impetuous and foolish dogs, imitating the first ones, raise a din and strive to deceive others. Around the so-called sophists, likewise, you will sometimes find such a great accompanying throng of simpletons, and you will discover that your sophist does not differ one whit from a lecherous eunuch.'

[36] On hearing this, Alexander wondered what his reason was for likening the sophist to a eunuch and asked him.

'Because,' came the reply, 'the most wanton eunuchs, protesting their virility and their passion for women, lie with them and annoy them, and yet nothing comes of it, not even if they stay with them night and day. [37] So too in the schools of the sophists you will find many growing old in their ignorance, wandering about in their discussions far more helplessly than Homer says Odysseus ever did upon the deep, and any one of them might sooner find his way to Hades as that hero did than become a good man by talking and listening. [38] And you, since you have been born with the right nature, if you come upon a man of understanding, will find a single day sufficient to get a grasp of his subject and art, and you will no longer have any need of subtle claptrap and discussions. But if you are not so fortunate as to have a disciple of Zeus or one like Zeus for your teacher to tell you forthwith and clearly what your duty is, then nothing comes of it for you, even if you waste your whole life in sleepless study and fasting in the schools of the miserable sophists. [39] I am not the first man to say this, but Homer said it before me. Or are you not acquainted with the Homeric poems?'

Now Alexander prided himself very greatly on knowing by heart the whole of the one poem, the *Iliad*, and much of the *Odyssey* likewise.[254] And so he said in surprise, 'Pray, where has Homer discoursed about these things?'

'In the passage,' came the reply, 'where he calls Minos[255] the consort of Zeus. [40] Or does not "to consort" mean "to associate"? Well then, he says that he was an associate of Zeus, which would virtually be calling him his disciple. Now do you imagine that he associated with Zeus as a pupil with any other object than to learn justice and the duties of a king? For mark you, Minos is said to have been the most righteous man in the world. [41] Once more, when he says that kings are "nurtured of Zeus" and "dear unto Zeus", do you think that he means any other nurture than the teaching and instruction which I called[256] divine? Or do you believe that he means that kings are nourished by Zeus as by a nurse, on milk and wine and various foods, and not on knowledge and truth? [42] And in the same way he means[257] that friendship also is nothing else than identity of wish and of purpose, that is, a kind of likemindedness. For this, I presume, is the view of the world too: that friends are most truly likeminded and are at variance in nothing. [43] Can anyone, therefore, who is a friend of Zeus and is likeminded with him by any possibility conceive any unrighteous desire or design what is wicked and disgraceful? Homer seems to answer this very question clearly also when in commending

---

[254] This information is found only here.
[255] *Odyssey* 19.178–9.
[256] In § 29 [above].
[257] That is, when he speaks of kings as 'dear unto Zeus'.

some king he calls him a "shepherd of peoples". [44] For the shepherd's business is simply to oversee, guard, and protect flocks, not, by heavens, to slaughter, butcher, and skin them. It is true that at times a shepherd, like a butcher, buys and drives off many sheep;[258] but there is a world of difference between the functions of butcher and shepherd, practically the same as between monarchy and tyranny. [45] For instance, when Xerxes[259] and Darius[260] marched down from Susa[261] driving a mighty host of Persians, Medes, Sacae,[262] Arabs, and Egyptians into our land of Greece to their destruction, were they functioning as kings or as butchers in driving this booty for future slaughter?'

[46] And Alexander said: 'Apparently you do not hold even the Great King to be a king, do you?'

And Diogenes with a smile replied, 'No more, Alexander, than I do my little finger.'

'But shall I not be a great king,' Alexander asked, 'when once I have overthrown him?'

'Yes, but not for that reason,' replied Diogenes; [47] 'for not even when boys play the game to which the boys themselves give the name "kings" is the winner really a king. The boys, anyhow, know that the winner who has the title of "king" is only the son of a shoemaker or a carpenter – and he ought to be learning his father's trade, but he has played truant and is now playing with the other boys, and he

---

[258] A shepherd may drive a flock to be butchered, just as a king may drive an army to its ruin: but the one is not a true shepherd but a butcher, and the other is not a true king but a tyrant.

[259] King of Persia, son of Darius and Atossa, invaded Greece in 480 BC and was defeated in the battle of Salamis.

[260] King of Persia, invaded Greece in 490 BC and was defeated at Marathon.

[261] Winter residence of Persian kings.

[262] One of the most powerful and warlike of the nomadic Scythian tribes. They lived on the steppes of Central Asia.

fancies that now of all times he is engaged in a serious business – [48] and sometimes the "king" is even a slave who has deserted his master. Now perhaps you kings are also doing something like that: each of you has playmates – the eager followers on his side – he his Persians and the other peoples of Asia, and you your Macedonians and the other Greeks. And just as those boys try to hit one another with the ball, and the one who is hit loses, so you now are aiming at Darius and he at you, and perhaps you may hit him and put him out; for I think you are the better shot. [49] Then, those who were on his side at first will be on yours and will do you obeisance, and you will be styled king over all.'

Now Alexander was again hurt and vexed, for he did not care to live at all unless he might be king of Europe, Asia, Libya, and of any islands which might lie in the ocean. [50] His state of mind, you see, was the opposite of what Homer says was that of Achilles' ghost. For that hero said that he preferred to live in bondage to

> Some man of mean estate, who makes scant cheer,
> Rather than reign o'er all who have gone down
> To death.[263]

But Alexander, I doubt not, would have chosen to die and govern even a third part of the dead rather than become merely a god and live forever – unless, of course, he became king over the other gods. [51] Perhaps, too, Zeus is the only one for whom he would have shown no contempt, and that because men call him king. This is the reason why Diogenes was bent on reproving him thoroughly.

The king replied, 'Diogenes, you seem to be joking. If I capture Darius and the king of the Indians to boot, there

---

[263] *Odyssey* 11.490 f.

will be nothing to prevent my being the greatest king that ever lived. For what is left for me when I have once become master of Babylon, Susa, Ecbatana, and the Empire of the Indies?'

[52] And the other, observing that he was aflame with ambition and that with all his heart he was being borne at full stretch in that direction, just as the cranes when flying stretch themselves out in whatever direction they are speeding, exclaimed, [53] 'Nay, in the state of mind in which you are, you will have not one whit more than anyone else, nor will you really be a king, no, not even if you leap over the walls of Babylon and capture the city in that way, instead of breaking through the walls from without or sapping them from beneath, nor even if you imitate Cyrus and glide in like a water-snake by the river-route,[264] and in the same way get inside the walls of Susa and Bactra, no, not even though you swim across the ocean and annex another continent greater than Asia.'[265]

[55] 'And what enemy have I still left,' said he, 'if I capture those peoples I have mentioned?'

---

[264] Cyrus, the founder of the Persian empire, who took Babylon in 583 BC, was said to have used this ruse, but the story is now discredited. See Herodotus 1.191.

[265] [At this point] the MSS. have §54: ἢ σὺ τοὺς ἀλεκτρυόνας οὐ καλεῖς νόθους, οἳ ἂν ὦσιν ἐξ ἀνομοίων; ἢ οὐ μείζων σοι δοκεῖ διαφορὰ θεοῦ πρὸς γυναῖκα θνητὴν ἢ γενναίου ἀλεκτρυόνος; εἰ οὖν γέγονας οὕτως καθάπερ φασί, καὶ σὺ νόθος ἂν εἴης ὥσπερ ἀλεκτρυών. τυχὸν δὲ καὶ μαχιμώτατος ἔσῃ τῶν ἄλλων διὰ ταύτην τὴν νοθείαν. – 'Or do you not call a cock a mongrel when it is from two different breeds? And do you not consider the inequality between a god and a mortal woman greater than it is in the case of a thoroughbred cock? Therefore, if your origin is as it is said to be, you too would be as much a mongrel as a cock in the same case. Perhaps, too, you will turn out to be the greatest fighter in the world, thanks to this mixture.' These words Geel puts after §19.

'The most difficult of all to conquer,' he answered, 'one who does not speak Persian or Median as Darius does, I presume, but Macedonian and Greek.'

At this Alexander was troubled and sore distressed for fear the other knew of someone in Macedonia or Greece who was preparing to make war on him, [56] and asked, 'Who is this enemy of mine in Greece or Macedonia?'

'Why, do you not know,' said he, 'you who think that you know more than anyone else?'

'In that case will you please tell me?' he asked; 'do not conceal it.'

'I have been trying to tell you for a long time, but you do not hear that you are yourself your own bitterest foe and adversary as long as you are bad and foolish. And this is the man of whom you are more ignorant than of any other person. [57] For no foolish and evil man knows himself; else Apollo would not have given as the first commandment, "Know thyself!"[266] regarding it as the most difficult thing for every man. [58] Or do you not think that folly is the greatest and most serious of all ailments and a blight to those that have it, and that a foolish man is his own greatest bane? Or do you not admit that he who is most harmful to a man and causes him the most ills is that man's greatest foe and adversary? In view of what I say rage and prance about,' said he, [59] 'and think me the greatest blackguard and slander me to the world and, if it be your pleasure, run me through with your spear; for I am the only man from whom you will get the truth, and you will learn it from no one else. For all are less honest than I and more servile.'

[60] Thus spoke Diogenes, counting it as nothing that he might be chastised, yet quite convinced that nothing would

---

[266] The first of three inscriptions known to have been upon the temple of Apollo at Delphi.

happen. For he knew that Alexander was a slave of glory and would never make a bad move where it was at stake. [61] So he went on to tell the king that he did not even possess the badge of royalty.

And Alexander said in amazement, 'Did you not just declare that the king needs no badges?'

'No indeed,' he replied; 'I grant that he has no need of outward badges such as tiaras and purple raiment – such things are of no use – [62] but the badge which nature gives is absolutely indispensable.'

'And what badge is that?' said Alexander.

'It is the badge of the bees,' he replied, 'that the king wears. Have you not heard that there is a king among the bees, made so by nature, who does not hold office by virtue of what you people who trace your descent from Heracles call inheritance?'

'What is this badge?' inquired Alexander.

[63] 'Have you not heard farmers say,' asked the other, 'that this is the only bee that has no sting, since he requires no weapon against anyone? For no other bee will challenge his right to be king or fight him when he has this badge. I have an idea, however, that you not only go about fully armed but even sleep that way. [64] Do you not know,' he continued, 'that it is a sign of fear in a man for him to carry arms? And no man who is afraid would ever have a chance to become king any more than a slave would.'

At these words Alexander came near hurling his spear.

[65] With these words Diogenes strove to encourage him to put his trust in well-doing and devotion to righteousness and not in arms. 'But you,' he continued, 'also carry in your soul a keen-whetted temper, a goad difficult to restrain, as we see, and compelling. [66] Will you not throw off this

armour which you now wear, don a worker's tunic,[267] and serve your betters, instead of going about wearing a ridiculous diadem? And perhaps before long you will grow a comb or tiara as cocks do? Have you never heard about the Sacian feast[268] held by the Persians, against whom you are now preparing to take the field?'

[67] And Alexander at once asked him what it was like, for he wished to know all about the Persians.

'Well, they take one of their prisoners,' he explained, 'who has been condemned to death, set him upon the king's throne, give him the royal apparel, and permit him to give orders, to drink and carouse, and to dally with the royal concubines during those days, and no one prevents his doing anything he pleases. But after that they strip and scourge him and then hang him. [68] Now what do you suppose this is meant to signify and what is the purpose of this Persian custom? Is it not intended to show that foolish and wicked men frequently acquire this royal power and title and then after a season of wanton insolence come to a most shameful and wretched end? [69] And so, when the fellow is freed from his chains, the chances are, if he is a fool and ignorant of the significance of the procedure, that he feels glad and congratulates himself on what is taking place; but if he understands, he probably breaks out into wailing and refuses to go along without protesting, but would rather remain in fetters just as he was. [70] Therefore, O perverse man, do not attempt to be king before you have attained to wisdom. And in the meantime,' he added, 'it is

---

[267] Short tunic open on right side; worn by slaves and artisans [ἐξωμίς].

[268] Strabo (C. 512.5) gives a different account of this feast. He says it was celebrated by the Persians with carousing in memory of a victory by Cyrus over the Sacae (called Σακαῖοι in Strabo 512 ff.). On the custom see Frazer, *Golden Bough*, II², p. 24).

better not to give orders to others but to live in solitude, clothed in a sheepskin.'

'You,' he objected, 'do you bid me, Alexander, of the stock of Heracles, to don a sheepskin – me, the leader of the Greeks and king of the Macedonians?'

[71] 'Surely,' he replied, 'just as your ancestor did.'

'What ancestor?' he asked.

'Archelaus.[269] Was not Archelaus a goatherd and did he not come into Macedonia driving goats? Now do you think he did this clad in purple rather than in a sheepskin?'

And Alexander calmed down, laughed, and said, 'Do you refer to the story about the oracle,[270] Diogenes?'

[72] The other puckered his face and said, 'Oracle indeed! All I know is that Archelaus was a goatherd. But if you will drop your conceit and your present occupations, you will be a king, not in word maybe, but in reality; and you will prevail over all women as well as all men, as did Heracles, whom you claim as an ancestor of yours.'

[73] Alexander said, 'Women indeed! Or am I to understand that you refer to the Amazons?'

'Nay, it was no hard matter to overcome them,' he replied. 'I refer to women of another kind, who are extremely dangerous and savage. Have you not heard the Libyan myth?[271]

---

[269] According to Hyginus (*Fabula* 219), Archelaus, a reputed ancestor of Alexander, after casting the treacherous Cisseus, Macedonian king, into the pit prepared for himself, followed a goat by Apollo's direction and founded the city of Aegae in Macedonia.

[270] The story of the oracle bidding Archelaus follow the goat.

[271] Told by Dio in the *Fifth Discourse*, [concerning a species of monster that haunted the uninhabited regions of Libya, that was especially fond of human flesh. These creatures had the dazzlingly beautiful faces and breasts of human women, with the scaly bodies of giant snakes. Their victims were beguiled by the beauty of their faces and of their breasts, which they would expose at the opportune moment, causing an intense

And the king replied that he had not.

[74] Then Diogenes told it to him with zest and charm, because he wanted to put him in a good humour, just as nurses, after giving the children a whipping, tell them a story to comfort and please them. [75] 'Be assured,' he continued, 'that you will never be king until you have propitiated your attendant spirit[272] and, by treating it as you should, have made it commanding, free-spirited and kingly, instead of, as in your present state, slavish, illiberal, and vicious.'

[76] Then was Alexander amazed at the courage and fearlessness of the man; yet deeming him to have greater knowledge than other men, he urgently besought him not to say him nay but to explain what his attendant spirit was and how he must propitiate it. For he assumed that he would hear some deity's name and of certain sacrifices or purifications that he would have to perform.

---

desire for sexual intercourse that no man could resist. The King of Libya took his army to destroy the beasts, but with only partial success; having killed the creatures in their den they fled in haste from the region, only to be pursued and wiped out by those remaining monsters who had been away hunting at the time of the army's attack. In the end, the creatures could only be destroyed by Heracles. Dio tells this myth to illustrate the irrational and brutish nature of the passions, explaining that the myth is an allegory to show that 'when the majority of men try to clear the trackless region of their souls, teeming with savage beasts, by rooting out and destroying the brood of lusts in the hope of then having got rid of them and escaped, and yet have not done this thoroughly, they are soon afterwards overwhelmed and destroyed by the remaining lusts; but that Heracles, the son of Zeus and Alcmene, carried the task through to completion and made his own heart pure and gentle or tame; and that this is what is meant by his taming, that is, civilizing the earth' (*Fifth Discourse* 22-3, trans. Cohoon) KS].

[272] The popular idea was of an indwelling spirit or genius by which a man was possessed or controlled. Heraclitus, fr. 119 (Diels), claims that character is each man's genius.

[77] So when Diogenes perceived that he was greatly excited and quite keyed up in mind with expectancy, he toyed with him and pulled him about in the hope that somehow he might be moved from his pride and thirst for glory and be able to sober up a little. [78] For he noticed that at one moment he was delighted, and at another grieved, at the same thing, and that his soul was as unsettled as the weather at the solstices when both rain and sunshine come from the very same cloud. He realised, too, that Alexander despised the way in which he argued with him, due to the fact that the prince had never heard a real master of discourse but admired the style of the sophists, as being lofty and distinguished. [79] So wishing to win his favour and at the same time to show that he was quite able, whenever he chose, to make his discourse step out like a well-trained and tractable horse, he spoke to him as follows about attendant spirits, showing that the good and the bad spirits that bring happiness and misery are not outside the man, [80] and that each one's intelligence – this and nothing more – is the guiding spirit of its owner, that the wise and good man's spirit is good, the evil man's evil, and likewise the free man's is free, the slave's slavish, the kingly and high-minded man's kingly, the abject and base man's abject. [81] 'However, not to provoke a tedious discussion,' he continued, 'by taking up each separate point, I shall mention the commonest and most noticeable spirits by which everybody, generally speaking, is actuated – tyrants and private citizens, rich and poor, whole nations and cities.' Thereupon he let out all his sails and delivered the following discourse with great loftiness and courage.

[82] 'Many, thou son of Philip, are the vices and corrupting influences that in all circumstances beset wretched

man, and they are well-nigh more numerous than tongue can tell. For in truth, as the poet says,

> No word is there so fraught with fear to speak,
> Nor sorrow, nor calamity god-sent,
> But mortal man might bear the weight thereof.[273]

[83] 'Now as there are, roughly speaking, three prevailing types of lives which the majority usually adopt, not after thoughtful consideration and testing, I assure you, but because they are carried away by chance and thoughtless impulse, we must affirm that there is just the same number of spirits whom the great mass of foolish humanity follows and serves – some men one spirit and some another – just as a wicked and wanton troop follows a wicked and frenzied leader. [84] Of these types of lives which I have mentioned, the first is luxurious and self-indulgent as regards bodily pleasures, the second, in its turn, is acquisitive and avaricious, while the third is more conspicuous and more disordered than the other two – I mean the one that loves honour and glory – and it manifests a more evident and violent disorder or frenzy, deluding itself into believing that it is enamoured of some noble ideal.

[85] 'Therefore, come, let us imitate clever artists. They put the impress of their thought and art upon practically everything, representing not only the various gods in human forms but everything else as well. Sometimes they paint rivers in the likeness of men and springs in certain feminine shapes, yes, and islands and cities and well-nigh everything else, like Homer, who boldly represented the Scamander[274] as speaking beneath his flood, [86] and

---

[273] Euripides, *Orestes* 1 f.
[274] In the *Iliad* (21.233 ff.) Homer depicts the battle between Achilles and the Scamander [KS].

though they cannot give speech to their figures, nevertheless do give them forms and symbols appropriate to their nature, as, for example, their river gods recline, usually naked, and wear long flowing beards and on their heads crowns of tamarisk or rushes.[275] [87] Let us then show ourselves to be no whit worse or less competent in the field of discourse than they in their several arts as we mould and depict the characters of the three spirits of the three lives, therein displaying an accomplishment the reverse of and complementary to the skill and prophetic power of the physiognomists, as they call them. [88] These men can determine and announce a man's character from his shape and appearance; while we propose to draw from a man's habits and acts, a type and shape that will match the physiognomist's work – that is, if we shall succeed in getting hold rather of the average and lower types. [89] Since our purpose is to show the absurdity existing in human lives, there is no impropriety or objection to our being seen imitating poets or artists or, if need be, priests of purification[276] and to our striving to furnish illustrations and examples from every source, in the hope of being able to win souls from evil, delusion, and wicked desires and to lead them to love virtue and to long for a better life; [90] or else we might follow the practice of some of those who deal with initiations and rites of purification,[277] who appease the wrath of Hecate[278] and undertake to make a person sound, and then before the cleansing process, as I understand, set forth and point to the

---

[275] Plants which grow in wet soil.
[276] The *kathartai* were regarded as charlatans, as we see from Hippocrates and Plutarch. They professed to cure diseases.
[277] Plato (*Phaedrus* 244e) refers to this same method of appeasing the wrath of a deity and had evidently influenced Dio here.
[278] Goddess of the lower world, who sends phantoms from it to vex and terrify those needing κάθαρσις.

many and various visions that, as they claim, the goddess sends when angry.

[91] 'Well, then, the avaricious spirit craves gold, silver, lands, cattle, blocks of houses, and every kind of possession. Would it not be represented by a good artist as downcast and gloomy of appearance, humble and mean of dress – aye, as squalid and ragged, loving neither children nor parents nor native land, and recognising no kinship but that of money, and considering the gods as nothing more than that which reveals to him many vast treasures or the deaths of certain kinsfolk and connections from whom he might inherit, regarding our holy festivals as sheer loss and useless expense, never laughing or smiling, [92] eyeing all with suspicion and thinking them dangerous, distrusting everybody, having a rapacious look, ever twitching his fingers as he computes his own property, I take it, or that of someone else – a spirit not only without appreciation or capacity for any other thing, but scoffing at education and literature except when they have to do with estimates and contracts, the still blinder lover of wealth, which is rightly described and portrayed as blind; [93] mad about every kind of possession and thinking that nothing should be thrown away; unlike the magnetic stone,[279] which they say attracts iron to itself, but amassing copper and lead as well, yes, even sand and rock if anyone gives them, and everywhere and in almost every case regarding possession as more profitable and better than non-possession. He is most frantic and eager, however, to get money, simply because success here is quickest and cheapest, since money goes on piling up day

---

[279] A magnetic iron ore said by Pliny the elder (*Natural History* 36.126 f.) to have been found in Magnesia, a district of Macedonia, and also near the city of Magnesia in Asia.

and night and outstrips, I ween, the circuits of the moon.[280] [94] He recks naught of dislike, hate, and curses and, besides, holds that while other kinds of possessions may be pretty baubles wherewith to amuse oneself, money, to put it succinctly, is the very essence of wealth. [95] This, therefore, is what he seeks and pursues from any and every source, never concerning himself at all to ask whether it is acquired by shameful or by unjust means, except insofar as, observing the punishments meted out to footpads, he lets cowardice get the better of him and becomes cautious. For he has the soul of a worthless cur, that snatches up things when it expects not to be noticed, and looks on other morsels with longing eyes but keeps away from them, though reluctantly, because the guards are by. [96] So let him be a man insignificant in appearance, servile, unsleeping, never smiling, ever quarrelling and fighting with someone, very much like a pander, who in garb as well as in character is shameless and niggardly, dressed in a coloured mantle, the finery of one of his harlots. [97] A foul and loathsome spirit is this, for he brings every possible insult and shame upon his own friends and comrades, or, rather, his slaves and underlings, whether he find them in the garb of private citizens or in that of royalty. [98] Or is it not plain to see that many who are called kings are only traders, tax-gatherers, and keepers of brothels? Shall we assert that Dromon and Sarambus,[281] because they keep shops in Athens and are called shopkeepers by the Athenians, come fairly by the name, but that the elder Darius,[282] who kept a shop in Baby-

---

[280] Interest was payable monthly; cf. Aristoph. *Clouds* 17.

[281] Mentioned as a shopkeeper in Plato, *Gorgias* 518b.

[282] The first Persian king of that name. The Persians called him a 'shopkeeper' as a compliment, doubtless because he organised the Empire and imposed a regular tribute. According to one etymology 'Darius' means 'possessing goods'. See Herodotus 3.89 f.

lon and in Susa, and whom the Persians still to this day call a shopkeeper, has not deserved this name? [99] Moreover, there is one peculiarity about this spirit, not shared by the others: although he sometimes rules and masters the soul, yet sometimes he seems to be compliant, the reason being that wealth is the handmaid and the willing ministrant to every appetite and interest. [100] I, however, am now speaking of the spirit that takes the lead himself and dominates the faculties of his unhappy possessor; he has neither pleasure nor glory as the motive for the acquisition of wealth, and does not intend to spend or to use what he has gotten together, but keeps his wealth out of circulation and useless, actually locked up in secret and sunless vaults.

[101] 'So far so good. The second man and the attendant spirit of that man is the one which proclaims the orgies of Pleasure and admires and honours this goddess, a truly feminine being. He is of many hues and shapes, insatiable as to things that tickle nostril and palate, and further, methinks, as to all that pleases the eye, and all that affords any pleasure to the ear, as to all things that are soothing and agreeable to the touch, such as warm baths taken daily, or rather, twice a day, anointings that are not for the relief of weariness [102] and, besides, the wearing of soft sweeping robes,[283] bolstered repose, and attentive service for every appetite and desire. He is passionately devoted to all these things, but especially and most unrestrainedly to the poignant and burning madness of sexual indulgence, through intercourse both with females and with males, and through still other unspeakable and nameless obscenities; after all

---

[283] Cf. Plato, *Alcibiades* 122c, ἱματίων ἕλξεις.

such indiscriminately he rushes and also leads others, abjuring no form of lust and leaving none untried.[284]

[103] 'At present, it should be explained, we are treating as one this spirit which is afflicted with all these maladies and excesses of the soul; for we do not want to assemble a huge gallery of lecherous, gluttonous, and bibulous spirits and others unnumbered, but to treat as simply one that spirit which is incontinent and enslaved to pleasure, [104] which – if only there is from some source an inflow of inexhaustible means, whether from royal coffers or from some great private estate – wallows in a deep and boundless slough of debauchery until old age comes; failing such resources, the man speedily squanders the fortune he began with, or is reduced to impotent and licentious penury, and in deprivation combined with craving falls terribly short of his desires. [105] And, further, this spirit has sometimes changed those possessed by it to the life and the garb of women, just as the myths relate of those who transformed human beings into birds or beasts, if they were unfortunate enough to have become enslaved to an appetite of such a nature.

'But here again we find a contrast in our examples. [106] There is, first in this class, the weak and unventuresome spirit, which easily leads men into effeminate vices and other kinds of misconduct which involve loss and disgrace, but, where certain indulgences are followed by punishments that inflict upon the culprit death or imprisonment or heavy fines, altogether avoids inciting the victim to those extremes. [107] There is, however, the more aggressive and audacious spirit, which compels its victim to overleap absolutely all bounds, both human and divine. Now while the

---

[284] The last part of this description bears a resemblance to the description which Diodorus Siculus (II.23) gives of Sardanapalus.

weak and unventuresome spirit no sooner gets involved than he acknowledges his shameful weakness by taking up no manly occupation, but leaving social and civic activities to those who have lived a better life, [108] the bold and impetuous spirit, after enduring many a rebuff and humiliation, by a sudden turn of fortune's wheel,[285] as they say, emerged as a general or as a popular leader with shrill and piercing voice, and, like actors on the stage, discards his feminine attire for the time being and then, having seized that of a general or an orator, stalks about as a blackmailer and an object of terror, looking all the world in the eye.

[109] 'Now does a manly and grave appearance befit such a spirit, or rather a weak and effeminate one? Therefore we shall dress him up in his proper attire, not in the brave and awe-inspiring clothes which he often assumes when playing a part. [110] So, by heavens, let him step forth luxurious, breathing of myrrh and wine, in a saffron robe, with much inordinate laughter, resembling a drunken reveller in a wanton midday riot and wearing faded garlands on his head and about his neck, reeling in his gait, dancing and singing an effeminate and tuneless song. Let him be led by brazen, dissolute women, [111] known as certain of the sensual lusts, each pulling him her own way, and he rebuffs none of them nor says her nay, but follows readily and eagerly enough. [112] And let them, with a great din of cymbals and flutes, come eagerly forth, escorting the frenzied fellow. And from the midst of the women let him utter shriller and more passionate cries than they; he is pale and effeminate in appearance, unacquainted with heaven's air or honest toil, lets his

---

[285] Literally, 'the shell having fallen underside uppermost'. This expression is borrowed from a game played with shards or shells in which the players ran away or pursued according as the shell fell with one or the other side uppermost. See Plato, *Phaedrus* 241b.

head droop, and leers lasciviously, with his watery eyes ever studying his fleshy self, but heedless of the soul and her mandates. [113] Were a statuary or a painter compelled to represent this man, he could create no better likeness of him than that of the Syrian king,[286] who spent his life in his harem with eunuchs and concubines without ever a sight of army or war or assembly at all. [114] Let his steps also be guided by Delusion, a very beautiful and enticing maid, decked out in harlot's finery, smiling and promising a wealth of good things and making him believe that she is leading him to the very embrace of happiness, till unexpectedly she drops him into the pit, into a morass of foul mud, and then leaves him to flounder about in his garlands and saffron robe. [115] In servitude to such a tyrant and suffering such tribulation those souls wander through life which, craven and impotent in the face of hardships, enslaved to pleasure, pleasure-loving, and carnally-minded, go on living a disgraceful and reprehensible life, not from choice, but because they have drifted into it.

[116] 'And now, leaving this spirit, my discourse is eager, as in a contest, to bring in the third spirit, as the herald to bring in a chorus[287] – I mean the ambitious one. He is not so very eager at present to contest, although he is naturally emulous about everything and demands to be first. However, the present trial is not concerned with the question of any fame or honour that may come to him, but with his abundant and merited dishonour. [117] So come, what garb and appearance shall we give to the ambitious spirit? Or is it manifest that he shall be winged and buoyant in keeping with his character and ambition, floating along with the

---

[286] The Assyrian king Sardanapalus seems to be meant. Syria and Assyria were sometimes confused.
[287] Cf. Aristoph. *Ach.* 11.

breezes like those sons of Boreas[288] whom artists have conceived and painted, lightly poised on high and running in company with their father's breezes? [118] But while they used to display a power of their own whenever they pleased, yet for a time they went voyaging with the other heroes on the Argo, serving as their shipmates and performing the regular tasks as much as anyone. But the spirit who presides over men who love glory is always aspiring and never touches the earth or anything lowly; no, he is high and lifted up [119] as long as he enjoys a calm and clear sky or a gently blowing zephyr, feeling ever happier and happier and mounting to the very heavens, but often he is enwrapped in a dark cloud when accompanied by some unpopularity or censure from the many people whom he courts and honours and has appointed to the mastery over his own happiness.

[120] 'As to his safety, this spirit is not at all to be classed with either eagles or cranes or any other feathered species; nay, one might rather liken his flight to the violent and unnatural soaring of Icarus,[289] whose father undertook to contrive a device that proved disastrous. [121] So then the lad, moved by the conceit of youth and desiring to soar above the stars, was safe enough for a short time, but when the fastenings became loose and the wax ran, he gave his name from this circumstance to the sea where he fell to be seen no more. [122] Just so with this spirit of ambition: When he also puts his faith in weak and truly airy wings – I mean the honours and plaudits bestowed at haphazard by the general crowd – he floats away on his perilous and unsteady voyage, taking with him the man, his admirer and henchman, who

---

[288] God of the north wind. His sons sailed on the Argo with Jason to get the Golden Fleece.
[289] Son of Daedalus, who essayed to fly with his father's wings. The portion of the Aegean Sea that lies between Myconos and the mainland of Asia Minor was called the Sea of Icarus.

now appears to many to be high and blessed, but now again seems low and wretched, not only to others, but first and foremost to himself. [123] But if there be anyone who does not care to conceive of and portray him as winged, let him liken him to Ixion,[290] constrained to cruel and violent gyrations as he is rapidly whirled round and round on a wheel. Indeed, the comparison of the wheel with reputation would not be unfitting nor far inferior in truth to the clever and brilliant metaphors of the rhetoricians: by its shifting movement it very readily turns round, and in its revolutions forces the soul to assume all kinds of shapes, more truly than the potter's wheel affects the things that are being shaped upon it. [124] Such a man, ever turning and revolving, a flatterer of peoples and crowds, whether in public assemblies or lecture halls, or in his so-called friendship with tyrants or kings and his courting of them – who would not feel pity for his character and manner of living? I am not speaking of the man, however, who, having managed his own life admirably, endeavours by the persuasion of speech combined with goodwill and a sense of justice to train and direct a great multitude of men and to lead them to better things.

[125] 'Let us, then, come to an end with this spirit, too, for I should prefer at the present time not to provide him with clothing and shape, and his other appurtenances, and thus add a great and endless throng of words. [126] Put briefly, then, he could be characterised as contentious, foolish, and conceited, and a prey to vainglory, jealousy, and all such difficult and savage emotions. For it is quite inevi-

---

[290] Ixion was a legendary king of Thessaly who committed the world's first parricide, and later, after Zeus had purified him, he attempted to rape Hera, the wife of Zeus. For these crimes he was punished by being crucified on a fiery wheel which revolves throughout eternity (this is presumably the sun) [KS].

table that all these unsociable and savage and difficult feelings should accompany the honour-seeking type of soul, [127] and it is natural that he should change his mind often and be inconsistent – inasmuch as he serves and courts so fickle a thing – alternating between joy and sorrow more often and continuously than hunters are said to do. For they say this is their especial and most continuous experience, when they sight the game and then lose it again. [128] So it is with the ambitious: When good repute and praise come their way, their souls are magnified and swell and show a wondrous burgeoning, just like the shoot of the sacred olive[291] that they tell of at Athens, which swelled and grew to full size in a single day. But, alas! they soon wither again and droop and die when censure and obloquy overtake them. [129] And Delusion, the most convincing thing imaginable, besets this spirit also. For while the miser's delusion and the hedonist's were not able to promise them definitely a brilliant fruition, and did not open the door for their dupes to exalted and splendid destinies, but merely whispered and suggested to them the names of the blessings in prospect, it is otherwise with the Delusion of ambition. Fascinating her victim with her charms and spells, she tells him he is a lover of all that is good and leads him towards notoriety as to some virtue or fair renown. [130] So I shall be tempted here again to make a second allusion to the same story of Ixion. 'Tis said that in his eagerness for the blissful union with Hera he embraced a dark and dismal cloud and became the parent of a useless and monstrous brood, the curious hybrid race of the centaurs. [131] And in the same way he who has been disappointed in his love for true fame and has then dallied with a lust for notoriety has

---

[291] Sacred to Athena, who according to one version is said to have planted the first one on the Acropolis of Athens. See Herodotus 8.55.

in reality been consorting with a cloud without knowing it instead of enjoying intercourse with the divine and august. And from such associations and unions nothing useful or serviceable can come, but only strange irrational creations that resemble the centaurs – [132] I mean the political acts of certain demagogues and the treatises of the sophists; for both sophists and demagogues are purely mercenary leaders. But in saying this I distinguish the generals and educators and statesmen from those whom I have just mentioned, all of whom may well be assigned to that spirit of ambition and be counted in its faction and following.

[133] 'And now I have described those who are under the sway of each of the spirits named; but very often two or all of them get hold of the same individual, make conflicting demands upon him, and threaten that, if he does not obey, they will inflict severe penalties upon him. [134] The pleasure-loving spirit bids him to spend money on pleasures and to spare neither gold nor silver nor anything else he has, while the avaricious and parsimonious spirit objects, and checks him and threatens that it will destroy him with hunger, thirst, and utter beggary and want, so surely as he heeds the other. [135] Again, the spirit that loves distinction counsels and encourages him to sacrifice all that he has for the sake of honour, but the other spirit opposes and blocks this one. And indeed, the lover of pleasure and the lover of fame can never be in accord or say the same thing; for the one despises fame, thinks it nonsense, and often cites the lines of Sardanapalus:

> What I have eaten and wantoned, the joys I have had of my amours,

> These alone have I now. The rest of my blessings have vanished.[292]

[136] And especially does this spirit ever keep death before his eyes, warning him that when dead he will be able to enjoy no pleasures any longer. But the spirit that courts fame leads, yea, drags him away from pleasure by keeping him in mind of the censure and reproach that will be his. [137] Not knowing, therefore, what to do or whither to turn and hide himself, he often runs away into the darkness and under its cover tries to please and serve the second spirit, [138] but the other finds him out and drags him into the open, and his soul, thus torn and distracted and ever in battle and ceaseless strife with itself, cannot but end its course in utter misery. For just as a complication of maladies, that often seem to conflict with one another, make the cure difficult and well-nigh hopeless, so, in my opinion, must the situation be when different affections of the soul are mingled and entwined into one.

[139] 'But come, let us attain a pure harmony, better than that which we enjoyed before, and extol the good and wise guardian spirit or god – us who the kindly Fates decreed should receive Him when we should have gained a sound education and reason.'

---

[292] See Preger, *Inscriptiones Graecae Metricae* 232.

APPENDIX 2

Epictetus: *Discourse* 3.22[293]

CYNIC PHILOSOPHY

[1] When one of his students, who seemed inclined to the Cynic way of life, enquired of Epictetus as to what kind of person a Cynic ought to be and what was the basic notion of the Cynic undertaking, Epictetus said:

Let us examine this at our leisure. [2] But this much I can tell you now, that he who attempts so great an affair without divine guidance is an object of divine wrath, and has no other purpose than to act indecently in public. [3] For in any well-managed house no man comes forward saying to himself, 'I ought to be manager here.' If he does so, when the master returns and sees him insolently giving orders, he will drag him out and flog him. [4] So it is also in this great city of the world; for here also there is a master of the house who assigns to everything its place. [5] 'You are the sun,' he says, 'and by going round the heavens you make the year and the seasons, and make the fruits grow and nourish them, and stir the winds and make them calm, and moderately warm the bodies of men: go, travel round, and so administer things from the greatest to the least. [6] *You*

---

[293] The text of Appendix 2 is extracted from my forthcoming edition of Epictetus, *Epictetus: The Discourses, Handbook and Fragments*. The translation is based on extensive revisions of the nineteenth-century editions translated by George Long and Thomas Wentworth Higginson.

are a calf and when a lion appears, do what is appropriate:[294] *for if you do not, you will suffer for it. You are a bull: advance and fight, for this is your business, and becomes you, and you can do it.* [7] *You can lead the army against Troy: be Agamemnon. You can fight Hector in single combat: be Achilles.'* [8] But if Thersites[295] had come forward and claimed the command, he would either not have obtained it, or if he did obtain it, he would have disgraced himself before a multitude of witnesses.

[9] So think carefully about this undertaking: it is not what it seems to you.

[10] *I wear a cloak now, and I shall wear it then. I sleep upon the hard ground now, and I shall sleep so then. I will take in addition a little bag and a staff, and I will go about and begin to beg and to abuse those whom I meet. And if I see any man plucking the hair out of his body, I will rebuke him; or if he arranges his curls, or walks about in purple, I will rebuke him.*

[11] If you imagine the thing to be such as this, keep far away from it: do not approach it, it is not at all for you. [12] But if your impression of it is correct, and you do not think yourself unworthy of it, consider what a great enterprise you are undertaking.

[13] First, with regard to yourself, you must no longer, in any instance, behave as you do now. You must accuse neither God nor man. You must altogether suppress desire, and must transfer aversion to only those things which are within

---

[294] That is, run away.
[295] Thersites was the ugliest man in Troy who fulminated against Agamemnon (Homer, *Iliad* 2.212 ff.) until faced down and beaten into silence by Odysseus (*Iliad* 2.243 ff.). Homer describes him as 'ugly ... beyond all men' (*Iliad* 2.216) with respect to whom 'there is no baser mortal ... among all those who [came to Troy]' (2.248; translations Murray and Wyatt). He is someone entirely unsuited for command.

the sphere of your moral character: you must not feel anger nor resentment nor envy nor pity; neither boy, nor girl, nor fame, nor dainties, must have appeal for you. [14] For you must know that other men indeed fence themselves with walls, and houses, and darkness, when they indulge in anything of this kind, and they have many means of concealment. A man shuts his door, he sets somebody before the chamber: and if anyone comes, they say that he is out, he is not available. [15] But the Cynic, instead of all these things, must use self-respect as his protection. If he does not, he will be naked under the open sky, his shame exposed. His self-respect is his house and his door: it is the slave before his bedchamber; it is his darkness. [16] For he ought not to wish to hide anything that he does: but if he does so, he is lost, he has destroyed his character as a Cynic, as a man who lives under the open sky, as a free man; for he has begun to fear some external thing, and he has begun to have need of concealment. Nor can he get concealment when he wants it, for where shall he now hide himself, and how? [17] And if by chance this educator, this pedagogue of the public, shall be detected, what kind of things will he be compelled to suffer? [18] How is it possible for a man who fears these things to have the confidence to devote himself wholeheartedly to supervising the conduct of others? It cannot be done: it is impossible.

[19] In the first place then you must purify your own ruling faculty, and hold to this way of life: [20] 'From now on, the material upon which I have to work is my own mind, as wood is to the carpenter, as leather to the shoemaker; and my business is the right use of impressions.'[296]

---

[296] 'impressions' (*phantasiai*; singular *phantasia*) are what we are aware of in virtue of having experiences. They are not limited only to what is sensed in perception, but include as well what we are aware of

[21] But my body is nothing to me: its parts are nothing to me. Death? Let it come when it chooses, either death of the whole or of a part. [22] Exile? Where? Can anyone turn me out of the world? They cannot. But wherever I go, there is the sun, there is the moon, there are the stars, dreams, omens, and conversations[297] with Gods.'

[23] Then, if he is thus prepared, the true Cynic cannot be satisfied with this; but he must know that he is sent as a messenger from Zeus to men about what is good and bad, to show them that they have gone astray and are seeking the true nature of good and evil where it is not, but where it is they never think; [24] and that he is a spy, like Diogenes when he was carried off to Philip after the battle of Chaeronea.[298] For in fact a Cynic is a spy of the things which are good for men and which are evil, [25] and it is his duty, after making accurate observations, to come and tell them the truth; not to be struck with terror so as to point out to them

---

when thinking abstractly, having memories, imagining things, and so forth. 'An impression is an imprint on the soul, its name being appropriately borrowed from the imprint on wax made by a seal' (DL 7.45). The notion of making proper use of impressions is for Epictetus a key component of his exposition of Stoic ethics, and someone makes proper use of their impressions by assenting to them correctly, by not judging good or bad anything external (goodness, for the Stoics, being confined exclusively to virtue). Whereas non-rational animals respond to their impressions automatically (thus 'using' them), over and above using our impressions, human beings, being rational, can 'understand their use' (*Discourses* 1.6.13, 2.14.15) and, with practice, assent or not assent to them as we deem appropriate. 'The use of impressions' (*hê chrêsis tôn phantasiôn*) in this wider sense is an essential component of making progress as a Stoic, and it is this capacity that Epictetus strives to teach his students (adapted from Seddon 2005, 226).

[297] Translating *homilia*.
[298] Diogenes of Sinope has already appeared at *Discourses* 1.24.3–10 as the spy (*kataskopos*) whose mission is to report on what is truly good and bad.

enemies where there are none; nor, in any other instance, to be troubled or confounded by his impressions.

[26] It is his duty then, if the occasion should arise, to be able to mount the tragic stage and say with a loud voice, like Socrates: 'Men, to where do you hurry? What are you doing, you wretches? Like blind people you are wandering up and down: you have strayed from the true road and are going by another; you seek for prosperity and happiness where they are not, and if another shows you where they are, you do not believe him.' [27] Why do you seek it in external things? In the body? It is not there. If you doubt this, look at Myro, look at Ophellius.[299] In possessions? It is not there. But if you do not believe me, look at Croesus:[300] look at those who are now rich, with what lamentations their life is filled. In power? It is not there. If it were, those who have been twice and thrice consuls must be happy; but they are not. [28] Whom shall we believe in these matters? You who from outside look upon their affairs and are dazzled by what you see, or the men themselves? [29] What do they say? Hear them when they groan, when they grieve, when on account of these very consulships and glory and splendour they think that they are more wretched and in greater danger. [30] Is it in royal power? It is not there. If it were, Nero[301]

---

[299] Oldfather conjectures that these men, otherwise unknown, were famous athletes or gladiators of their day.

[300] Croesus (c.560–546 BC) was the last king of Lydia, famed for his enormous wealth. His armies were defeated by the Persians, and his riches were of no avail to him.

[301] Nero (AD 37–68) was emperor of Rome from AD 54. His reign is often associated with tyranny and extravagance. Surviving sources for Nero's reign – Tacitus, Suetonius and Cassius Dio – portray him as the emperor who 'fiddled while Rome burned' and an early persecutor of the Christians. He perpetrated a number of murders (including that of his mother Agrippina and his adoptive brother Britannicus) and ordered the executions of his political opponents (including that of the Stoic philosopher Seneca for his supposed involvement in the Pisonian conspiracy).

would have been happy, and Sardanapalus.[302] But neither was Agamemnon[303] happy, although he was a better man than Sardanapalus and Nero; but while others are snoring, what is he doing?

> Much from his head he tore his rooted hair.[304]

And what does he say himself?

> I wander bewildered ...
> my heart leaps forth from my bosom.[305]

[31] Poor man! Which of your affairs goes badly?[306] Your possessions? No. Your body? No. For you have gold and bronze in abundance. What then is the matter with you? You have neglected and corrupted that part of you, whatever it is called, with which we desire, with which we avoid, with which we choose and with which we reject things.

[32] —*How neglected?*

You remain ignorant of the true nature of the good for which you were born, and of the nature of evil, and what is your own, and what belongs to another; and when anything that belongs to others goes badly, you say:

—*I am undone; the Greeks are in danger!*

[33] Wretched is your ruling faculty, alone neglected and uncared for!

His end came when the Senate sentenced him to death and sent the Praetorian Guard to arrest him, forcing him to commit suicide at the age of 30.

[302] Sardanapalus, according to the Greek writer Ctesias of Cnidus, was the last king of Assyria.

[303] Agamemnon, king of Mycenae, in Homer's *Iliad* was the commander of the Greek army that besieged the city of Troy for ten years, attempting to recover King Menelaus' wife Helen who had been abducted by Paris.

[304] Homer, *Iliad* 10.15.

[305] Homer, *Iliad* 10.91-4.

[306] Epictetus imagines that he is addressing Agamemnon.

—The Greeks will be slain by the swords of the Trojans!

And if the Trojans do not kill them, will they not die anyway?

—Yes, but not all at once.

What difference does that make? For if death is an evil, whether men die altogether, or if they die singly, it is equally an evil. Is anything else going to happen, then, other than the separation of the soul from the body?

—Nothing.

[34] And if the Greeks should all perish, is the door closed against you, and is it not in your power to die?[307]

—It is.

Why then do you lament, you who are a king and hold the sceptre of Zeus? A king can no more be made unfortunate than a god. [35] What are you, then? You are a mere shepherd, rightly called so; for you weep, just as shepherds do when the wolf seizes any of their sheep; and they who are governed by you are mere sheep. [36] But why did you come here? Was your desire in any danger? Was your aversion? Was your capacity to choose or reject?

—No, he answers, *but my brother's wife was carried off.*

[37] Was it not then a great gain to be rid of an adulterous wife?

—Shall we be held in contempt by the Trojans?

What kind of people are the Trojans, wise or foolish? If they are wise, why do you fight them? If they are fools, why do you take any notice of them?

[38] *—Where, then, does our good lie, since it does not lie in these things? Tell us, sir, you who are our messenger and spy.*

---

[307] Following such a complete and utter military failure, with his armies destroyed, Agamemnon would be expected to commit suicide.

It is neither where you think that it is, nor where you choose to seek it: for if you chose to seek it, you would have found it in yourselves; nor would you be wandering out of the way, nor seeking what belongs to others as if it were your own. [39] Turn your thoughts into yourselves: observe the preconceptions that you have. What kind of a thing do you imagine the good to be?

—*That which flows easily, that which is happy, that which is not impeded.*

Come, do you not imagine it to be something naturally great? Do you not imagine it to be something precious? Do you not imagine it to be something free from harm? [40] In what kind of material then ought you to seek for that which flows easily, for that which is not impeded? In that which is enslaved, or in that which is free?

—*In that which is free.*

Is your body, then, enslaved or free?

—*We do not know.*

Do you not know that it is the slave of fever, of gout, ophthalmia, dysentery; of a tyrant, of fire, of iron, of everything that is stronger than itself?

—*Yes, it is a slave.*

[41] How then is it possible for anything that belongs to the body to be free from hindrance? And how can what is naturally lifeless, a thing of earth or clay, be something great or precious? Well then, do you possess nothing which is free?

[42] —*Perhaps nothing.*

And who is able to compel you to assent to that which appears false?

—*No one.*

And who can compel you *not* to assent to that which appears true?

—*No one.*

Here, then, you see that there *is* something in you that is naturally free. [43] But who among you can desire or avoid something, choose or reject something, prepare yourself for something, or propose to set about something, unless you have first conceived an impression of what is advantageous and appropriate?

—*No one.*

You have then in these things also something which is unhindered and free. [44] Wretched men, cultivate this, take care of this, seek here for your good.

[45] *—And how is it possible for a man who has nothing, who is naked, without a house, without a hearth, squalid, without a slave, without a city, to live a life that flows easily?*

[46] See, God has sent you a man to show you that it is indeed possible. [47] Look at me, I have no city, I have no house, I have no possessions, I have no slave; I sleep on the ground; I have no wife, no children, no governor's petty mansion, but only earth and heaven, and one poor cloak. [48] Yet what do I lack? Am I not without sorrow? Am I not without fear? Am I not free? Did any of you ever see me disappointed in my desire, or suffering anything to which I am averse? Did I ever blame God or man? Did I ever accuse anyone? Did any of you ever see me with a sorrowful countenance? [49] And how do I face those before whom you stand in fear and awe? Do I not treat them like slaves? Who, when they see me, does not think that they see their own king and master? [50] This is the language of a Cynic, this their character, this their purpose. But no, you say – what makes a Cynic is his little wallet and staff, his great jaws, and the way he devours everything that you give him, or stows it away, or his reviling tactlessly everyone he meets, or showing off his fine shoulders. [51] Is this the spirit in

which you are going to undertake so great an endeavour? First take a mirror: look at your shoulders; observe your back, your thighs. You are going, my man, to be enrolled as a competitor in the Olympic Games, not any old cheap and miserable contest. [52] At the Olympic Games you cannot simply be defeated then make your departure. You must first be disgraced in the sight of all the world, not in the sight of those from Athens only, or from Sparta or from Nicopolis; and next if you enter the contest carelessly you must be whipped:[308] and before being whipped, you must suffer thirst and heat, and swallow quantities of dust.[309]

[53] Reflect more carefully, know yourself, consult the divinity; without God attempt nothing; for if he advises you (to do this or anything), be assured that he intends you to become a great man or suffer many blows. [54] For there is this fine circumstance woven into the Cynic's destiny, that he must be beaten like an ass, and yet, when beaten, must love those who beat him as the father, as the brother of all. [55] You say no – if a man flogs you, you stand out in a public place, calling, *Caesar, am I to suffer such things in breach of your peace? Let us bring the offender before the proconsul.* [56] What has the Cynic to do with Caesar or a proconsul or anyone else? His concern is with Zeus, who sent him into the world, and whom he serves. Does he call upon any other than Zeus? Is he not convinced that whatever hardship he suffers, it is Zeus who is exercising him? [57] Heracles, when

---

[308] This probably refers to the punishment meted out to sprinters caught committing false starts, that is, caught 'entering the contest carelessly'.

[309] This is probably a reference to a defeated wrestler who ends up having his face pushed into the sand.

he was exercised by Eurystheus,[310] did not think himself wretched, but without hesitation he attempted to fulfil all that he was appointed to do. And is he who is trained to the contest and exercised by Zeus going to call out and complain, he who is worthy to bear the sceptre of Diogenes? [58] Hear what Diogenes said to the passers-by when he was in a fever, *Miserable wretches, will you not stay? Are you going on so long a journey to Olympia to see the contest of worthless athletes? Will you not choose to see the struggle between a fever and a man?* [59] Would such a man accuse God who sent him down as if God were treating him unworthily, a man who gloried in his circumstances, and claimed to be an example to those who were passing by? For what accusation could he bring? That he maintains a decency of behaviour, that he displays his virtue more conspicuously? [60] Well, and what does Diogenes say regarding poverty, regarding death, regarding pain? How did he compare his own happiness with that of the great king of Persia?[311] Or rather, he thought that there was no comparison between them. [61] For where there are perturbations, and griefs, and fears, and desires not satisfied, and aversions of things which you cannot avoid, and envies and jealousies, how can there be a road to happiness in all this? But where there are corrupt judgements, there these things must of necessity be.

[62] When the young man asked whether the Cynic who has fallen sick should accept the invitation of a friend who asks him to come to his house so that he can take care of him in his sickness, Epictetus replied, And where will you

---

[310] Eurystheus was the king of Mycenae, at whose commands Heracles undertook the twelve labours for which he is most famed. See Heracles in the Glossary of Names.

[311] Presumably Darius I, 'Darius the Great', king of Persia.

find me the friend of a Cynic? [63] For to be worthy of being counted his friend, such a person must be another Cynic himself. He must to be a partner in the Cynic's sceptre and his kingdom, and a worthy minister, if he intends to be considered worthy of a Cynic's friendship, as Diogenes was a friend of Antisthenes, as Crates was a friend of Diogenes. [64] Or do you think that if a man comes to a Cynic and salutes him, that he is the Cynic's friend, [65] and that the Cynic will think him worthy of being received into his house? If such a thought comes into your head, rather look round for some convenient dunghill on which you can bear your fever and which will shelter you from the north wind that you may not be chilled. [66] But it seems to me that all you want is to get into some man's house and to be well fed there for a time. What business have you then, even to attempt so important an undertaking as this?

[67] —*But,* said the young man, *will the Cynic seek to marry and have children as matters of prime importance?*

If you grant me a city of sages, Epictetus replied, perhaps no one there will readily take up the Cynic's profession. For on whose account would he undertake this way of life? [68] However, if we suppose that he does, nothing will prevent him from marrying and having children; for his wife will be another person like himself, and his father-in-law another person like himself, and his children will be brought up like himself. [69] But as the state of things is now, like that of the battlefield, is it not necessary that a Cynic should be free from distractions, entirely attentive to his service to God, at liberty to walk among mankind, not tied down to common duties nor entangled in relationships which he cannot disregard if he is to keep the character of a wise and good man, relationships which, if he maintains them, will in fact destroy his character as the messenger, and spy, and herald of the gods? [70] For consider, there are some duties due to his father-in-law, some to the other relatives of his wife, and some to his wife herself: finally, he is excluded from his profession of Cynic by his having to become a nurse when his own family is sick, and from having to provide for their support. [71] And what about all the other things? He must have a vessel in which to warm water, to wash his child in the bath; there must be wool, oil, a bed, a cup for his wife after her delivery. And thus his possessions increase. [72] More business, more distractions. Where now is this king whose time is devoted to the public good?

> The people's guardian and so full of cares.[312]

This is the king whose duty it is to look after others, the married and those who have children; to see who is treating his wife well, and who uses her badly; who is quarrelling; which household is well administered, and which not; going about as a physician does, feeling the pulses of his patients. [73] He says to one, *you have a fever*, to another *you have a headache*, or *you have the gout*: he says to one, *abstain from food*; to another he says, *eat*; or *do not use the bath*; to another, *you must have an incision made*, or *you need to be cauterised*. [74] Where will he find time for this when he is tied down to the duties of everyday life? Must he not provide little cloaks for his children, and to send them to the schoolmaster with little writing tablets, writing equipment and little notebooks? And must he not also get ready their little beds? For they cannot be Cynics from the moment they are born. It would have been better to expose the children as soon as they were born than to fail to make proper provision for them, and kill them in that way. [75] Do you

---

[312] Homer, *Iliad* 2.24–5.

see to what we bring down our Cynic? How we deprive him of his kingdom?

[76] —*Yes, but Crates was married.*

The case of which you speak was a particular one, arising from love, concerning a wife who was another Crates.[313] But we are enquiring about ordinary marriages which are liable to distraction, and making this enquiry we do not find that marriage in this state of the world is something especially suited to the Cynic.

[77] —*How then*, he asked, *will he keep society going?*

In the name of God, are those men greater benefactors to society who introduce into the world to occupy their own places two or three snivelling children, or those who watch over as far as they can all mankind, and see what they do, how they live, what they attend to, what they neglect contrary to their duty? [78] Did they who left little children to the Thebans do them more good than Epaminondas[314] who died childless? And did Priam[315] who begat fifty worthless sons or Danaus or Aeolus contribute more to the community than Homer?[316] [79] Shall then a military command or the writing of a book prevent a man from marrying and becoming a father, so that he shall not be judged to have accepted the condition of childlessness for nothing, yet the kingdom of a Cynic not thought a comparable compensa-

---

[313] See DL 6.96, p. 115, above.

[314] Epaminondas was a Theban general, renowned for his great victories. The benefit he provided for Thebes lay in these victories. It would not have been better for the city if, instead of winning battles, he had had children.

[315] Priam was king of Troy at the time of his city's defeat by Agamemnon.

[316] Danaus was the father of 50 daughters, and Aeolus had six sons and six daughters. Homer is offered as another example of someone like Epaminondas, whose worth rests on something other than providing children to their communities.

tion for the lack of children? [80] Perhaps we do not understand his grandeur, nor properly represent to ourselves the character of Diogenes; but instead we think of Cynics as they are now,

> dogs that wait at tables and guard the gates[317]

who in no respect imitate the Cynics of old except perhaps in breaking wind in public, but in nothing else. [81] If this were not so, then the things that you have mentioned would not have moved us, nor should we have been astonished that a Cynic will not marry or have children. Man, the Cynic is the father of all mankind; all men are his sons, and all women are his daughters. Thus he attends to all; thus takes care of all. [82] What! Do you think it is from impertinence that he rebukes those he meets? No, he does it as a father, as a brother, and as the servant of Zeus, who is father of us all.

[83] If you like, ask me also if a Cynic will engage in administration of the state. [84] Fool, do you seek a greater form of administration than that in which he is already engaged? Do you ask if he should appear before the Athenians and say something about revenues and taxes, he who must talk with all mankind, Athenians, Corinthians, and Romans alike, not about taxes and revenues, nor about peace and war, but about happiness and misery, good fortune and bad fortune, about slavery and freedom? [85] When a man has undertaken the administration of such a state as this, why do you ask me if he should engage in the administration of a state? Ask me also if he should hold public office, and again I will say to you, fool, what greater office could he exercise than that which he already holds?

---

[317] Homer, *Iliad* 22.69.

[86] It is necessary also for the Cynic to have a certain kind of body: for if he appears to be consumptive, thin and pale, his testimony will no longer have the same authority. [87] For he must not only give a proof to the uneducated person, by the constancy of his mind, that it is possible to be a good and excellent man without those things that they set such store by; but he must show, too, by the state of his body, that his plain and simple way of living in the open air does no harm even to his body. [88] *See*, he says, *I and my body bear witness to this*. This is what Diogenes used to do, for he used to go about with a radiant complexion, and he attracted the notice of the masses by his mere physical presence. [89] But a Cynic who arouses pity is regarded as a mere beggar: all persons turn away from him, all are offended by him; for neither ought he to appear dirty so that he shall not also in this respect drive people away, but his very roughness ought to be clean and attractive.

[90] Much natural charm and a keen wit are similarly necessary in a Cynic (otherwise he becomes a mere driveller, and nothing else), and he must have these qualities so that he may respond to whatever befalls him. [91] So it was that Diogenes replied to someone who said, *Are you the Diogenes who does not believe in the existence of the gods?* by saying, *How can this be so when I believe that you are hated by the gods?*[318] [92] And on another occasion in reply to Alexander, who stood over him while he was sleeping, and quoted Homer's line,

> To sleep all night long does not become a man who gives counsel,[319]

he answered, when he was half asleep,

---

[318] DL 6.42.
[319] Homer, *Iliad* 2.24.

The people's guardian and so full of cares.[320]

[93] But above everything, the Cynic's ruling faculty must be purer than the sun; and if it is not, he must necessarily be a common cheat and a man of no principle, since while he himself is entangled in some vice he will reprove others. [94] See how the matter stands. Kings and tyrants have their guards and arms, giving them the power to reprove and punish those who do wrong, no matter how wicked they are themselves. But to a Cynic, instead of arms and guards, it is his conscience which gives him this power.[321] [95] When he knows that he has watched and laboured for mankind, that his sleep has been pure, and that awakening from sleep he is purer still, and that he thought whatever he has thought as a friend of the gods, as a servant, as one who shares the power of Zeus, and that on all occasions he is ready to say

Lead me, Zeus, and thou, O Destiny,[322]

and also,

[96] If it thus pleases the gods, thus let it be,[323]

---

[320] Homer, *Iliad* 2.24-5, already quoted above, at *Discourses* 3.22.72. Oldfather observes in his footnote: 'The only point in the anecdote seems to be that Diogenes could say something more or less apposite even when only half awake; for the completion of the quotation is in no sense a real answer to the reproach.'

[321] Matheson, in his translation of Epictetus' *Discourses*, includes this footnote, quoting from Edwin A. Abbott, *The Son of Man* (p. 3143): 'The Cynic is a natural king; he goes about like a Heracles destroying noxious beasts, and like Aesculapius healing diseases – Warrior and Physician in one. In both these capacities he receives from God authority over men, and men recognize it in him, because they perceive him to be their benefactor and deliverer.'

[322] Epictetus, *Handbook* 53.1. At *Discourses* 4.4.34, Epictetus attributes this line to the early Stoic Cleanthes.

[323] Epictetus, *Handbook* 53.3. This line is from Plato, *Crito* 43d, and is spoken by Socrates who has awoken in prison to see that Crito has come

why should he not have confidence to speak freely to his own brothers, to his children, in a word to his kinsmen? [97] For this reason, the man whose mind is thus disposed is neither impertinent nor a busybody; for he is not meddling in what concerns other people when he oversees human affairs, but he is looking after his own interests. If that is not so, you would have to say that the general is a busybody when he inspects his soldiers and examines them and watches them and punishes the disorderly. [98] But if while you have a cake under your arm, you rebuke others, I will say to you: Wouldn't you rather go away into a corner and eat what you have stolen? [99] What have you to do with the affairs of others? For who are you? Are you the bull of the herd, or the queen of the bees? Show me the tokens of your authority, such as they have from nature. But if you are a drone claiming the kingship over the bees, do you not suppose that your fellow citizens will drive you out, just as the bees do the drones?

[100] The Cynic also ought to have such power of patient endurance that to the multitude he will seem as unfeeling as a stone. No one reviles him, no one strikes him, no one insults *him*,[324] but he gives his body to anyone to do with as they please. [101] For he bears in mind that the inferior, in whatever respect it is the inferior, must be overpowered by the superior; and the body is inferior to the multitude, the weaker to the stronger. [102] Thus, he never enters such a contest in which he can be overpowered, but he immediately gives up what belong to others, and makes no claim upon what is slavish and dependent. [103] But where moral

---

to visit him. What he is happy to let happen if it pleases the gods is, of course, his own pending execution.

[324] In the sense that no one *can*, since being so treated means nothing to the Cynic.

character and the use of impressions are concerned, there you will see that he has so many eyes that compared with him you would say that Argos[325] was blind. [104] Is his assent ever hasty, his impulse rash, does his desire ever fail in its objective, does that which he would avoid befall him, is his purpose unaccomplished, does he ever find fault, is he ever dejected, is he ever envious? [105] It is upon these things that he directs all his attention and energy. As for everything else, he lies back and snores, in perfect peace. For no one can steal away his moral character, or stand as tyrant over it.

—But they can when it comes to his body?
Indeed they can.
[106] —And so also regarding his paltry possessions?
Certainly.
—And what about public offices and honours?

But what does he care for these things? When therefore anyone tries to frighten him with them, he says to them, *Go away and look for children – your masks may be frightening to them, but I know that they are made of pot, behind which lies nothing.*

[107] Such is the affair upon which you deliberate. Therefore I urge you in God's name to defer the matter, and first consider whether you are really prepared for it. [108] Take notice of what Hector says to Andromache:[326]

> Hasten home and tend to the loom.
> War is the work of men,
> Of all indeed, but specially 'tis mine.[327]

---

[325] Argos features in Greek mythology as a giant with a hundred eyes.
[326] Hector is the son of King Priam of Troy, and the greatest of the Trojan heroes: Andromache is his wife.
[327] This is a paraphrase of Homer, *Iliad* 6.490-3.

Such was his recognition of his own capacities, and of her weakness.

APPENDIX 3

Pseudo-Lucian: *The Cynic*[328]

LUCIAN Give an account of yourself, my man. You wear a beard and let your hair grow; you eschew shirts; you exhibit your skin; your feet are bare; you choose a wandering, outcast, beastly life; unlike other people, you make your own body the object of your severities; you go from place to place sleeping on the hard ground where chance finds you, with the result that your old cloak, neither light nor soft nor gay to begin with, has a plentiful load of filth to carry about with it. Why *is* it all?

CYNIC It meets my needs. It was easy to come by, and it gives its owner no trouble. It is the cloak for me.
 [2] Pray tell me, do you not call extravagance a vice?

LUCIAN Oh, yes.

CYNIC And economy a virtue?

LUCIAN Yes, again.

---

[328] The text of Appendix 3 is taken from volume 4 of the Clarendon Press edition of *The Works of Lucian of Samosata*, translated by H. W. Fowler and F. G. Fowler (in four volumes), published in 1905, and now in the public domain. This particular discourse, reprinted here in its entirety, has been transmitted along with Lucian's other works, but is now recognised as spurious. Desmond (2008, 5) remarks that it is 'perhaps the most eloquent single summary of the Cynic outlook.' The notes to this text are mine.

CYNIC Then, if you find me living economically, and others extravagantly, why blame me instead of them?

LUCIAN I do not call your life more economical than other people's; I call it more destitute – destitution and want, that is what it is; you are no better than the poor who beg their daily bread.

[3] CYNIC That brings us to the questions, What is want, and what is sufficiency? Shall we try to find the answers?

LUCIAN If you like, yes.

CYNIC A man's sufficiency is that which meets his necessities; will that do?

LUCIAN I pass that.

CYNIC And want occurs when the supply falls short of necessity – does not meet the need?

LUCIAN Yes.

CYNIC Very well, then, I am not in want; nothing of mine fails to satisfy my need.

[4] LUCIAN How do you make that out?

CYNIC Well, consider the purpose of anything we require; the purpose of a house is protection?

LUCIAN Yes.

CYNIC Clothing – what is that for? Protection too, I think.

LUCIAN Yes.

CYNIC But now, pray, what is the purpose of the protection, in turn? The better condition of the protected, I presume.

LUCIAN I agree.

CYNIC Then do you think my feet are in worse condition than yours?

LUCIAN I cannot say.

CYNIC Oh, yes; look at it this way; what have feet to do?

LUCIAN Walk.

CYNIC And do you think my feet walk worse than yours, or than the average man's?

LUCIAN Oh, not that, I dare say.

CYNIC Then they are not in worse condition, if they do their work as well.

LUCIAN That may be so.

CYNIC So it appears that, as far as feet go, I am in no worse condition than other people.

LUCIAN No, I do not think you are.

CYNIC Well, the rest of my body, then? If it is in worse condition, it must be weaker, strength being the virtue of the body. Is mine weaker?

LUCIAN Not that I see.

CYNIC Consequently, neither my feet nor the rest of my body need protection, it seems; if they did, they would be in bad condition; for want is always an evil, and deteriorates the thing concerned. But again, there is no sign, either, of my body's being nourished the worse for its nourishment's being of a common sort.

LUCIAN None whatever.

CYNIC It would not be healthy, if it were badly nourished; for bad food injures the body.

LUCIAN That is true.

[5] CYNIC If so, it is for you to explain why you blame me and depreciate my life and call it miserable.

LUCIAN Easily explained. Nature (which you honour) and the Gods have given us the earth, and brought all sorts of good things out of it, providing us with abundance not merely for our necessities, but for our pleasures; and then you abstain from all or nearly all of it, and utilise these good things no more than the beasts. Your drink is water, just like theirs; you eat what you pick up, like a dog, and the dog's bed is as good as yours; straw is enough for either of you. Then your clothes are no more presentable than a beggar's. Now, if this sort of contentment is to pass for wisdom, God must have been all wrong in making sheep woolly, filling grapes with wine, and providing all our infinite variety of oil, honey, and the rest, that we might have food of every sort, pleasant drink, money, soft beds, fine houses, all the wonderful paraphernalia of civilisation, in fact; for the productions of art are God's gifts to us too. To live without all these would be miserable enough even if one could not help it, as prisoners cannot, for instance; it is far more so if the abstention is forced upon a man by himself; it is then sheer madness.

[6] CYNIC You may be right. But take this case, now. A rich man, indulging genial kindly instincts, entertains at a banquet all sorts and conditions of men; some of them are sick, others sound, and the dishes provided are as various as the guests. There is one of these to whom nothing comes amiss; he has his finger in every dish, not only the ones within easy reach, but those some way off that were intended for the invalids; this though he is in rude health, has not more than one stomach, requires little to nourish him, and is likely to be upset by a surfeit. What is your opinion of this gentleman? Is he a man of sense?

LUCIAN Why, no.

CYNIC Is he temperate?

LUCIAN No, nor that.

[7] CYNIC Well, then there is another guest at the same table; he seems unconscious of all that variety, fixes on some dish close by that suits his need, eats moderately of it and confines himself to it without a glance at the rest. You surely find him a more temperate and better man than the other?

LUCIAN Certainly.

CYNIC Do you see, or must I explain?

LUCIAN What?

CYNIC That the hospitable entertainer is God, who provides this variety of all kinds that each may have something to suit him; this is for the sound, that for the sick; this for the strong and that for the weak; it is not all for all of us; each is to take what is within reach, and of that only what he most needs.

[8] Now you others are like the greedy unrestrained person who lays hands on everything; local productions will not do for you, the world must be your storehouse; your native land and its seas are quite insufficient; you purchase your pleasures from the ends of the earth, prefer the exotic to the home growth, the costly to the cheap, the rare to the common; in fact you would rather have troubles and complications than avoid them. Most of the precious instruments of happiness that you so pride yourselves upon are won only by vexation and worry. Give a moment's thought, if you will, to the gold you all pray for, to the silver, the costly houses, the elaborate dresses, and do not forget their conditions precedent, the trouble and toil and danger they cost – nay, the blood and mortality and ruin; not only do numbers perish at sea on their account, or endure miseries in

the acquisition or working of them; besides that, they have very likely to be fought for, or the desire of them makes friends plot against friends, children against parents, wives against husbands.

[9] And how purposeless it all is! Embroidered clothes have no more warmth in them than others, gilded houses keep out the rain no better, the drink is no sweeter out of a silver cup, or a gold one for that matter, an ivory bed makes sleep no softer; on the contrary, your fortunate man on his ivory bed between his delicate sheets constantly finds himself wooing sleep in vain. And as to the elaborate dressing of food, I need hardly say that instead of aiding nutrition it injures the body and breeds diseases in it.

[10] As superfluous to mention the abuse of the sexual instinct, so easily managed if indulgence were not made an object. And if madness and corruption were limited to that – but men must take nowadays to perverting the use of everything they have, turning it to unnatural purposes, like him who insists on making a carriage of a couch.

LUCIAN Is there such a person?

CYNIC Why, he is you; you for whom men are beasts of burden, you who make them shoulder your couch-carriages, and loll up there yourselves in luxury, driving your men like so many asses and bidding them turn this way and not that; this is one of the outward and visible signs of your happiness.

[11] Again, when people use edible things not for food but to get dye out of – the murex-dyers, for instance – are they not abusing God's gifts?

LUCIAN Certainly not; the flesh of the murex[329] can provide a pigment as well as food.

CYNIC Ah, but it was not made for that. So you can *force* a mixing-bowl to do the work of a saucepan; but that is not what it was made for. However, it is impossible to exhaust these people's wrong-headedness; it is endless. And because I will not join them, you reproach me. My life is that of the orderly man I described; I make merry on what comes to hand, use what is cheap, and have no yearning for the elaborate and exotic.

[12] Moreover, if you think that because I need and use but few things I live the life of a beast, that argument lands you in the conclusion that the Gods are yet lower than the beasts; for they have no needs at all. But to clear your ideas on the comparative merits of great and small needs, you have only to reflect that children have more needs than adults, women than men, the sick than the well, and generally the inferior than the superior. Accordingly, the Gods have no needs, and those men the fewest who are nearest Gods.

[13] Take Heracles, the best man that ever lived, a divine man, and rightly reckoned a God; was it wrong-headedness that made him go about in nothing but a lion's skin, insensible to all the needs you feel? No, he was not wrong-headed, who righted other people's wrongs; he was not poor, who was lord of land and sea. Wherever he went, he was master; he never met his superior or his equal as long as he lived. Do you suppose he could not get sheets and shoes, and therefore went as he

---

[329] murex: 'any of the marine snails constituting the family Muricidae (subclass Prosobranchia of the class Gastropoda). ... Most species exude a yellow fluid that, when exposed to sunlight, becomes a purple dye. The dye murex (*Murex brandaris*) of the Mediterranean was once a source of royal Tyrian purple ... ' (*Encyclopædia Britannica. Encyclopædia Britannica 2007 Deluxe Edition.* Chicago: Encyclopædia Britannica, 2007).

did? Absurd! He had self-control and fortitude; he wanted power, and not luxury.

[14] And Theseus his disciple – king of all the Athenians, son of Poseidon, says the legend, and best of his generation – he too chose to go naked and unshod; it was his pleasure to let his hair and beard grow; and not *his* pleasure only, but all his contemporaries'; they were better men than you, and would no more have let you shave them than a lion would; soft smooth flesh was very well for women, they thought; as for them, they were men, and were content to look it; the beard was man's ornament, like the lion's, or the horse's mane; God had made certain beautiful and decorative additions to those creatures; and so he had to man, in the beard. Well, I admire those ancients and would fain be like them; I have not the smallest admiration for the present generation's wonderful felicity – tables! clothes! bodies artificially polished all over! Not a hair to grow on any of the places where nature plants it!

[15] My prayer would be that my feet might be just hoofs, like Chiron's in the story,[330] that I might need bedclothes no more than the lion, and costly food no more than the dog. Let my sufficient bed be the whole earth, my house this universe, and the food of my choice the easiest procurable. May I have no need, I nor any that I call friend, of gold and silver. For all human evils spring from the desire of these, seditions and wars, conspiracies and murders. The fountain of them all is the desire of more. Never be that desire mine; let me never wish for more than my share, but be content with less.

[16] Such are our aspirations – considerably different from other people's. It is no wonder that our get-up is

---

[330] Chiron, who dwelt on Mount Pelion, was the wise Centaur who raised the boy Achilles, and therefore had the hoofs of a horse, and not human feet.

peculiar, since the peculiarity of our underlying principle is so marked. I cannot make out why you allow a harpist his proper robe and get-up – and so the flute-player has his, and the tragic actor his – but will not be consistent and recognise any uniform for a good man; the good man must be like everyone else, of course, regardless of the fact that everyone else is all wrong. Well, if the good are to have a uniform of their own, there can be none better than that which the average sensual man will consider most improper, and reject with most decision for himself.

[17] Now my uniform consists of a rough hairy skin, a threadbare cloak, long hair, and bare feet, whereas yours is for all the world that of some minister to vice; there is not a pin to choose between you – the gay colours, the soft texture, the number of garments you are swathed in, the shoes, the sleeked hair, the very scent of you; for the more blessed you are, the more do you exhale perfumes like his. What value can one attach to a man whom one's nose would identify for one of those minions? The consequence is, you are equal to no more work than they are, and to quite as much pleasure. You feed like them, you sleep like them, you walk like them – except so far as you avoid walking by getting yourselves conveyed like parcels by porters or animals; as for me, my feet take me anywhere that I want to go. I can put up with cold and heat and be content with the works of God – such a miserable wretch am I – whereas you blessed ones are displeased with everything that happens and grumble without ceasing; what is is intolerable, what is not you pine for, in winter for summer, in summer for winter, in heat for cold, in cold for heat, as fastidious and peevish as so many invalids; only their reason is to be found in their illness, and yours in your characters.

[18] And then, because we occasionally make mistakes in practice, you recommend us to change our plan and

correct our principles, the fact being that you in your own affairs go quite at random, never acting on deliberation or reason, but always on habit and appetite. You are no better than people washed about by a flood; they drift with the current, you with your appetites. There is a story of a man on a vicious horse that just gives your case. The horse ran away with him, and at the pace it was going at he could not get off. A man in the way asked him where he was off to; 'wherever this beast chooses,' was the reply. So if one asked you where you were bound for, if you cared to tell the truth you would say either generally, wherever your appetites chose, or in particular, where pleasure chose today, where fancy chose tomorrow, and where avarice chose another day; or sometimes it is rage, sometimes fear, sometimes any other such feeling, that takes you whither it will. You ride not one horse, but many at different times, all vicious, and all out of control. They are carrying you straight for pits and cliffs; but you do not realise that you are bound for a fall till the fall comes.

[19] The old cloak, the shaggy hair, the whole get-up that you ridicule, has this effect: it enables me to live a quiet life, doing as I will and keeping the company I want. No ignorant uneducated person will have anything to say to one dressed like this; and the soft livers turn the other way as soon as I am in sight. But the refined, the reasonable, the earnest, seek me out; they are the men who seek me, because they are the men I wish to see. At the doors of those whom the world counts happy I do not dance attendance; their gold crowns and their purple I call ostentation, and them I laugh to scorn.

[20] These externals that you pour contempt upon, you may learn that they are seemly enough not merely for good men, but for Gods, if you will look at the Gods' statues; do those resemble you, or me? Do not confine your attention to Greece; take a tour round the foreign

temples too, and see whether the Gods treat their hair and beards like me, or let the painters and sculptors shave them. Most of them, you will find, have no more shirt than I have, either. I hope you will not venture to describe again as mean an appearance that is accepted as godlike.

GLOSSARY OF NAMES[331]

[References within the Glossary are indicated by **Bold Type**.]

Achaicus is mentioned at DL 6.99 as the author of a book on ethics. He is otherwise unknown.

Agesilaus II (c.445–359 BC) was a king of Sparta. (He is mentioned at DL 6.39 as exemplifying someone who has outstanding merit.) See OCD 'Agesilaus II'.

Alexander the Great, Alexander III, or Alexander of Macedonia (356–323 BC), king of Macedonia from 336 BC, was possibly the greatest military commander of all time having never been defeated in battle and, by the time of his death in the palace of Nebuchadrezzar II of Babylon, having overthrown the Persian Empire and conquered most of the known world (known to the ancient Greeks, that is). His short-lived empire stretched from Macedonia and Greece in the west to the Indus valley in the east. His father was Philip II of Macedonia, and his mother was Olympias, who belonged to the royal house of Epirus, and through her he traced his descent from the great hero Achilles. When a teenager, he was tutored by the philosopher Aristotle. (He appears many times in Diogenes Laertius Book Six, at 6.32, 6.38, 6.44, 6.45, 6.60, 6.63, 6.68, 6.79, 6.84, 6.88, 6.93; he appears as Diogenes' interlocutor in Dio Chrysostom's *Fourth Discourse on Kingship* – see Appendix 1, above – where he is

---

[331] The following sources were consulted in the preparation of this Glossary: Curnow 2006, *Encyclopædia Britannica* 11th edition 1910–11 (via Wikipedia), *Encyclopædia Britannica 2007 Deluxe Edition*, OCD, Smith 1867 and 1870, Wikipedia, Zeyl 1997.

told that kingship does not reside in power and dominion, but in the quality of one's mind and character; Epictetus also mentions a meeting between Alexander and Diogenes, at *Discourses* 3.22.92 – see Appendix 2, above, pp. 170–1.)

Anaximenes of Lampsacus (c.380–320 BC) was a historian and rhetorician, a pupil of the Cynic philosopher Zoïlus. (He is mentioned at DL 6.57, where **Diogenes of Sinope** accosts him for being too fat, and hijacks his lecture by holding up a piece of salt fish.)

Antipater (c.397–319 BC) was a Macedonian statesman who governed Macedonia during the Danubian campaign of **Alexander the Great** (335 BC). (He is mentioned at DL 6.44 as the recipient of a letter sent to him by Alexander. The person mentioned at DL 6.66, who gave **Diogenes of Sinope** a cloak, is probably the same individual.)

Antisthenes of Athens (mid-5th–mid-4th century BC) was an associate of **Socrates** and, according to Diogenes Laertius, the founder of the Cynic school (DL 1.19). He was present at Socrates' final discussion (on the immortality of the soul, recounted in the *Phaedo* of Plato) which took place on the last day of Socrates' imprisonment in the hours before his execution by drinking hemlock. Diogenes Laertius devotes a short section to Antisthenes (DL 6.1–19), where we learn that he held that virtue is sufficient for happiness, that it is found in actions and not words (DL 6.11), that it can be taught (DL 6.10/105), and that it cannot be taken away (DL 6.12/105) – doctrines which would be taken up by both Cynics and Stoics. He was responsible for the exile from Athens of **Anytus** and the execution of Meletus, the two men who had brought accusations against Socrates (DL 6.10). He inaugurated the Cynic way of life by holding to the austerity and hardiness that he learned from Socrates, and he would walk from where he lived in the Piraeus the five miles to Athens every day to hear Socrates speak (DL 6.2). (He is also mentioned at DL 6.21, 6.103, 6.104, and 6.105.) Antisthenes was from ancient times recognised as the founder and head of the Cynic school (Reale 1987, 268). Even so, whether it is right to regard Antisthenes, rather than Diogenes of Sinope, as the true founder of the Cynic tradition has been much debated. Dudley (1998, 1–4), for instance, rejects Antisthenes as the founder, contrary to the views of Navia (2001) and Reale (1987, 263–9), for instance.

Antisthenes of Rhodes (*fl.* early 2nd century BC) was a Peripatetic philosopher who wrote a history of the philosophical schools which is cited at DL 6.77 and 6.87. (He is also mentioned at DL 6.19.)

Anytus and **Meletus** had brought the accusations against Socrates which resulted in the latter's execution in 399 BC from drinking hemlock. Antisthenes was later responsible for the exile from Athens of Anytus and the execution of Meletus (DL 6.9–10).

Aristogiton, *see* **Harmodius and Aristogiton**.

Aristippus (born c.435 BC, Cyrene, Libya, died 366 BC, Athens) an associate of **Socrates**, reputedly the founder of the Cyrenaic school, though the true founder may in fact have been his grandson. The Cyrenaics held that only sense impressions are knowable, and that the supreme good is sensory pleasure in the present moment. The hedonistic Cyrenaic outlook anticipated the philosophy of Epicurus. See OCD 'Cyrenaics'. (Aristippus is mentioned at DL 6.19, 6.25 and 6.32.)

Aristo of Chios (4th–3rd century BC) was a pupil of Zeno, whose Stoic philosophy he developed in a way later regarded as unorthodox. He focused exclusively on ethics, rejecting physics and logic as unimportant, holding that the proper end of life was to maintain a perfect indifference to everything that is neither virtue nor vice (opposing the orthodox view of **Zeno of Citium**, Chrysippus, and the later Stoics, who hold that some indifferent things are preferred, and some dispreferred).

Diogenes Laertius devotes a short section to him at DL 7.160-4. (He is mentioned at DL 6.103 and 6.105.)

Asclepius was a God of healing, a son of Apollo. His healing powers were so great that he was even able to raise people from the dead, which provoked Zeus into killing him with his thunderbolt. (He is mentioned at DL 6.38.)

Athenodorus of Tarsus (1st century BC) was a Stoic philosopher, and a friend of Cicero and Strabo. He was one of Augustus' court philosophers (along with Arius Didymus). He was probably the pupil of the Stoic teacher Posidonius of Apamea, a summary of whose views he sent to Cicero who wanted them for his book *On Duties*. (He is mentioned at DL 6.81 for having described **Diogenes of Sinope** as having a 'shining appearance' as a consequence of applying oil to his skin.)

Bryson of Achaea (4th century BC) was one of **Crates** teachers, according to **Hippobotus** (DL 6.85). He was the pupil of **Stilpo** (DL 9.61) and of Clinomachus (*Suda*, 'Pyrrho') in the Megarian school. He was also the teacher of Pyrrho (DL 9.61; *Suda*, 'Pyrrho') and Theodorus the Atheist (*Suda*, 'Theodorus').

Callisthenes of Olynthus (died 327 BC) was a historian and a nephew of the philosopher Aristotle. (He is mentioned at DL 6.45 with reference to his being well treated as a guest of **Alexander the Great**.)

Cercidas of Megalopolis (*fl.* 225 BC) was a statesman, lawgiver, and poet. (His account, in verse, of the death of **Diogenes of Sinope** is quoted at DL 6.76-7.)

Cleomenes (4th-3rd century BC) is mentioned as the author of a book entitled *The Schoolmaster* (DL 6.75), and as having been the pupil of **Metrocles of Maroneia** and the teacher of Timarchus of Alexandria and Echecles of Ephesus (DL 6.95). Nothing further is known of him.

Craterus (died 321 BC) was one of **Alexander the Great's** senior officials. (He is mentioned at DL 6.57.)

Crates of Thebes (c.368/365–288/285 BC) was a Cynic philosopher and poet who went to Athens as a young man and became a pupil of **Diogenes of Sinope**. He is famous for giving all his wealth to the poor at the point he became a philosopher, though an alternative story tells that he threw all of his money into the sea (DL 6.87). When **Zeno of Citium**, the founder of the Stoic school, first came to Athens (according to Diogenes Laertius at DL 7.2–4), Crates was his first teacher. Crates has his own section at DL 6.85–93. (He is also mentioned at DL 6.15, 6.82, 6.94, 6.96, 6.98, 6.105.)

Cyrus the Elder (6th century BC) was the founder of the Persian Empire. (He is mentioned at DL 6.2 and 6.84.)

Demetrius of Magnesia (*fl.* 50 BC) was a Greek author who wrote on concord, and on homonymous towns and writers. (His work is cited at DL 6.79, 6.84, and 6.88.)

Demosthenes (384–322 BC) was the greatest orator in Athens. He both defended and prosecuted in the law courts, and led an active public life. Some of his *Orations* are extant. (He is mentioned at DL 6.34) See OCD 'Demosthenes (2)'.

Diagoras of Melos (*fl.* late 5th century BC) was a lyric poet. Cicero, in his *On the Nature of the Gods*, reports that he was an atheist, though no traces of atheism are found in the surviving fragments of his poetry. (He is mentioned at DL 6.59.)

Didymon is a flute-player, referred to at DL 6.51 as an adulterer and as someone who had already attained notoriety for his immortality. This is presumably that same Didymon also mentioned as an adulterer at DL 6.68. He is otherwise unknown.

Dio Chrysostom (c. AD 40–120) from Prusa (modern Bursa) in the Roman province of Bithynia (present-day north-western Turkey) was an orator, writer, philosopher and historian, having been the student of the Roman Stoic teacher Musonius Rufus. His name 'Chrysostom' derives from the Greek *chryso-*

stomos, meaning 'golden-mouthed'. Much of his writing survives, including eighty *Discourses* (or *Orations*), a few brief letters, an essay 'In Praise of Hair', and a few other fragments. Probably in AD 82, for his frank criticisms he was banished from both Bithynia and Italy by the emperor Domitian. For 14 years he wandered the coastal lands of the Black Sea, embracing poverty and adopting the life of a Cynic. Upon Domitian's death in 96, his exile ended, and he returned to Rome where he established himself as an orator and philosopher. In the early years of the second century he returned to his native Prusa, after which the historical record remains silent. The content and style of several of his *Discourses* are strongly Cynic in character (see *Discourses* 1, 3, 4, 6, 7, 8, 9 and 10, all of which appear in volume 1 of the Loeb edition of Dio Chrysostom). (His *Fourth Discourse on Kingship* is included in this volume as Appendix 1.) For more on Dio Chrysostom, see especially Jones 1978 and Swain 2000.

Diocles of Magnesia (mid to late 1st century BC) was a historian of philosophy. His doxographical *Survey of the Philosophers* and his biographical *Lives of the Philosophers* were important sources for Diogenes Laertius. (His work is cited or quoted at DL 6.12, 6.13, 6.20, 6.36, 6.87, 6.91, 6.99, 6.103.)

Diodorus of Aspendos (4th century BC) was a Pythagorean philosopher who probably lived after the time of **Plato**. (He is mentioned at DL 6.13 as the first person, according to **Sosicrates**, to wear his cloak doubled over – a style of dress associated with the Cynics).

Diogenes of Sinope (on the Black Sea) (c.412/403–324/321 BC) was a Cynic philosopher. He was exiled from Sinope for 'defacing the currency', living afterwards in Athens and Corinth (where he died). He taught **Crates**, who taught **Zeno of Citium**. Diogenes Laertius devotes a substantial section to him at DL 6.20–81. His report at DL 6.21 that Diogenes of Sinope had been a pupil of **Antisthenes** (a follower of **Socrates**) is disputed. Dudley (1998, 1–4) is of the opinion that Diogenes did not arrive in Athens until after Antisthenes' death, and that the account that he was Antisthenes' pupil was concocted in order to establish an 'apostolic succession', Socrates–Antisthenes–Diogenes–Crates–Zeno, favoured by the Stoics as grounding their tradition to the greatest of all philosophers, Socrates himself: 'Any sect that professed φιλοσοφία must trace back its pedigree to Socrates' (Dudley 1998, 4). Navia, by contrast, is reluctant to view the association between Antisthenes and Diogenes as a mere fiction, pointing out that 'Nothing ... should force us to disregard the testimony of Diogenes Laertius (VI, 21) with respect to the master–disciple relationship between Antisthenes and Diogenes, because there is no contradictory evidence, while there is much supporting doxographical and anecdotal confirmation' (Navia 1996, 18). On this specific topic see also Navia 1998, 52, 90–1, and Navia 2001, 27–31.

Dionysius of Heraclea (on the Pontus) (c.328–248 BC), the 'deserter', was a pupil of **Zeno of Citium**. He wrote poetry and also philosophical works. He is called 'deserter' at DL 7.23 because when sick in old age he rejected the Stoic view that pain is not an evil because it is not morally bad. He is accorded a very brief section at DL 7.166–7, and is mentioned at DL 7.37 where the illness that caused his change of mind is identified as some sort of eye disease. (He is mentioned at DL 6.43 for relating that **Diogenes of Sinope** was brought to Philip after being taken prisoner at the battle of Chaeronea. The Dionysius mentioned at DL 6.100 is probably the same person.)

Dionysius the Younger (c.396–343 BC), the 'tyrant of Syracuse', at first ruled under the supervision of his uncle, Dion, who invited Plato to tutor Dionysius in the hope of making him the archetypal philosopher-king. The scheme failed, and both Dion and Plato were dismissed in 366 BC. But nine years later in 357 BC, Dion deposed Dionysius, who was exiled to Locri (in southern Italy). In 346 BC, eight years after Dion's assassination, Dionysius was able to regain power in Syracuse only to have to surrender to Timoleon of Corinth in 344 BC. He lived privately in Corinth for only a year before he died. (He is mentioned at DL 6.26, 6.50, and 6.58.)

Dioxippus (mentioned at DL 6.43) was an ancient Greek athlete, renowned for his Olympic victories in the pancratium. His fame and skill were such that he was crowned Olympic champion by default in 336 BC when no other pancratiast dared meet him on the field. This kind of victory was called *akoniti* ('without getting dusty') and remains the only one ever recorded in the Olympics in this discipline.

The most famous story of Dioxippus is his defeat of Coragus of the Macedonian army. It was during a banquet hosted by **Alexander the Great** (who was a friend and sponsor of Dioxippus) that a powerful Macedonian warrior of distinction named Coragus challenged Dioxippus to single combat. Dioxippus accepted the challenge.

Despite his friendship with Dioxippus, Alexander and his Macedonians supported Coragus, while the Athenians in attendance supported their champion Dioxippus. Coragus came on the field resplendent in full combat armour and carrying a full complement of weapons, including javelins, a spear, and a sword. Dioxippus carried only a club, and wore no armour. Coragus threw his javelin, which was dodged by the pancratist, and then his spear was shattered by Dioxippus' club. Before Coragus could draw his sword, however, Dioxippus used his techniques to unbalance his opponent and throw him to the ground. With one foot on Coragus' neck, he looked to the crowd of spectators. Alexander signalled that Coragus be spared, and the Athenians celebrated the victory, much to the chagrin of the embittered Macedonians.

This victory was also Dioxippus' ultimate defeat. Alexander continued to be more and more hostile to him for the embarrassing situation, and his friends and other Macedonians in his court conspired to embarrass Dioxippus by putting a golden cup underneath his pillow and accusing him of theft. Dioxippus, put in such a situation and realising that the Macedonians had framed him, wrote a letter to Alexander describing the conspiracy, and committed suicide. Whether Coragus of Macedonia was involved in the conspiracy is not known (adapted from the article 'Dioxippus' at Wikipedia <http://en.wikipedia.org/wiki/Dioxippus> accessed 2008-03-03).

Epaminondas (died 362 BC) was a Theban general, famous for significant victories. (He is mentioned at DL 6.39 as an example of someone having outstanding merit, and by Epictetus at *Discourses* 3.22.78 as an example of someone who, although childless, was nevertheless of great benefit to his city.) See OCD 'Epaminondas'.

Epictetus (c. AD 55–135) was a teacher of Stoic philosophy, active during the latter decades of the first century and the early decades of the second century, basing his teachings especially on those of **Zeno of Citium** (who founded the Stoic school in about 300 BC) and of Chrysippus, the third head of the school. Whilst still a slave in Rome, Epictetus attended the lectures of the famous and acclaimed Roman Stoic teacher Gaius Musonius Rufus (also the teacher of **Dio Chrysostom**). He had probably made the transition from student to teacher by the time the Emperor Domitian banished all philosophers from Rome in about AD 93 when he went to Nicopolis in Greece to open his own school. One of his students in the early years of the second century was Lucius Flavius Arrian, who composed the *Discourses* and *Handbook* through which we are acquainted with Epictetus' philosophy and the style of his teaching. (Chapter 22 of Book 3 from the *Discourses*, on Cynic philosophy, is included in this volume as Appendix 2.) For more on Epictetus, see especially Long 2002, Seddon 2005 and forthcoming, and the introduction to Oldfather 1925.

Epicurus (born 341 BC on Samos, died 270 BC in Athens) was the founder of the philosophical school that bears his name –

sometimes called the Garden because of its location in the garden of his house in Athens – teaching that happiness is found in tranquillity (*ataraxia*) and the absence of pain (*aponia*). He was a close associate of the New Comedy poet **Menander**.

Eratosthenes of Cyrene (c.285–194 BC) was a Greek mathematician, poet, athlete, geographer and astronomer, who wrote on all these subjects. In 236 BC, Ptolemy III Euergetes I appointed him as librarian of the library at Alexandria, succeeding Zenodotos, the first librarian. (He is Diogenes Laertius' source for his account of **Crates**' son Pasicles at DL 6.88–9.)

Eubulides of Miletus (mid-4th century BC) was a dialectician associated with the Megarian school, a critic of Aristotle, and reputedly the inventor of several logical puzzles, including the Sorites ('How many grains are required for making a heap?'), the Liar Paradox ('If I say, "I am lying," is this true and false?'), the Horned Argument ('Have you lost your horns?'), and the Veiled Man. (He is mentioned at DL 6.20.)

Eubulus (4th century BC) was a distinguished comic poet of the middle comedy. A work no longer extant (mentioned at DL 6.30), entitled *The Sale of Diogenes*, recounts how Diogenes was sold as a slave to **Xeniades** and became the tutor to his two sons.

Euclides of Megara (c.450–380 BC) was the founder of the Megarian school. He was an associate of Socrates, and was present at his death, afterwards providing accommodation for Plato and others of Socrates' circle. Such was his dedication to philosophy and to Socrates that even after the Athenian authorities banned from the city all citizens of Megara under pain of execution, he risked his life by slipping into the city after dark disguised as a woman in a long tunic, his face concealed by a veil, in order to hear Socrates teach; then just before dawn, he would set off for home, back to Megara, some twenty miles away (Gell. 7.10). He is mentioned at DL 6.24

GLOSSARY OF NAMES ☙ 197

where **Diogenes of Sinope** remarks that his school was 'bilious', and at DL 6.89 we learn that he was the teacher of Pasicles, **Crates'** brother. Diogenes Laertius devotes a short section to him at DL 2.106–12, where we read: 'He used to teach that the supreme good is one thing, but that it is known by different names, sometimes called wisdom, sometimes God, sometimes intellect (*nous*), and so on. But everything that was contrary to good, he rejected, denying its existence' (DL 2.106).

Euthycrates appears at DL 6.90 as possibly being the person who flogged and dragged **Crates** from a gymnasium by his feet. This may be Euthycrates the sculptor (*fl. c.*300 BC), the most distinguished of Lysippus' three sons, famous for his Heracles at Delphi, an Alexander the Great, a cavalry battle, a Trophonius at Lebadea, and several chariot groups. But the attribution is at best only very tentative.

Favorinus (*c.* AD 85–155) was a sophist who may have studied with the philosopher and orator **Dio Chrysostom** in Rome. Amongst others, he was the friend of the writers Plutarch and Aulus Gellius (and is quoted frequently in the latter's work, *Attic Nights*). His works are cited at DL 6.25, 6.73, and 6.89.

Gorgias of Leontini (*c.*485–380 BC) was one of the most influential of the sophists, said to have been a pupil of Empedocles. He was one of **Antisthenes'** teachers (DL 6.1). He lived beyond the age of 100, and attributed his longevity to never having done anything for anyone else.

Harmodius and **Aristogiton**, both of the family of Gephyraei, plotted, along with others, to assassinate the Athenian tyrant Hippias at the Panathenaic festival of 514 BC. The plot failed (though Hippias' younger brother Hipparchus was killed), and Harmodius and Aristogiton were executed. After the expulsion of Hippias in 510 BC by Sparta, Harmodius and Aristogiton were praised as heroes, and bronze statues of them were made by the Athenian sculptor Antenor. (The statues are mentioned at DL 6.50 with reference to their being made from the best bronze.)

Hecato of Rhodes (*fl. c.*100 BC) was a Stoic philosopher, a pupil of Panaetius (head of the Stoic school from *c.*129 BC), who wrote mainly on ethics. He is mentioned a number of times by Seneca in his essay *On Benefits*. (His volume of *Anecdotes* is cited at DL 6.4, 6.32 and 6.95.)

Hegesias of Sinope was a pupil of **Diogenes of Sinope**. (He is mentioned at DL 6.48 and 6.84.)

Heracles was a demigod, the son of Zeus and the mortal woman Alcmene, fathered by Zeus with the intention that his son would aid the gods in their war with the Titans. Blinded by a rage inflicted upon him by the goddess Hera, Heracles killed two of his nephews and six of his own children. To atone for his crime, he was told by Apollo's oracle at Delphi to dedicate himself to the service of Eurystheus, king of Mycenae, at whose commands he undertook the twelve labours for which he is most famed. Smith (1867, 2.393) informs us that '[Heracles was] the most celebrated of all the heroes of antiquity. The traditions about him are not only the richest in substance, but also the most widely spread; for we find them not only in all the countries round the Mediterranean, but his wondrous deeds were known in the most distant countries of the ancient world.'

It was the aim of Cynic to live like Heracles, as someone who chooses to live a life of hardship, enduring pain and despising death, setting an example for the good of others. In Diogenes Laertius' Book Six, Heracles' name occurs in the titles of four books: in three from **Antisthenes** (DL 6.16/18), and in one from **Diogenes of Sinope** (6.80).[332] He is offered as an example when Antisthenes argues that labour is something good (6.2); Diogenes of Sinope swears by Heracles when he is

---

[332] See also DL 6.104/5 where one of Antisthenes' books on Heracles is cited twice in the brief account of Menedemus.

struck by someone (6.41); his name appears on an inscription that Diogenes defaces (6.50); and Diogenes is reported as saying that he was adopting Heracles' way of life, 'preferring freedom above everything' (6.71).

In **Dio Chrysostom's** *Fourth Discourse on Kingship* (at 26–33, in Appendix 1 above, pp. 129–31) Heracles appears as an example of the person who possesses the art of kingship, imparted to him by Zeus himself, in whom the art originates, referred to as that 'good education' which comes from heaven, as opposed to mere human education which is 'small and weak and full of pitfalls and no little deception'. In his *First Discourse on Kingship* (50–84), Dio recounts that once he had been lost in the woods one day when he met a woman who told him the tale of how Heracles was taken by the god Hermes to a fantastical landscape in which stand two mountains, Peak Royal and Peak Tyrannous. Upon Peak Royal, the highest peak, dwelt Lady Royalty, a daughter of Zeus, accompanied by three others as beautiful as she, Justice, Civic Order, and Peace, along with Law, a grey-haired man. Hermes then took Heracles to the lower peak, Peak Tyrannous, to Tyranny, the place to which most people come. Tyranny was sitting upon a throne higher and more splendid than that of Lady Royalty, but as she moved, it rocked and swayed on shaky foundations. With her were Cruelty, Insolence, Lawlessness, Faction, and Flattery. When Heracles told Hermes that he liked Royalty the best, Hermes took this news to Zeus, who entrusted Heracles with kingship over all mankind.[333]

And in **Epictetus'** *Discourses* (at 3.22.57, in Appendix 2 above, pp. 164–5), Heracles is offered as an example of the Cynic outlook which embraces hardship as an exercise sent by Zeus to those who wish to train themselves for the rigors of being in his service. (For more on the myth of Heracles, see the references in Hard 2004, especially 244–86.)

---

[333] This brief summary of the Heracles and Hermes story, with minor amendments, has been taken from Seddon 2005, 179–80.

Hermippus of Smyrna (3rd century BC) wrote biographies of philosophers, writers and lawgivers. He delighted in sensationalist but falsified reports, particularly of death scenes. (He is referred to at DL 6.2, 6.29, 6.99.) See OCD 'Hermippus (2)'.

Hipparchia of Maronea (4th–3rd century BC) married the Cynic **Crates of Thebes**, and adopted the Cynic way of life. Her brother **Metrocles** was a pupil of Crates. (She has her own brief section at DL 6.96–8.)

Hippobotus (late 3rd–early 2nd century BC) was a philosophical historian. He divided philosophy into nine schools, but refused to admit the Cynics (along with the Sceptic, Dialectician and Elian schools; DL 1.19–20). His *On Sects* and *Catalogue of Philosophers* were sources for Diogenes Laertius (in Book Six, at DL 6.85 and 6.102).

Lysanias appears at DL 6.23 as someone who attested to **Diogenes of Sinope** carrying his wallet and leaning on his staff as he made his way along the roads outside Athens. He is otherwise unknown.

Lysimachus (*c*.355–281 BC) was a Macedonian from Pella. He became the bodyguard of **Alexander the Great** in 328 BC, and is possibly the person mentioned at DL 6.97 who hosts a dinner at which **Hipparchia** faces up to **Theodorus**.

Meletus *see* **Anytus and Meletus**, above.

Menander of Athens (born 342 BC) was the most distinguished New Comedy poet. He was a close associate of the philosophers **Theophrastus** and **Epicurus**. (He is quoted at DL 6.83 and 6.93.) (Menander Drymus, mentioned at DL 6.84 as a pupil of **Diogenes of Sinope**, appears to be a different person.)

Menedemus of Eretria (*c*.339-265 BC) was sent by his city on military service to Megara where he was attracted to philosophy, becoming the pupil of **Stilpo**. He became a member of Phaedon's school after moving to Elis, and when he later became its head, he transferred the school to Eretria. (He is mentioned at DL 6.91 as possibly being the person who dragged **Crates** from a gymnasium by his feet. This is not the Menedemus named at DL 6.95, and who is mentioned briefly in the final section of Book Six of the *Lives* at DL 6.102.)

Menippus of Gadara (3rd century BC), was a Cynic and satirist. The Menippean satire genre is named after him. His works (written in a mixture of prose and verse) are all lost. He discussed serious subjects in a spirit of ridicule, and especially delighted in attacking the Epicureans and Stoics. Strabo and Stephanus call him the 'earnest-jester' (*spoudogeloios*). In Diogenes Laertius' account (DL 6.99–101), he was born a slave, but as a money-lender he amassed a fortune, which he then lost, and committed suicide through grief. (Menippus of Sinope, mentioned at DL 6.95, is a different person.) (Adapted from the article 'Menippus' at Wikipedia <http://en.wikipedia.org/wiki/Menippus> accessed 2008-05-17.)

Metrocles of Maronea (4th–3rd century BC) was the brother of **Hipparchia** and student of **Crates**. His *Anecdotes* is cited at DL 6.33. He has his own brief section at DL 6.94–5, and is mentioned at DL 2.102 where we learn that once when he was washing vegetables he rebuked **Aristippus** for the large crowd of students he had in tow, saying that he would have no need of so many pupils if he had washed vegetables instead. This seems to be a reference to Aristippus being the first of Socrates' associates to charge a fee for teaching.

Midias is mentioned at DL 6.42, where he punches **Diogenes of Sinope**, and appears to be the same Midias who struck the Athenian orator Demosthenes in the face in 348 BC at the Dionysia (one of the festivals of Dionysus). Demosthenes settled out of court. Diogenes, with respect to his own assault it seems, also settled the matter out of court by giving Midias a taste of his own medicine. See OCD 'Demosthenes'.

Monimus of Syracuse (4th century BC) has a brief section at DL 6.82–3, where we learn that he was the slave of a money-changer, and wishing to be dismissed in order to follow **Diogenes of Sinope**, pretended to be mad by throwing all the money about. After he was dismissed, his master learned that he had indeed taken up with Diogenes, and this convinced him all the more that his former slave had really succumbed to madness.

Neanthes of Cyzicus (3rd century BC) was a historian and pupil of Philiscus of Miletus. Amongst other works, mostly historical, he wrote a series of biographies (which Diogenes Laertius draws on at DL 6.13 in his account of **Antisthenes**). At DL 6.13 he reports that Antisthenes was the first person to wear his cloak doubled over.

Odysseus is mentioned at DL 6.27 as the person whose misfortunes were investigated by the grammarians whilst they remained ignorant of their own. He was the husband of Penelope, one of the main heroes at the siege of Troy, and the eponymous hero of Homer's *Odyssey*.

Olympiodorus was apparently an Athenian magistrate, and is mentioned at DL 6.23 as testifying that **Diogenes of Sinope** used to walk the roads around Athens carrying his wallet and leaning on his staff – which accoutrements from that time became especially associated with Cynics. He is otherwise unknown.

Onesicritus of Aegina (or possibly of Astypalaea; see DL 6.84) (4th century BC) was a historian who accompanied **Alexander the Great** on his campaigns in Asia, writing a history of them which is frequently cited by later authors. He was the father of two sons who took up philosophy after hearing the lectures of **Diogenes of Sinope**, and who himself took up philosophy as a pupil of Diogenes when he came to Athens looking for his sons (DL 6.75–6). (He has his own very brief section at DL 6.84.) See **Philiscus of Aegina**, below. (Some scholars are of the opinion that Onesicritus of Aegina and Onesicritus of Astypalaea are not the same person; see Curnow 2006, 201.)

Orpheus was a mythical singer, the son of Apollo (or possibly Oeagrus, a king of Thrace) and a Muse (probably Calliope, the patron of epic poetry), whose song had magical power over rocks, trees and wild beasts, and who used this power to overcome the song of the Sirens and thereby save the Argonauts. Later on the expedition he lulled to sleep the dragon that guarded the golden fleece. His wife was a nymph named Eurydice (or in some accounts, Agriope), and when she died from the bite of a snake, Orpheus followed her into the underworld where he used his songs to charm the ferryman Charon and the dog Cerberus (guardians of the River Styx) to gain admittance. Hades, king of the underworld, was so moved by the charms of Orpheus' singing and the depth of his grief for Eurydice that he allowed the couple to return to the world of the living on the condition that as they departed Orpheus should not look back at his wife. As they approached the world above, Orpheus was so overjoyed to see the sun again that he looked back to share his delight, and at that moment Eurydice disappeared. (In other accounts, it was Orpheus' love for Eurydice and his wish to see that she was following him that made him look back.) The myth of Orpheus gave rise to a mystery cult – into which, Diogenes Laertius tells us (at DL 6.4), **Antisthenes** was initiated – which emphasised the divinity of the human soul that was destined to be reborn through successive lives, the cycle of which could be broken by the candidate who undergoes secret initiation rites and adopts an ascetic way of life. (For the Orpheus myth, see the references to Orpheus in Hard 2004, especially 550-3. For the Orphic mystery cult, see for instance Guthrie 1993.)

Phanias (*fl.* c.300 BC) was a Peripatetic, having been a pupil of Aristotle. He wrote on history, botany, the poets, and the Socratic philosophers. (He is cited at DL 6.8.)

Philemon (368/60-267/63 BC) was a New Comedy poet from Syracuse, later granted Athenian citizenship. He wrote 97 comedies, and may have lived to the age of 101. (He is quoted at DL 6.87.) See OCD 'Philemon (2)'.

Philiscus of Aegina (4th century BC), according to the *Suda*, was a pupil of **Diogenes of Sinope** (or, according to Hermippus, a pupil of **Stilpo**), was the author of dialogues (one was entitled *Kodros*), and a tutor of **Alexander the Great**. A second entry in the *Suda* probably refers to the same person, and reports that after he travelled from Aegina to Athens to see the city, having heard Diogenes of Sinope, he stayed and became a philosopher. His father sent his brother to fetch him back, but the same thing happened to *him*, and he too became a philosopher. Finally, the father himself came to Athens in search of his sons, and he also became a philosopher. A variation of this story features at DL 6.75-6, in which Philiscus appears as the second brother who becomes a philosopher when he is sent by the father, **Onesicritus of Aegina**, to bring back from Athens his younger brother Androsthenes, who had been the first to convert to philosophy. As in the *Suda* account, finally the father himself goes to Athens, and follows his sons in taking up the study of philosophy. (Philiscus is mentioned at DL 6.73, 6.75, 6.80 and 6.84.)

Phocion (402-318 BC) was an Athenian statesman and general. According to Plutarch he studied under **Plato** and Xenocrates. (He is mentioned at DL 6.76, where we learn that he was also a pupil of **Diogenes of Sinope**.) See OCD 'Phocion'.

Phryne (4th century BC) was one of the most celebrated Athenian courtesans (*hetaira*, as opposed to *pornê*, common prostitute) whose beauty secured her so much wealth that when **Alexander's** army had pulled down the walls of Thebes, she offered to have them rebuilt at her own expense, so long as she was allowed to add her own inscription: *Alexander destroyed them, but Phryne the hetaira rebuilt them.* 'The orator Hyperides was one of her lovers, and he defended her when she was accused by Euthias on one occasion of some capital charge; but when the eloquence of her advocate failed to move the judges, he bade her uncover her breast, and thus ensured her acquittal' (Smith 1867, 3.358). She was called *phrunê*, which means toad, on account of her sallow complexion. Phryne was the mistress of the sculptor Praxiteles, and according to Athenaeus she modelled for his statue of the Cnidian Aphrodite, copies of which survive in the Vatican and elsewhere.[334] (She is mentioned at DL 6.60 for having dedicated a golden statue to Aphrodite at Delphi, upon which **Diogenes of Sinope** wrote 'From the licentiousness of the Greeks.')

Plato (c.429–347 BC) is mentioned at DL 6.3 as having spoken ill of **Antisthenes**, and at DL 6.7 where Antisthenes likens Plato to a horse – on account of his pride – and where on another occasion he remarks that he could not see Plato's conceit in the bowl into which he had just vomited, only the bile. (He is also mentioned at DL 6.24, 6.25, 6.26, 6.40, 6.41, 6.53, 6.54, 6.58, 6.67 and 6.98.)

Polyeuctus was an Athenian orator. He is mentioned at DL 6.23 for attesting to **Diogenes of Sinope's** custom of walking the roads around Athens with his staff and wallet, and is mentioned also at DL 2.39 for delivering a speech against **Socrates** at his trial that was in fact composed by someone else. (He is otherwise unknown.)

Scirpalus is the pirate who sold **Diogenes of Sinope** into slavery, by which means Diogenes came to manage the household of **Xeniades** and tutor his two sons (DL 6.74). Nothing further is known of him.

Socrates (469–399 BC) was a philosopher in Athens who, despite writing nothing, can be credited with laying the foundations for Western philosophy. We know about him primarily from the work of **Plato**, **Xenophon**, and Aristophanes. He famously

---

[334] See *Encyclopædia Britannica. Encyclopædia Britannica 2007 Deluxe Edition*. Chicago: Encyclopædia Britannica, 2007.

maintained that 'the unexamined life is not worth living' (Plato, *Apology* 38a), and that what matters most is the quality of one's character. All the Hellenistic schools have a legitimate claim to consider themselves heirs to the Socratic tradition in one sense or another. He was charged with impiety and corrupting the youth of Athens, and sentenced to death by drinking hemlock. Diogenes Laertius devotes a section to him at DL 2.18–47. (He is mentioned at DL 6.1, 6.2, 6.8, 6.10, 6.11, 6.14, 6.54 and 6.103. He is mentioned by Epictetus at *Discourse* 3.22.26 – see Appendix 2, p. 159.) See Long 1996 and 1999.

Sosicrates (*fl.* mid-2nd century BC) was a historian and biographer. He wrote a *Succession of Philosophers* detailing philosophers' biographies, following the teacher–pupil relationship. He also wrote a history of Crete. (He is mentioned at DL 6.13, 6.80 and 6.82.) See OCD 'Sosicrates'.

Sotion of Alexandria (possibly early second century BC) was a Peripatetic who wrote a *Succession of the Philosophers* in thirteen books, which was an important source for Diogenes Laertius. (He is mentioned by name at DL 6.26 and 6.80.)

Stilpo of Megara (died early 3rd century BC) was probably the last head of the Megarian school (which was influenced by both Socrates and Parmenides, focusing on ethics and metaphysics). He was one of **Zeno's** teachers, and the teacher of **Menedemus**, founder of the Eretrian school. The *Suda* reports that Stilpo wrote twenty dialogues, no fragments of which survive. A small section is devoted to him at DL 2.113–20. (He is mentioned at DL 6.76 as having been a pupil of **Diogenes of Sinope**.)

Theodorus (4th–3rd century BC) is mentioned at DL 6.42 and at DL 6.97–8, and possibly both references relate to the same person. The latter reference specifically identifies him as 'the Atheist', a philosopher of the Cyrenaic school, to one branch of which he gave the name 'Theodorians'. He is mentioned at DL 2.97–103, where we learn that, 'He considered joy and grief to be the supreme good and evil, the one brought about by wisdom, the other by folly. Wisdom and justice he called goods, and their opposites evils, pleasure and pain being intermediate to good and evil. Friendship he rejected because it did not exist between the unwise nor between the wise; with the former, when the want is removed, the friendship disappears, whereas the wise are self-sufficient and have no need of friends' (DL 2.98, trans. Hicks). He is mentioned at DL 6.97, where having no response to **Hipparchia's** argument, he resorts to simply roughing her up a bit.

Theophrastus of Eresus in Lesbos (c.372–286 BC) was an associate of Aristotle whom he succeeded as head of the Lyceum when Aristotle left Athens on the death of **Plato**. (He is mentioned at DL 6.22, 6.94 and 6.95. The Theophrastus at DL 6.90, who is wearing fine linen in a barber's shop, is probably the same individual.)

Theopompus of Chios (4th century BC) was an important Greek historian. Only a few fragments survive of his extensive output. (He is cited at DL 6.14.)

Timon of Phlius (c.320–230 BC) was a Sceptic and follower of Pyrrho. He staved off poverty in his early life by working as a dancer until he went to Megara to study with **Stilpo**, and later going to study with Pyrrho in Elis. Only fragments of his large output survive, most of which come from the *Silloi* (*Lampoons*), in which he ridicules all the philosophers. A modest section is devoted to him at DL 9.109–16. (This may be the Timon mentioned at DL 6.18.)

Xanthus was an author whose work was abridged by Menippus (not **Menippus of Gadara**, the Cynic), the author of a work entitled *History of the Lydians* (DL 6.101). He is otherwise unknown.

Xeniades purchased **Diogenes of Sinope** when he was sold as a slave, and made him the tutor of his two sons (DL 6.30–1).

(Xeniades is also mentioned at DL 6.36, 6.74, and 6.82.) Is it doubtful that he is the philosopher, also from Corinth, who is mentioned by Sextus Empiricus as holding ultra sceptical opinions.

Xenophon (c.431–350 BC) wrote works on history and other topics, and also three books on **Socrates** and his philosophy (*Apology*, *Symposium*, and *Memorabilia*) which offer a different view of Socrates from that found in the writings of his contemporary, **Plato**. Diogenes Laertius devotes a section to Xenophon at DL 2.48–59. (Xenophon's *Symposium* is mentioned at DL 6.14. He is mentioned again in the next paragraph, at DL 6.15, and also at DL 6.84.)

Zeno of Citum (335–263 BC) founded the Stoic school in Athens in about 300 BC. He studied with several philosophers including **Crates of Thebes**, **Antisthenes of Athens**, and the Academics Xenocrates of Chalcedon and Polemo of Athens. Zeno taught in the *Stoa Poecile* ('Painted Colonnade') from which the Stoic school derives its name. Diogenes Laertius devotes a considerable section to him at DL 7.1–160 (see Yonge and Seddon 2007). (He is mentioned at DL 6.15, 6.104 and 6.105, and he is cited at DL 6.91.)

Zoilus of Perga is mentioned at DL 6.37 as the source for the story of **Diogenes of Sinope** addressing the woman who had 'fallen down before the Gods in an unbecoming attitude'. He is otherwise unknown.

Zopyrus of Colophon (4th–3rd century BC), with one Dionysius (probably Dionysius of Heraclea), may have written the books attributed to **Menippus of Gadara** (DL 6.100). He is otherwise unknown.

SELECT BIBLIOGRAPHY

TRANSLATIONS OF DIOGENES LAERTIUS

Hicks, R. D. 1938 [1925]. *Lives of Eminent Philosophers*. vol. 1. Cambridge, MA: Loeb Classical Library, Harvard University Press. [This 1938 revised reprint of the 1st 1925 edition of volume 1 includes Hick's Preface and Introduction.]

———. 1931 [1925]. *Lives of Eminent Philosophers*. vol. 2. Cambridge, MA: Loeb Classical Library, Harvard University Press. [The Cynics are in Book 6, and Zeno and the Stoics are in Book 7, both Books included in volume 2 of Hicks' translation.]

———. 1972 [1925]. *Lives of Eminent Philosophers*. vol 1. Cambridge, MA: Loeb Classical Library, Harvard University Press. [This 1972 revised reprint of the 1st 1925 edition of volume 1 includes a Preface and Introduction by Herbert S. Long, and omits Hick's Preface and Introduction from the first printing and subsequent reprintings to 1966.]

Yonge, C. D. 1853. *The Lives and Opinions of Eminent Philosophers by Diogenes Laërtius*. London: Bohn. [The edition upon which this present revised translation of Book Seven is based.]

Yonge, C. D. and Keith Seddon. 2007. *A Summary of Stoic Philosophy: Zeno of Citium in Diogenes Laertius Book Seven*. Morrisville, NC: Lulu. [A revised translation based, as is this present volume, on the relevant sections of Yonge's 1853 edition of Diogenes Laertius.]

HOMER[335]

Fagles, Robert. 1991. *Homer: The Iliad*. with introduction and notes by Bernard Knox. Harmondsworth: Penguin.

———. 1997. *Homer: The Odyssey*. with introduction and notes by Bernard Knox. Harmondsworth: Penguin.

Fitzgerald, Robert. 1992. *Homer: The Iliad*. with an introduction by Gregory Nagy. London: Everyman's Library.

———. 1992. *Homer: The Odyssey*. with an introduction by Seamus Heaney. London: Everyman's Library.

Jones, Peter and D. C. H. Rieu. 2003. *Homer: The Iliad*. London: Penguin. [A revised and updated edition of E. V. Rieu's 1950 translation, edited with an introduction by Peter Jones.]

Murray, A. T. and George E. Dimock. 1998, 2004. *Homer: Odyssey*. 2 vols. Cambridge, MA: Loeb Classical Library, Harvard University Press. [A revised edition of Murray's 1919 translation.]

Murray, A. T. and William F. Wyatt. 2003, 1999. *Homer: Iliad*. 2 vols. Cambridge, MA: Loeb Classical Library, Harvard University Press. [A revised edition of Murray's 1924/25 translation.]

Pope, Alexander. 1902. *The Iliad of Homer*. with notes and introduction by Rev. Theodore Alois Buckley. New York: A. L. Burt.

Rieu, D. C. H. 2003 [1991]. *Homer: The Odyssey*. London: Penguin. [A revised edition of E. V. Rieu's 1946 translation, with an introduction by Peter Jones.]

OTHER ANCIENT SOURCES

Attridge, Harold W. 1976. *First-Century Cynicism in the Epistles of Heraclitus*. Missoula, MT: Scholars Press.

Cahoon, J. W. 1932. *Dio Chrysostom*. 1st of 5 vols. Cambridge, MA: Loeb Classical Library, Harvard University Press. [Six *Dis-*

---

[335] Not all editions of Homer include the traditional numbering notation of Book and Line (e.g., Homer, *Iliad* 5.375–9) based on the original Greek of early editions. Those that do, from the items listed in this Bibliography, are: Jones and Rieu, Murray and Dimock, Murray and Wyatt, and Rieu.

courses, the *Fourth, Sixth, Seventh, Eighth, Ninth* and *Tenth*, discuss Cynic themes. The *Fourth Discourse* is included in this present edition: see Appendix 1, above.]

Davie, John. 2005. *Euripides: The Bacchae and Other Plays*. with introduction and notes by Richard Rutherford. London: Penguin. [Includes *Phoenician Women, Orestes* and others.]

Fowler, H. W. and F. G. Fowler. 1905. *The Works of Lucian of Samosata*. 4th of 4 vols. Oxford: Clarendon Press. [Includes the dialogue *The Cynic*, which is not in fact now generally attributed to Lucian, but to a pseudo-Lucian. This dialogue is included in this present edition: see Appendix 3, above.]

Frazer, J. G. 1921. *Apollodorus: The Library*. 2 vols. Cambridge, MA: Loeb Classical Library, Harvard University Press.

Higginson, Thomas Wentworth. 1890. *The Works of Epictetus Consisting of His Discourses, in Four Books, The Enchiridion, and Fragments*. Boston: Little, Brown, & Company. [See Appendix 2 for *Discourse* 3.22 on Cynic philosophy.]

Hine, Daryl. 2005. *The Works of Hesiod and the Homeric Hymns*. Chicago: University Press of Chicago.

Lamb, W. R. M. 1924. *Plato: Laches, Protagoras, Meno, Euthydemus* [vol.2 of Loeb Plato]. Cambridge, MA: Loeb Classical Library, Harvard University Press.

Long, George. 1877. *The Discourses of Epictetus with the Encheiridion and Fragments*. London: George Bell. [See Appendix 2 for *Discourse* 3.22 on Cynic philosophy.]

Malherbe, Abraham J. ed. 1977. *The Cynic Epistles: A Study Edition*. Missoula, MT: Scholars Press.

Oldfather, W. A. 1925, 1928. *Epictetus: The Discourses as Reported by* Arrian, *The Manual, and Fragments*. 2 vols. Cambridge, MA: Loeb Classical Library, Harvard University Press. [See Appendix 2 for *Discourse* 3.22 on Cynic philosophy.]

O'Neil, Edward N. 1977. *Teles: The Cynic Teacher*. Missoula, MT: Scholars Press.

Rolfe, John C. 1946, 1948, 1952. *Aulus Gellius: The Attic Nights*. 3 vols. Cambridge, MA: Loeb Classical Library, Harvard University Press.

Seddon, Keith. 2005. *Epictetus' Handbook and the Tablet of Cebes.* Abingdon: Routledge. [Translations and Commentaries.]

———. forthcoming. *Epictetus: The Discourses, Handbook and Fragments.* Morrisville, NC: Lulu.

Todd, O. J. 1923. *Xenophon: Symposium.* In E. C. Marchant and O. J. Todd. 1923. *Xenophon: Memorabilia, Oeconomicus, Symposium, Apology.* Cambridge, MA: Loeb Classical Library, Harvard University Press, 527–635.

Trapp, M. B. 1997. *Maximus of Tyre: The Philosophical Orations.* Oxford: Clarendon Press. [*Oration* 36 discusses Cynic philosophy.]

Vellacott, Philip. 1963. *Euripides: Medea and Other Plays.* London: Penguin.

Wilson, N. G. 1997. *Aelian: Historical Miscellany.* Cambridge, MA: Loeb Classical Library, Harvard University Press.

Wright, Wilmer Cave. 1913. *Julian: To the Uneducated Cynics* (= *Oration* 6) (with others) [vol. 2 of Loeb Julian]. Cambridge, MA: Loeb Classical Library, Harvard University Press. [*Oration* 7 (*To the Cynic Heracleios*) also addresses Cynic themes.]

ANTHOLOGY OF HELLENISTIC PHILOSOPHY

Malherbe, Abraham J. 1986. *Moral Exhortation: A Greco–Roman Sourcebook.* Philadelphia: Westminster Press. [Primary source extracts with commentaries.]

SECONDARY LITERATURE

Algra, Keimpe, et al. eds. 1999. *The Cambridge History of Hellenistic Philosophy.* Cambridge: Cambridge University Press.

Aune, David E. 2008. The Problem of the Passions in Cynicism. In Fitzgerald 2008, 48–66.

Branham, R. Bracht and Marie-Odile Goulet-Cazé. eds. 1996. *The Cynics: The Cynic Movement in Antiquity and Its Legacy.* Berkeley: University of California Press.

Brickhouse, Thomas C. and Nicholas D. Smith. 2000. *The Philosophy of Socrates*. Boulder, CO : Westview Press.

Curnow, Trevor. 2006. *The Philosophers of the Ancient World: An A–Z Guide*. London: Duckworth.

Cutler, Ian. 2005. *Cynicism from Diogenes to Dilbert*. Jefferon, NC: McFarland.

Cynic. 2008. article at Wikipedia. [At <http://en.wikipedia.org/wiki/Cynic> accessed 2008-06-29.]

Dawson, Doyne. 1992. *Cities of the Gods: Communist Utopias in Greek Thought*. Oxford: Oxford University Press.

Desmond, William P. 2006. *The Greek Praise of Poverty: Origins of Ancient Cynicism*. Notre Dame, IN: University of Notre Dame Press.

———. 2008. *Cynics*. Stocksfield: Acumen.

Downing, F. Gerald. 1992. *Cynics and Christian Origins*. Edinburgh: T&T Clark.

Dudley, Donald R. 1998 [1937]. *A History of Cynicism: From Diogenes to the 6th Century AD*. 2nd edition. with a foreword and bibliography by Miriam Griffin. London: Bristol Classical Press.

Fitzgerald, John T. ed. 2008. *Passions and Moral Progress in Greco-Roman Thought*. Abingdon: Routledge.

Guthrie, W. K. C. 1993 [1952]. *Orpheus and Greek Religion: A Study of the Orphic Movement*. Princeton, NJ: Princeton University Press.

Hadot, Pierre. 1995. *Philosophy as a Way of Life*. trans. Michael Chase. edited with an introduction by Arnold I. Davidson. Oxford: Blackwell.

———. 2002. *What is Ancient Philosophy?* trans Michael Chase. Cambridge, MA: Harvard University Press.

———. 2009. *The Present Alone is Our Happiness: Conversations with Jeannie Carlier and Arnold I. Davidson*. trans. Marc Djaballah. Stanford, CA: Stanford University Press.

Hard, Robin. 2004. *The Routledge Handbook of Greek Mythology*. London: Routledge.

Hope, Richard. 1930. *The Book of Diogenes Laertius: Its Spirit and its Method*. New York: Columbia University Press.

Hornblower, Simon and Antony Spawforth. 1996. *The Oxford Classical Dictionary*. 3rd ed. Oxford: Oxford University Press.

Irwin, Terence. 1995. *Plato's Ethics*. Oxford: Oxford University Press.

———. 2007. *The Development of Ethics: A Historical and Critical Study*. vol. 1. Oxford: Oxford University Press.

Jones, C. P. 1978. *The Roman World of Dio Chrysostom*. Cambridge, MA: Harvard University Press.

Liddell, Henry George, Robert Scott, Henry Stuart Jones, and Roderick McKenzie. 1996 [1843]. *A Greek–English Lexicon*. Oxford: Clarendon Press.

Long, A. A. 1996. The Socratic Tradition: Diogenes, Crates, and Hellenistic Ethics. In Branham and Goulet-Cazé 1996, 28–46.

———. 1999. The Socratic Legacy. In Algra 1999, 617–41.

———. 2002. *Epictetus: A Stoic and Socratic Guide to Life*. Oxford: Oxford University Press.

Lovejoy, Arthur O. and George Boas. 1997 [1935]. *Primitivism and Related Ideas in Antiquity*. Baltimore: John Hopkins Press.

Mansfeld, Jaap. 1986. Diogenes Laertius on Stoic Philosophy. *Elenchos* 7, 295–382. Also in Mansfeld 1990, 343–428.

———. 1990. *Studies in the Historiography of Greek Philosophy*. Assen/Maastricht: Van Gorcum.

Moles, John. 2000. The Cynics. In Christopher Rowe et al. eds. 2000. *The Cambridge History of Greek and Roman Political Thought*. Cambridge: Cambridge University Press, 415–34.

Morison, William. 2006. Cynosarges. *Internet Encyclopedia of Philosophy*. [At <http://www.iep.utm.edu/ancillaries/small-articles/cynosarg.htm> accessed 2008-06-29.]

Navia, Luis E. 1996. *Classical Cynicism: A Critical Study*. Westport, CT: Greenwood Press.

———. 1998. *Diogenes of Sinope: The Man in the Tub*. Westport, CT: Greenwood Press.

———. 2001. *Antisthenes of Athens: Setting the World Aright.* Westport, CT: Greenwood Press.

———. 2005. *Diogenes the Cynic: The War Against the World.* Amherst, NY: Humanity Books. [This is a reissue of Navia 1998 with new typesetting, slightly revised.]

Piering, Julie. 2006a. Antisthenes. *Internet Encyclopedia of Philosophy.* [At <http://www.iep.utm.edu/a/antisthe.htm> accessed 2008-06-29.]

———. 2006b. Cynics. *Internet Encyclopedia of Philosophy.* [At <http://www.iep.utm.edu/c/cynics.htm> accessed 2008-06-29.]

———. 2006c. Diogenes of Sinope. *Encyclopedia of Philosophy.* [At <http://www.iep.utm.edu/d/diogsino.htm> accessed 2008-06-29.]

Reale, Giovanni. 1985. *A History of Ancient Philosophy: 3. The Systems of the Hellenistic Age.* ed. & trans. John R. Catan. Albany, NY: State University of New York Press.

———. 1987. *A History of Ancient Philosophy: 1. From the Origins to Socrates.* ed. & trans. John R. Catan. Albany, NY: State University of New York Press.

———. 1990. *A History of Ancient Philosophy: 4. The Schools of the Imperial Age.* ed. & trans. John R. Catan. Albany, NY: State University of New York Press.

Riley, Woodridge. 2004 [1929]. *Men and Morals: The Story of Ethics.* Whitefish, MT: Kessinger. [Facsimile reprint of the Doubleday, Doran & Company edition of 1929.]

Russo, M. 2002. Cynicism. component of *The Problem of Happiness,* one of the Sophia On-Line Philosophy Courses. [At <http://www.molloy.edu/sophia/ancient_lit/happiness/cynicism.htm> accessed 2008-06-29.]

Sayre, Farrand. 1948. *The Greek Cynics.* Baltimore: J. H. Furst.

Smith, William. ed. 1867. *Dictionary of Greek and Roman Biography and Mythology.* 3 vols. Boston: Little, Brown, and Company. [At <http://www.ancientlibrary.com/smith-bio> accessed 2007-11-19.]

———. ed. 1870. *Dictionary of Greek and Roman Antiquities*. 2nd edition. Boston: Little, Brown, and Company. [At <http://www.ancientlibrary.com/smith-dgra> accessed 2008-01-28.]

Striker, Gisela. 1990. *Ataraxia*: Happiness as Tranquillity. *The Monist* 73-1, 97–110. Also in Striker 1996, 183–95.

———. 1991. Following Nature: A Study in Stoic Ethics. *Oxford Studies in Ancient Philosophy* 9, 1–73. Also in Striker 1996, 221–80.

———. 1996. *Essays on Hellenistic Epistemology and Ethics*. Cambridge: Cambridge University Press.

Swain, Simon. ed. 2000. *Dio Chrysostom: Politics, Letters, and Philosophy*. Oxford: Oxford University Press.

Trapp, Michael. 2007. *Philosophy in the Roman Empire: Ethics, Politics and Society*. Aldershot: Ashgate.

Warren, James. 2007. Diogenes Laertius, Biographer of Philosophy. In Jason König and Tim Whitmarsh. eds. 2007 *Ordering Knowledge in the Roman Empire*. Cambridge: Cambridge University Press, 133–40.

Zeller, E. 2007 [1885]. *Socrates and the Socratic Schools*. trans. Oswald J. Reichel. 3rd edition. Whitefish, MT: Kessinger. [Facsimile reprint of the Longmans Green edition of 1885.]

Zeyl, Donald. ed. 1997. *Encyclopedia of Classical Philosophy*. London: Fitzroy Dearborn.

INDEX

Achaicus
  on Menippus, 117
Achilles, 156, 188
Aelian
  on Diogenes and the mouse, 64n.102
  on Diogenes of Sinope being Antisthenes' pupil, 63n.101
Aeolus, 168
Agamemnon, 156, 160, 161–2
Agesilaus II, 74, 187
Alexander the Great, 28–9, 32, 91, 187–8
  admires Diogenes of Sinope, 69
  amazed at courage and fearlessness of Diogenes of Sinope, 140
  death of, 101
  envied Diogenes of Sinope for his courage and endurance, 124
  expedition, 106
  lodged with Crates, 109
  meets Diogenes of Sinope, 73, 89, 94, 123–42, 170
  said to be son of Ammon/Zeus, 127, 129
  sends letter to Athens, 77
  talks to Crates, 111

Alexander the Great (*cont.*)
  treatment of Callisthenes, 78
  ambition, 123n.240, 135, 149, 150, 153
  delusion of, 152
Ammon, 127
Anaximenes of Lampsacus, the orator, 87, 188
Andromache, 173
Androsthenes of Aegina, 99
anger, 127, 157
animals, 65
  live simply, 33
Antipater, 77, 93, 188
Antisthenes of Athens, 22–4 *passim*, 49–61, 120, 166, 188–9
  'absolute dog', 24, 56
  accused of babbling, 60
  accused of intimacy with wicked men, 52
  asked for a coat, 53
  asked to sing, 53
  attendant spirit, 140
  bitter dog, 60
  books by Antisthenes, 57–60
  carried staff and wallet, 56
  criticises Plato's admiration of horse, 53
  death of, 60

Antisthenes of Athens (*cont.*)
  defined the proposition, 51
  Diogenes of Sinope his pupil, 63
  Diogenes of Sinope told to double his cloak, 53
  doubles his cloak, 56
  drives away pupils with silver rod, 51
  envy is like rust, 52
  exposes rent in cloak, 53–4
  favourite themes, 55
  few disciples, 51
  finds philosophy advantageous, 52
  founder of Cynic school, 50, 188
  founder of Stoic school, 57
  ill repute a good thing, 55
  initiated into mysteries, 51
  labour a good thing, 50
  laughed at/criticised Plato's conceit, 53
  lectured in Cynosarges, 56
  on appointing generals, 53
  on bronze priding itself, 54
  on crows and flatterers, 52
  on education, 120
  on suffering slander, 53
  on wealth, 31n.47
  on wisdom, 56
  on worthless/wicked citizens, 52
  praised by the wicked, 52, 53, 55n.89
  'prepare a fortress', 56
  shun bad habits, 54
  spoken ill of by Plato, 51
  suffering is good, 55
  temperate, 57
  urged Athenians to vote that asses were horses, 53

Antisthenes of Athens (*cont.*)
  virtue a matter of deeds, 55
  virtue can be taught, 55, 121
  virtue same in women as in men, 56
  virtue sufficient for happiness, 55
  virtues cannot be lost, 56
  wise man alone knows what is deserving of love, 55
  'would rather go mad than feel pleasure', 51
  wrestler, 51
Antisthenes of Rhodes, 61, 108, 189
  on death of Diogenes of Sinope, 99
Anytus (with Meletus, Socrates' accuser), 54, 188, 189
  wiser than Socrates, 54
Aphrodite, 95
Apollo, 136, 139n.269
  oracle at Delphi, 23, 26, 30n.45, 63, 139
Apollodorus, 118
Apollonides the Sceptic, 18, 20
Archelaus, 139
Argonauts, 150
Argos, 173
Aristippus, 61, 69, 189
Aristo of Chios, 120, 121, 189–90
Aristogiton, 81, 197
Aristotle, 25, 36n.62, 188, 190, 196, 203, 207,
Asclepiades the Phliasian friend of Crates, 111
Asclepius/Aesculapius, 73, 171n.321, 190
Athena/Athene, 50n.76, 94n.192, 152n.291
Athenaeus
  on Stoics, 57

Athenians, 50, 145, 164, 169, 182
  claim freedom of speech,
    94n.194
  descended from Erichthonius,
    50n.76
  disparaged by Socrates, 49–50
  give Diogenes of Sinope a new
    wine jar, 76
  pressed by Antisthenes to vote
    that asses be horses, 53
  urge Diogenes of Sinope to be
    initiated, 74
  vote honour to Alexander, 91
Athenodorus of Tarsus, 103, 190

bag, 81
  leather bag, *see* wallet
bath
  public, dirty, 79
beard, *see* hair and beard
beauty, 54
bees, 137, 172
beetroot, 78, 90
begging, 23, 45, 46, 73, 81, 86, 88,
  93, 117, 156, 170
body, 160, 161, 170, 172, 173, 177
Boreas
  sons of, 150
boys, 78
  in Lacedaemon, 67
Bryson of Achaea, 190
  possibly tutor of Crates, 107
bull, 156, 172

calamities, 30–1
calf, 156
Callisthenes of Olynthus, 78, 190
Celotes of Lampsacus
  teacher of Menedemus, 119
Centaurs, 82, 88n.175, 152–3
Cerberus, 203

Cercidas of Megalopolis
  on Diogenes of Sinope's death,
    99, 190
character, 26–7, 29, 34, 38, 40, 47,
  123n.240, 140n.272, 143, 145,
  149, 151, 157, 163, 166, 169,
  183, 188, 206
  excellent (*kalokagathos*), 67;
    (*kratistos*), 92
  'moral character' (*prohairesis*),
    157, 172–3
Charon, 203
Charybdis, 82, 82n.157
children, 97, 166–9 *passim*
Chiron, 82, 88, 182
Cicero, 190, 191
Cisseus, 139n.269
Cleanthes, 171n.322
Cleomenes, 98, 190
  pupil of Metrocles, 114
cloak
  doubled by Cynics, 53, 56, 64,
    99, 121, 192
  worn by Cynics, 26, 28, 45, 90,
    93, 100, 111, 112, 156, 163, 167,
    175, 183, 184
clock, 120
clothes, 33, 43, 79, 115, 116, 148,
  178, 180, 182
  stealing, 83
convention (*nomos/nomikos*), 73
  rejection of, 32, 34, 43–7
    passim, 96; *see also* custom
Corinth, 50n.77, 98, 100, 110, 125,
  126n.244, 192, 194, 208
  where Diogenes of Sinope
    died, 101, 101n.208
cottabos (drinking game), 79
courage, 38, 43, 47, 53, 124, 126,
  137, 140, 141, 153
  opposed to fortune, 73

courtesans/prostitutes, 91, 93, 110;
    see also women
Craneum/Craneion, 99, 126
Craterus, 87, 190
Crates of Thebes, 107–12, 121, 166,
    191
  accused of wearing fine linen,
    110
  Alexander the Great his guest,
    109
  buried at Boeotia, 116
  death of, 111
  deliberately provoked abuse,
    110
  disposes of wealth, 108–9
  'Door-opener', 108
  hunchbacked in old age, 111
  influences Monimus, 104
  letters, 116
  married, 168
  Pasicles his son, 109
  possibly flogged and dragged
    by feet, 110
  relationship with Hipparchia,
    115, 168
  saves Metrocles from suicide,
    113
  sewed sheepskin into cloak, 111
  strips naked, 115
  temperance instilled by
    Antisthenes, 57
  threw money into sea, 109
  touches man's hips/thighs, 110,
    111
  tragedy, specimen lines from,
    116
  ugly, 111
  visits Metrocles, 113
  water-drinker, 110
Croesus, 159

currency
  defacing (*paracharassô*), 23–4,
    30n.45, 62–3, 86, 96
cushions
  Diogenes of Sinope tramples
    on, 66
custom (*nomos/nomikos*), 24, 30,
    31, 32n.48, 45, 46, 97; *see
    also* convention
Cynic conduct, 42–5
Cynic doctrine, 26–47, 120–1
  modern relevance, 46–7
Cynic outlook
  just a way of life, 24–6, 119
  short road to virtue, 121
Cynic training/practice (*askêsis*),
    29, 34, 35n.56, 65, 80, 95, 96
Cynic/Cynics
  conceived as educators, 157
  conceived of as messenger or
    spy from Zeus, 158, 161, 166
  father of all mankind, 169
  in service to God, 164, 166, 169
  shares power of God, 171
  wrote books, 25
Cynosarges, 22, 56
Cyrus the Elder, 50–1, 106, 135,
    138n.268, 191

dagger, 60, 90, 93
Danaus, 168
Darius Codomannus, 127, 133, 134,
    145–6, 165n.311
death, 47, 51, 52, 78, 84, 87, 94,
    134, 147, 154, 158, 161, 165
Delphi
  Apollo's oracle at, 23, 26,
    30n.45, 63, 139
Demeter, 74n.125, 95, 101n.208
Demetrius of Alexander
  pupil of Theombrotus, 114

Demetrius of Magnesia, 191
    affirms that Onesicritus was a native of Astypalaea, 106
    on Crates' money, 109
    on Diogenes of Sinope's death, 101
    on Onesicritus' birthplace, 106
Demetrius of Phalerum
    sends loaves and wine to Crates, 110
Demosthenes, 191
    dines in inn, 70–1
desire, 29, 30–1, 33, 36–7, 42, 45, 47, 132, 143, 146, 147, 160, 161, 163, 165, 173, 180, 182
    'suppress desire', 156
    wicked people are slaves to, 93
Diagoras of Melos, 88, 191
Didymon the adulterer, 94, 101
Didymon the flute-player, 83, 94, 191
Dio Chrysostom, 191–2
Diocles of Magnesia, 192
    on Antisthenes' sayings, 56
    on cheese story, 72
    on Crates, 109, 110–11
    on Diogenes of Sinope, 62, 72, 120
    on Menippus, 117
Diodorus of Aspendos, 192
    first to adopt Cynic dress, 56
Diogenes of Sinope, 22–4, 26, 44, 57, 62–103, 120, 166, 169, 171n.320, 192–3
    asks Antisthenes for coat, 53
    asks Plato for wine, 66
    associate of Crates, 112
    bathes in dirty bath, 79
    begs from statue, 81
    binds hand with cestus, 76
    books by Diogenes of Sinope, 101–3

Diogenes of Sinope (*cont.*)
    buried by gates of Corinth, 100
    called 'dog', 75, 86, 89, 99
    called son of Zeus by Cercidas, 99
    calls for men, 69
    calls Plato's lectures a waste of time, 65
    can 'govern men', 68
    carries staff and wallet, 64
    celebrates conclusion of boring book, 73
    condemns popular leaders, 75
    condemns Plato's pride, 66
    conquers men, 76
    criticises professionals, 67
    death of, 99–101
    died same day as Alexander the Great, 101
    dispenses with cup and spoon, 72
    doubles his cloak, 53n.85, 64, 99
    drags bottle, 71
    eats in marketplace, 87
    eats lupins, 80
    eats octopus and dies, 99
    embraces statues, 65
    envied by Alexander the Great for his courage and endurance, 124
    gives pupil fish to carry, 72
    gives someone cheese to carry, 72
    glare like a lion's, 126
    goes into theatre as everyone else comes out, 45, 92
    goes barefoot in snow, 70
    holds breath and dies, 99
    holds up salt fish to interrupt lecture, 87
    invited to banquet, 70

Diogenes of Sinope (*cont.*)
  invites passers-by to witness his struggle with illness, 165
  laughed at, 85, 87
  lives in public buildings, 64
  lives in wine jar, 45, 65, 121
  loved by Athenians, 76
  mankind the wisest and most foolish of all animals, 65
  meets Alexander the Great, 123–54
  on holding up finger, 71
  on sheep and children, 75
  on supper-time, 75
  on values, 71
  on washing, 76
  opposes custom (*nomos*) to nature (*phusis*), 30, 73, 96
  passed over for praise, 90
  perfumes his feet, 73–4
  persuades Crates to throw away possessions, 109
  possibly a tutor of Crates, 107
  praised by unworthy men, 70
  praises those who change their minds, 67–8
  prefers freedom above all, 28
  proved that simple life was not injurious to health of body, 170
  regarded by Plato as 'A Socrates gone mad,' 84
  right reason is thing most needed, 65
  searches for a man by lamplight, 44, 75
  sees mouse living simply, 33, 64
  sits next to target, 94
  sold as slave, 71, 98
  sold to Xeniades, 68, 98
  spits, 69

Diogenes of Sinope (*cont.*)
  stands under fountain, 75
  superior to Alexander the Great, 28–9, 32
  taken to Philip, 77, 158
  teaches philosophy, 45
  reproached for banishment, 80
  tramples on Plato's cushions, 66
  tutor to Xeniades' sons, 28, 98
  urged to retire, 70
  urinates like a dog, 79
  whistles, 67
  wishes to be buried face-down, 69
Dionysian Games, 65
Dionysius of Heraclea, 76–7, 193
  on Diogenes of Sinope, 76–7
  possibly wrote works attributed to Menippus, 118
Dionysius the Younger, 66, 81, 87, 193–4
  said by Diogenes of Sinope to treat his friends like bags, 81
Dionysus
  mystery cult, 91
Dioxippus the Athenian athlete, 70n.117, 76, 89n.179, 194–5
distractions
  Cynic should be free from, 166–8 *passim*
dog/dogs/doglike, 22, 43, 60, 75, 78, 89, 90, 99, 100, 131, 145, 169, 178, 182
Domitian (emperor), 192, 195
dreams, 76
Dromon, 145

easy life, 28, 77
eating, 97
Echcles of Ephesus
  pupil of Cleomenes, 114

education, 94, 120, 144, 153, 154, 157
  two sorts, divine and human, 129–30
effeminacy, 78–9, 90, 92, 146–9, 156
Eiclides' school
  criticised by Diogenes of Sinope, 65
Elusinian Mysteries, 74, 74n.125
Empedocles, 197
end (*telos*), *see* goal
envy, 52
Epaminondas, 74, 168, 195
Epictetus, 26, 195
  on correct use of impressions, 157n.296
Epicurus, 25, 195–6
Eratosthenes of Cyrene, 196
  on Crates' son, 109
Erichthonius
  mythical first Athenian king, 50n.76
ethics
  ancient Greek, 27
Eubulides of Miletus, 196
  on Diogenes of Sinope
    defacing the currency, 62
Eubulus, 196
  on Diogenes of Sinope
    teaching children, 68–9
Euclides of Megara, 65, 109, 196–7
eudaimonia, *see* happiness
eunuchs, 131
Euripides, 116n.231
Eurystheus, 165
Euthycrates, 197
  possibly flogged Crates, 110
everyday life
  duties of, 166–7
evil, 94, 120, 128, 136, 141, 143, 158, 160, 161, 169, 182

evil (*cont.*)
  'Let no evil enter here,' 73, 81
exile, 29, 64, 73, 109, 123, 124, 158, 188, 189, 192, 193
externals, 27, 41, 50, 157, 158n.296, 159, 184

Favorinus, 197
  on Crates, 109–10
  on Pasiphon, 97–8
  on Plato eating olives and figs, 66
fear/fearlessness, 43, 86, 94, 98, 137, 140, 157, 163, 165, 184
feet, 176–7
fig tree, 89
figs
  debauched men resemble, 88
  painted, 80
finger
  holding up, 71
flattery, 125, 126, 151
flute-player, *see* Didymon
foolishness, 136, 138, 142
freedom (*eleutheria*), 28, 96, 162–3, 166, 169
freedom of speech (*parrhêsia*), 94
friendship, 121, 132, 166

gallows, 78
global warming, 32n.48
goal (*telos*), 26, 27, 30, 37, 37n.62, 44, 120
goblet
  theft by stewards, 77-88
God/Gods, 28, 47, 49n.73, 50n.76, 93, 94–5, 127–8, 134, 144, 154, 161, 163–7 *passim*, 170, 171, 178–85 *passim*
  as master of the house, 155
  artists depict, 142–3

God/Gods (*cont.*)
   attempt nothing without God, 164
   Celotes of Lampsacus prepares his report for, 119
   Cynic converses with, 158
   Cynic in service to, 164, 166, 169
   Cynic shares power of, 171
   Diogenes of Sinope lived in shrines dedicated to, 126
   divine guidance, 155
   'everything belongs to', 72, 96
   good men bear the image of, 82
   have given mankind an easy life, 77
   'may be behind you', 73
   praying to, 76
   sacrificing to, 67, 91
   statues of resemble the Cynic, 184
   those who wish for nothing resemble, 121
   want nothing, 121
   'wise men are friends of', 72, 96
gold/golden, 83, 89, 90, 107, 125, 144, 153, 160, 179, 180, 182, 184, 194–5, 205
golden fleece, 79, 150n.288, 203
good, 28, 36–41 *passim*, 44, 46, 55n.91, 57, 76, 94, 120, 131, 154, 158, 160, 161–3, 169, 170, 178, 189, 197, 198, 207
   good man deserves to be loved, 56
   good men, 56, 67, 128, 131, 141, 183, 184
   good men are the image of God, 82
Gorgias of Leontini
   sophist Rhetorician, 50, 197

grammar/grammarians, 67, 76
Greek schools of philosophy address happiness (*eudaiminia*), 27n.35

Hades, 74n.125, 100, 111, 131, 203
   Celotes of Lampsacus prepared his report for, 119
hair and beard, 175, 182, 183–5 *passim*
happiness (*eudaimonia*), 23, 24, 27, 27nn.34–5, 29, 31, 34–5, 41, 43, 44, 100, 111, 120n.237, 123n.240, 125, 141, 149, 150, 159–60, 162, 165, 169, 179, 184
   Plato on, 37–9
   virtue is sufficient for, 34–41, 55, 188
Harmodius, 81, 197
harp-players, 79–80
health, 36–8 *passim*, 40 43, 67, 68, 95, 162, 177, 178, 181
heavenly bodies, 73
Hecate, 143–4
Hecato of Rhodes, 198
   on Antisthenes, 52
   on Diogenes of Sinope seeking for men, 69
   on Metrocles' burning his writings, 113
Hector, 156, 173
Hegesias of Sinope, 198
   a pupil of Diogenes of Sinope, 106
   asked Diogenes of Sinope for one of his books, 80
Hegesias, 80
Helen, 160n.303, 161
helmet, 76, 85
Hephaestus, 50n.76, 114
Hera, 151n.290, 152

Heracles, 76, 78n.140, 80n.149, 81, 81n.151, 88n.175, 130, 139n.271, 164–5, 171n.321, 181, 198–9
    forbear of Alexander the Great, 137, 139
    model for Diogenes of Sinope, 96
    offered as example by Anthistheses for goodness of labour, 50–1
    statue made by Euthycates, 197
Hermippus of Smyrna, 68n.114, 200
    on Antisthenes, 50
    on Menippus, 117
    on sale of Diogenes of Sinope, 68
Hicesias
    defaces the currency, 62
    father of Diogenes of Sinope, 23, 62
Hipparchia of Maronea, 115–16, 200
    attacks Theodorus at Lysimachus' dinner party, 115
    sister of Metrocles, 115
    wife of Crates, 109
Hippobotus, 200
    on Crates, 107
    on Menedemus, 119
Homer, 123n.240, 128, 131, 134, 142, 160n.303, 168, 170–1
horns argument, 73
horse/horses, 53, 55, 85n.168, 141, 182, 184, 205

Icarus, 150
immortality, 52
impressions (*phantasiai*)
    right use of, 157–8, 157n.296, 159

indifferent things, 121, 189
insults, 23
intention, 41
Isles of the Blessed, 74
Isthmian Games, 50
Ixion, 151, 152

Julian (emperor), 25n.31, 27
justice, 38, 47, 67, 132, 151, 199, 207

kingship, 128–9, 132–5, 137–41, 145, 161, 163, 167, 171, 172
kosmopolitês, 91n.184
Kunosarges, 22–3, 56n.92

labour, 55n.90; *see also* suffering something good, 50–1
Lacedaemon/Lacedaemonians, 50, 67, 88; *see also* Sparta
law, 97
lawyers, 85
lion, 98, 156, 182
    Diogenes of Simope's glare like that of, 126
    lion's skin, 78, 181
    Nemean lion, 80n.149
living in accordance with nature, *see* nature
living simply, 33–4, 45, 72, 121
    in public, 41, 43, 44, 95, 115, 126, 170; *see also*, public, living in public
love, 55, 56, 82, 108, 121
lupins, 80, 108, 113
lust, 139n.271, 148
luxury, 29, 30, 55, 64n.102, 124, 128, 142, 148, 180, 182
    'May the children of your enemies live in luxury,' 54
Lysanius, 200
    on Diogenes of Sinope's staff and wallet, 64

Lysias the drug-seller
  derided by Diogenes of Sinope, 76
Lysimachus, 200
  holds dinner party where Hipparchia attacks Theodorus, 115

Manes (Diogenes of Sinopes' slave)
  runs away, 85
marriage, 81, 84–5, 97, 109, 112, 115, 166–8
mass extinction, 32n.48
masterbation, 78, 95
mathematicians, 67, 196
Megara, 75
Meleager
  writing resembles that of Menippus of Gadara, 117
Meletus (with Anytus, Socrates' accuser), 54, 188, 189
men
  sought for by Diogenes of Sinope, 67, 69, 74–5, 88
Menander Drymus
  pupil of Diogenes of Sinope, 106
Menander the comic poet of Athens, 104–5, 112, 200
Menedemus of Eretria, 200–1
  drags Crates by feet, 110–11
Menedemus the Cynic, 119–21
  dresses as Fury, 119
  pupil of Theombrotus, 114
Menippus of Gadara, 117–18, 201
  books by Menippus, 118
Menippus of Sinope
  pupil of Metrocles, 114
messenger or spy from Zeus, 158, 161, 166–7

Metrocles of Maroneia, 113–14, 201
  brother of Hipparchia, 115
  on Diogenes of Sinope appearing half shaved, 70
Midias, 201
  strikes Diogenes of Sinope, 76
mind, 51, 52, 127
Minos, 132
mirror
  Cynic should examine himself in, 164
money, 31n.47, 67, 78, 81n.152, 104, 108, 109, 114, 124, 144–5, 153; *see also* wealth
  Menippus a money-lender, 117
Monimus of Syracuse, 104–5, 201–2
  essays by Monimus, 105
'moral character' (*prohairesis*), *see* character, 'moral character'; virtue
motion argument, 73
mouse, 33, 64
  mice are Diogenes of Sinope's hangers-on, 74
Muses, 108
music/musicians, 67, 98, 120; *see also* Didymon the flute-player, harp-players, Nicodromus
Myndus, 86
Myro, 159
Mysteries, *see* Eleusian Mysteries; Orpheus, mysteries of

nature, 73, 172, 178
  living in accordance with (*kata phusin*), 27, 27n.35, 29, 30, 33, 34, 42–4 *passim*, 92, 96
Neanthes of Cyzicus, 202
  on Antisthenes' doubling his cloak, 56

Nemean Games, 80
Nero, 159–60
Nicodromus
  harp-player, provoked by Crates, 108
Nicopolis, 164, 195
nomikos, see convention

octopus, 99
Odysseus, 67, 131, 156n.295, 202
olive tree, 83
olives, 82, 85
Olympias, 127, 129
Olympic Games, 76, 80, 88, 89, 101, 164, 165
Olympiodorus, 202
  on Diogenes of Sinope's staff and wallet, 64
Onesicritus of Aegina, 98–9, 106, 202, 204
  taught Diogenes of Sinope, 106
Ophellius, 159
oracle
  at Delos, 63
  at Delphi, 23, 30n.45, 63
orator/orators, 64, 67, 70, 79, 87, 148, 191, 192, 197, 201, 204, 205
Orpheus, 203
  mysteries of, 51

Pasicles
  son of Crates, 109
Pasiphon, 97–8
Peloponnesian War, 49
people pray for wrong things, 76
Perdicas
  threatens Diogenes of Sinope, 77
Persephone, 74n.125
Phanias, 54, 203
  on Antisthenes' virtue, 54

Philemon the comic poet, 108–9, 203–4
Philip of Madedon, 77, 127, 141, 158, 187, 194
  lodges with Hipparchia, 109
Philiscus of Aegina, 97, 99, 102, 106, 204
philosophers, 86, 87, 109
  deserve little, 107
philosophic life, 25–6
philosophical sects, 24–5
philosophy, 87, 90, 92, 111, 113, 116, 119–20
  its advantages, 53, 108
Phocion, 204
  pupil of Diogenes of Sinope, 99
Phryne, 89, 204–5
Piraeus, 50
Plato, 18, 35, 171n.323, 205
  Academy, 25
  calls Diogenes of Sinope a dog, 75
  criticised by Antisthenes for admiring horse, 53
  criticised by Diogenes of Sinope, 65–6
  eats olives and figs, 65
  Euthydemus, 37–40
  his cushions trampled by Diogenes of Sinope, 66
  ideas, 84
  sees Diogenes of Sinope washing vegetables, 87
  speaks ill of Antisthenes, 51
pleasure, 30, 96, 124, 146, 147, 149, 153, 178, 179, 183, 184
  rejected by Cynics, 29, 51
  the end, 27n.34
Polyeuctus the Athenian orator, 205
  on Diogenes of Sinope staff and wallet, 64

Poseidon, 101n.208
possessions, 29, 30, 46–7, 144–5, 160, 167, 173
   Antisthenes' are great, 31n.47
   happiness the most esteemed, 27
   rejection of, 28, 42, 159, 163
poverty, 29, 31n.47, 124, 125, 141, 165, 176
power, 45, 47, 182
   political, 29, 30, 31, 37, 38, 40, 69, 123n.240, 124, 138, 159, 171
practice; *see* training
pray/prayer, 28, 76, 179, 182
Priam, 168
proposition (*logos*)
   Antisthenes' definition, 51
prostitutes, *see* courtesans/prostitutes, women
pseudo-Diogenes, 27
public
   living in public, 23, 41, 42, 155, 157, 164; *see also*, living simply, in public
public office, 169, 173
purification, 74n.125, 143, 157, 171
Pythian Games, 70

reason, 34, 65, 73
Rhea, 49, 73
ruling faculty, 157, 160, 171

Samothrace
   temple at, 88
Sarambus, 145
Sardanapalus, 147n.284, 149n.286, 153–4, 160
Saturninus, 13, 17
Satyrus, 102
Scirpalus, 98, 205
Scylla, 82n.157
seafarers, 35–6

self-control, 47, 128, 182
self-respect, 157
self-sufficiency (*autarkeia*), 28, 69, 77, 100; *see also* sufficiency
Seneca, 159n.301, 198
Serapis, 91
sheep, 79
   wearing skins, whilst children go naked, 75
shepherd, 133, 161
shoes, 77
silver, 125, 144, 153, 179, 180, 182
silver rod
   Antisthenes uses one to drive away pupils, 51
simplicity, *see* living simply
slave/slaves, 72n.122, 128, 134, 141, 145
   as slaves obey masters, the wicked are slaves to desires, 93
   Cynic has no slave, 163
   Diogenes of Sinope's slave Manes runs away, 85
   Monimus the Cynic was a slave, 104
   runaway slaves, 83, 85
   slaves see masters eating, but do not lay hands on the food, 67
slavery, 162, 169
   Diogenes of Sinope sold as a slave, 68, 98, 104
Socrates, 26, 35–40 *passim*, 46, 49, 50, 53–7 *passim*, 84, 120, 159, 171n.323, 188, 192–3, 196, 201, 205–6, 208
   on happiness and virtue, 35–40
   sees rent in Antisthenes' cloak, 53–4
sophists, 130–2, 141, 153

Sosicrates, 102, 104, 192, 206
   on the Cynic's appearance, 56
Sotion of Alexandria, 102, 206
   on Diogenes of Sinope
      trampling on cushions, 66
soul, 147, 149, 152, 154, 161
Sparta, 164, 187, 197; see also
   Lacedaemon
speech, 82, 151; see also freedom
   of speech
spirits
   attendant, 140–51, 153–4
staff (carried by Cynics), 26, 28,
   56, 63, 64, 69, 93, 99, 109,
   119, 156, 163
statues, 29, 30, 65, 81
   Diogenes of Sinope embraces,
      65
   of Aphrodite at Delphi, 89
   of Gods resemble the Cynic,
      184
   of the Muses, 94
Stilpo of Megara, 190, 200, 204,
   206, 207
   pupil of Diogenes of Sinope, 99
Stoic/Stoics, 25, 26, 27n.35, 42, 57,
   76, 120, 121, 158n.296,
   159n.301, 188, 189, 190, 191,
   193, 195, 198, 201, 208
suffering, 55; see also labour
sufficiency, 176, 182; see also self-
   sufficiency
supper
   appropriate time for, 75, 120

target
   sitting next to is safest place,
      94
telos, see goal
Telesterion (Hall of Initiation),
   74n.125
temperance, 38, 57

theatre
   Diogenes of Sinope goes in as
      everyone else comes out, 45,
      92
Thebans, 50, 168
Thebes, sown men of, 128
theft, 83, 97
Theodorus the Atheist, 76, 190,
   200, 206–7
   attacked by Hipparchia, 115–16
Theombrotus
   pupil of Metrocles, 114
Theophrastus of Eresus, 14, 200,
   207
   Crates shows him wearing fine
      linen, 110
   notes taken at his lectures
      burnt by Metrocles, 113–14
   on Diogenes of Sinope seeing a
      mouse, 64, 74
   teacher of Metrocles, 113
Theopompous of Chios, 207
   praises Antisthenes, 56–7
Thersites, 156
Theseus, 182
'thrice human', 79
Timarchus of Alexandria
   pupil of Cleomenes, 114
Timon of Phlius, 207
   accuses Antisthenes of
      babbling, 60
training (*askêsis*), 34–5, 35n.56,
   95–6
Trajan (emperor), 123n.240
Troy, 91n.186, 156, 156n.295,
   160n.303, 168n.315, 173n.326,
   202
truth, 126, 132, 136, 158, 162
tutor, 28, 98, 193, 196, 204, 205,
   207

uncleanliness, 92

values, Cynic rejection of, 24
virtue, 34–5, 35n.56, 40, 41, 43–5
    passim, 85, 95, 143; *see also*
    character, 'moral character'
  a matter of deeds, 55
  can be taught, 55, 121
  cannot be lost, 56, 121
  four cardinal virtues, 38; *see
    also* courage, justice,
    temperance, wisdom
  live according to, 120
  of the body, 177
  pretended, 92
  same in women as in men, 56
  sole good, 57
  sufficient for happiness, 34–40, 55

wallet (*pera*), 26, 28, 56, 64, 70, 72, 104, 107, 156, 163
wealth, 31, 31n.47, 36–42 *passim*, 115, 121, 124, 125, 141, 144, 145, 146; *see also* money
whistling, 120
  Diogenes of Sinope attracts crowd by, 67
wine jar (*pithos*), 45, 65, 121
  Diogenes of Sinope's jar is broken by a youth, 76
wisdom, 36, 38, 40, 46, 56, 65, 92, 96–7, 99, 120, 124, 130, 138, 154
wise man, 56, 141, 166; *see also* good man
  alone knows what is deserving of love, 55
  cannot commit error, 121
  deserves to be loved, 121
  friend to all like himself, 121
  friend to the Gods, 72, 96
women, 51, 54–5, 56, 72, 83, 85, 88, 89, 91, 97, 116, 131, 139, 148–9, 182; *see also* courtesans/prostitutes
wrestler, 90, 96, 164n.309
  Anthisthenes claims to be a good one, 51
wretchedness, 82

Xanthus, 207
  works abridged by the historian Menippus, 118
Xeniades, 207–8
  buys Diogenes of Sinope, 68, 71–2
  extols excellence of Diogenes of Sinope, 104
  his sons tutored by Diogenes of Sinope, 98
  master of Diogenes of Sinope, 28, 68, 69, 98
Xenophon, 57, 106, 205, 208
  Symposium, 31n.47
Xerxes, 133

Zeno of Citium, 25, 42n.65, 57, 111, 121, 189, 191–3 *passim*, 195, 208
  on Crates, 111
Zeus, 42, 43, 49n.73, 82n.157, 99, 131, 132, 134, 164–5, 169
  created race of heroes, 74n.126
  crucifies Ixion, 151n.290
  Cynic is messenger from, 158; *see also* Cynic/Cynics
  Cynic shares power of Zeus, 171
  father of gods and men, 128
  kings are 'nurtured of Zeus', and 'dear unto Zeus', 132
  sends Cynic into world, 164
Zoilus of Perga, 72, 208
Zopyrus of Colophon
  works attributed to Menippus, 118

Outline of Cynic Philosophy
Antisthenes of Athens and Diogenes of Sinope in
Diogenes Laertius Book Six
C. D. Yonge and Keith Seddon
Revised edition published by Keith Seddon at Lulu 2008
© 2008 Keith Seddon
ISBN 978-0-9556844-8-7 (hardback)
ISBN 978-0-9556844-4-9 (paperback)

Typeset in Constantia and Maiandra by the author using Microsoft Word 2007. Proofs checked and reviewed in Portable Document Format created using open source PDFCreator 0.9.8.

NOTE ON THE TYPEFACES

Cover text, display text, and running headers are set in Maiandra GD, designed by Dennis Pasternak

'The Maiandra typeface is based on Oswald Cooper's hand-lettering, as seen in an advertisement for a book on home furnishing, c.1909. [Oswald Cooper, 1879–1940, was an American typographer and creator of the Cooper Old Style and Cooper Black typefaces.] Cooper's design was inspired by examples of Greek inscriptions, and combines ancient forms with design styles characteristic of his time. The result was an attractive design possessing subtle irregularities, or 'meanders' in his skilled brushwork. Maiandra, derived from the Greek 'maiandros', meaning 'meander', is intended for extended text use, as well as for informal subject matter, such as business correspondence, brochures and broadsides.'

(Abridged from http://www.galapagosdesign.com/original/maiand.htm)

Main text is set in Microsoft Constantia, designed by John Hudson

Microsoft informs us: 'Constantia is a modulated wedge-serif typeface designed primarily for continuous text in both electronic and paper publishing. The design responds to the recent narrowing of the gap between screen readability and traditional print media, exploiting specific aspects of the most recent advances in ClearType rendering, such as subpixel positioning. The classic proportions of relatively small x-height and long extenders make Constantia ideal for book and journal publishing, while the slight squareness and open counters ensure that it remains legible even at small sizes. This font is suitable for book typesetting, email, web design, and magazines.'

(http://www.microsoft.com/typography/ctfonts/ConstantiaPoster.xps)